COMPUTER
BOOK SERIES
FROM IDG

Intranet & Web Data___
For Dummies®

D1761311

Microsoft Database Publishing Tools

Product	What It Is	Comments
Access 97	A desktop database that includes a nifty wizard, the Publish to the Web Wizard, which generates static IDC, and ASP pages	Data must be stored in Access; because Access is the database engine, dynamic formats work only with small Web sites
SQL Server 6.5	A server database that includes a nice wizard, the Web Assistant, which produces static HTML pages	Data must be stored in SQL Server; no dynamic formats supported; includes advanced scheduling capabilities
Visual InterDev	An advanced Web application development tool	Includes helpful wizards; product focuses on building robust Web sites using any ODBC database and ASP technology

Microsoft Internet Servers

Server Class	Operating System	Product Name	Product Versions
Internet	Windows NT Server 4.0	Internet Information Server	1.0, 2.0, 3.0, and 4.0
Intranet	Windows NT Workstation 4.0	Peer Web Services/ Personal Web Server*	2.0, 3.0, 4.0
Intranet	Windows 95	Personal Web Server	1.0, 4.0
Intranet	Macintosh OS	Personal Web Server	1.0, 4.0

Microsoft renamed Peer Web Services for Windows NT Workstation to Personal Web Server for Version 4.0.

Microsoft Access Publish to the Web Wizard Template Tokens

HTML Template Token	Replaced with
`<!-AccessTemplate_Title-->`	Name of published object
`<!-AccessTemplate_Body-->`	Published detail
`<!-AccessTemplate_FirstPage-->`	Hyperlink to the first published page (reports)
`<!-AccessTemplate_PreviousPage-->`	Hyperlink to the previous published page (reports)
`<!-AccessTemplate_NextPage-->`	Hyperlink to the next published page (reports)
`<!-AccessTemplate_LastPage-->`	Hyperlink to the last published page (reports)
`<!-AccessTemplate_PageNumber-->`	Page number of current page

IDG
BOOKS
WORLDWIDE

...For Dummies: #1 Computer Book Series for Beginners

Intranet & Web Databases
For Dummies®

Cheat Sheet

ANSI* and Access Wildcard Characters

ANSI Character	Returns Values Where	Equivalent Access Character
%	One or more characters	*
_	Exactly one character	?

* You must use the ANSI version of the wildcard character when you construct SQL statements using the Internet Database Connector (IDC) or Active Server Pages (ASP).

Active Server Pages Objects

Object	Description
Application	Shares information among all users of an application. An ASP application is defined as all the .ASP files in a virtual directory and its subdirectories.
Request	Retrieves values from the client browser. Contains five collections (ClientCertificate, Cookies, Form, QueryString, and ServerVariables).
Response	Sends output to the client browser. Contains one collection, Cookies. You can use the Response object's Write method to write text to the browser.
Server	Provides access to several methods and properties of the server, including utility functions such as HTMLEncode. Using the Server object's CreateObject method, you can create objects on the server, including the ADODB object for performing data access and the MS.TextStream object for reading and writing information to files.
Session	Stores information about a user session that persists between pages. The Session object has several properties and methods, including the SessionID property.

...For Dummies: #1 Computer Book Series for Beginners

INTRANET &
WEB DATABASES
FOR
DUMMIES®

INTRANET & WEB DATABASES FOR DUMMIES®

by Paul Litwin

IDG Books Worldwide, Inc.
An International Data Group Company

Foster City, CA ♦ Chicago, IL ♦ Indianapolis, IN ♦ Southlake, TX

Intranet & Web Databases For Dummies®

Published by
IDG Books Worldwide, Inc.
An International Data Group Company
919 E. Hillsdale Blvd.
Suite 400
Foster City, CA 94404
www.idgbooks.com (IDG Books Worldwide Web site)
www.dummies.com (Dummies Press Web site)

Library of Congress Catalog Card No.: 97-80737

ISBN: 0-7645-0221-2

Printed in the United States of America

10 9 8 7 6 5 4 3 2 1

1B/RS/RR/ZX/IN

Distributed in the United States by IDG Books Worldwide, Inc.

Distributed by Macmillan Canada for Canada; by Transworld Publishers Limited in the United Kingdom; by IDG Norge Books for Norway; by IDG Sweden Books for Sweden; by Woodslane Pty. Ltd. for Australia; by Woodslane Enterprises Ltd. for New Zealand; by Longman Singapore Publishers Ltd. for Singapore, Malaysia, Thailand, and Indonesia; by Simron Pty. Ltd. for South Africa; by Toppan Company Ltd. for Japan; by Distribuidora Cuspide for Argentina; by Livraria Cultura for Brazil; by Ediciencia S.A. for Ecuador; by Addison-Wesley Publishing Company for Korea; by Ediciones ZETA S.C.R. Ltda. for Peru; by WS Computer Publishing Corporation, Inc., for the Philippines; by Unalis Corporation for Taiwan; by Contemporanea de Ediciones for Venezuela; by Computer Book & Magazine Store for Puerto Rico; by Express Computer Distributors for the Caribbean and West Indies. Authorized Sales Agent: Anthony Rudkin Associates for the Middle East and North Africa.

For general information on IDG Books Worldwide's books in the U.S., please call our Consumer Customer Service department at 800-762-2974. For reseller information, including discounts and premium sales, please call our Reseller Customer Service department at 800-434-3422.

For information on where to purchase IDG Books Worldwide's books outside the U.S., please contact our International Sales department at 415-655-3200 or fax 415-655-3295.

For information on foreign language translations, please contact our Foreign & Subsidiary Rights department at 415-655-3021 or fax 415-655-3281.

For sales inquiries and special prices for bulk quantities, please contact our Sales department at 415-655-3200 or write to the address above.

For information on using IDG Books Worldwide's books in the classroom or for ordering examination copies, please contact our Educational Sales department at 800-434-2086 or fax 817-251-8174.

For press review copies, author interviews, or other publicity information, please contact our Public Relations department at 415-655-3000 or fax 415-655-3299.

For authorization to photocopy items for corporate, personal, or educational use, please contact Copyright Clearance Center, 222 Rosewood Drive, Danvers, MA 01923, or fax 508-750-4470.

About the Author

Paul Litwin is an internationally recognized author, speaker, programmer, and trainer. Paul is a senior consultant and principal at MCW Technologies focusing on application development and mentoring services for Microsoft Access, Visual Basic, Microsoft Office, SQL Server, and Internet technologies.

He and his cohorts at MCW Technologies were responsible for creating the Visual InterDev Wizards and the Access 97 Upsizing Tools under contract for Microsoft.

Paul has written numerous articles for publications, including *Smart Access, Visual Basic Programmer's Journal,* and *PC World.* He also wrote the Jet Engine White Paper for Microsoft. Paul authored *VBA For Dummies Quick Reference* and has coauthored several books on Microsoft Access. He trains developers for Application Developers Training Company and is a regular speaker at conferences, including Tech*Ed, Windows Solutions, and Access Advisor DevCon. Paul is also a Microsoft Access MVP (Most Valuable Professional) specializing in helping users with Access and Internet integration problems.

In what little spare time he has, Paul enjoys spending time with his family and running.

Reach him at plitwin@mcwtech.com or www.mcwtech.com.

ABOUT IDG BOOKS WORLDWIDE

Welcome to the world of IDG Books Worldwide.

IDG Books Worldwide, Inc., is a subsidiary of International Data Group, the world's largest publisher of computer-related information and the leading global provider of information services on information technology. IDG was founded more than 25 years ago and now employs more than 8,500 people worldwide. IDG publishes more than 275 computer publications in over 75 countries (see listing below). More than 60 million people read one or more IDG publications each month.

Launched in 1990, IDG Books Worldwide is today the #1 publisher of best-selling computer books in the United States. We are proud to have received eight awards from the Computer Press Association in recognition of editorial excellence and three from *Computer Currents'* First Annual Readers' Choice Awards. Our best-selling ...*For Dummies*® series has more than 30 million copies in print with translations in 30 languages. IDG Books Worldwide, through a joint venture with IDG's Hi-Tech Beijing, became the first U.S. publisher to publish a computer book in the People's Republic of China. In record time, IDG Books Worldwide has become the first choice for millions of readers around the world who want to learn how to better manage their businesses.

Our mission is simple: Every one of our books is designed to bring extra value and skill-building instructions to the reader. Our books are written by experts who understand and care about our readers. The knowledge base of our editorial staff comes from years of experience in publishing, education, and journalism — experience we use to produce books for the '90s. In short, we care about books, so we attract the best people. We devote special attention to details such as audience, interior design, use of icons, and illustrations. And because we use an efficient process of authoring, editing, and desktop publishing our books electronically, we can spend more time ensuring superior content and spend less time on the technicalities of making books.

You can count on our commitment to deliver high-quality books at competitive prices on topics you want to read about. At IDG Books Worldwide, we continue in the IDG tradition of delivering quality for more than 25 years. You'll find no better book on a subject than one from IDG Books Worldwide.

John Kilcullen
CEO
IDG Books Worldwide, Inc.

Steven Berkowitz
President and Publisher
IDG Books Worldwide, Inc.

WINNER

Eighth Annual
Computer Press
Awards ≥1992

WINNER

Ninth Annual
Computer Press
Awards ≥1993

WINNER

Tenth Annual
Computer Press
Awards ≥1994

WINNER

Eleventh Annual
Computer Press
Awards ≥1995

Dedication

For Alicia and Geoff.

Author's Acknowledgments

Neil Charney and David Lazar at Microsoft probably don't realize it, but by inviting me to speak at the 1997 Tech*Ed conference in Orlando, Florida, on the topic of Access and the Internet, they were ultimately responsible for the sequence of events that became this book. Thanks, guys.

I'd like to thank the many fine people at IDG Books who helped make this book a reality, particularly my acquisitions editor, Jill Pisoni, my ever-helpful project editor, Kelly Ewing, and my copy editor, Patricia Yuu Pan.

My sincere thanks to David Shank, who improved the technical accuracy of the book immensely by his technical editing diligence. Thanks for helping me once again ship a great book, David.

I'd also like to thank the following Microsoft people: Michael Corning, Richard Dickinson, and James Sturms. At one time or another, they helped provide technical information or software for the book's CD-ROM.

A special thanks goes out to Richard Knudson and Stephen Forte. Although they may not realize this fact, they were both instrumental in furthering my knowledge of Internet technologies over the past couple of years.

Thanks always to my business associates and good friends at MCW Technologies: Mary Chipman, Ken Getz, Mike Gilbert, and Mike Gunderloy.

And I can't forget Rod Paddock, who saved my neck one September night in a New Jersey hotel when I couldn't get my modem to cooperate enough to upload the last few chapters of this book to the publisher. Thanks, Rod, for the use of one modem.

Of course, a very special thanks go to my personal support team, Alicia and Geoff. Once again, thanks for putting up with me in my crabbier moments when I was too focused on this book to be much of a husband or father. I'm back!

Publisher's Acknowledgments

We're proud of this book; please register your comments through our IDG Books Worldwide Online Registration Form located at http://my2cents.dummies.com.

Some of the people who helped bring this book to market include the following:

Acquisitions, Development, and Editorial

Project Editor: Kelly Ewing

Senior Acquisitions Editor: Jill Pisoni

Media Development Manager: Joyce Pepple

Permissions Editor: Heather H. Dismore

Copy Editor: Patricia Yuu Pan

Technical Editor: David Shank

Editorial Manager: Colleen Rainsberger

Editorial Assistant: Donna Love

Production

Associate Project Coordinator: Karen York

Layout and Graphics: Steve Arany, Lou Boudreau, Linda M. Boyer, J. Tyler Connor, Maridee V. Ennis, Angela F. Hunckler, Anna Rohrer, Brent Savage

Proofreaders: Sarah Fraser, Christine Berman, Kelli Botta, Nancy Price, Rebecca Senninger, Janet M. Withers

Indexer: Liz Cunningham

Special Help

Stephanie Koutek, Proof Editor
Access Technology

General and Administrative

IDG Books Worldwide, Inc.: John Kilcullen, CEO; Steven Berkowitz, President and Publisher

IDG Books Technology Publishing: Brenda McLaughlin, Senior Vice President and Group Publisher

Dummies Technology Press and Dummies Editorial: Diane Graves Steele, Vice President and Associate Publisher; Kristin A. Cocks, Editorial Director; Mary Bednarek, Acquisitions and Product Development Director

Dummies Trade Press: Kathleen A. Welton, Vice President and Publisher; Kevin Thornton, Acquisitions Manager

IDG Books Production for Dummies Press: Beth Jenkins, Production Director; Cindy L. Phipps, Manager of Project Coordination, Production Proofreading, and Indexing; Kathie S. Schutte, Supervisor of Page Layout; Shelley Lea, Supervisor of Graphics and Design; Debbie J. Gates, Production Systems Specialist; Robert Springer, Supervisor of Proofreading; Debbie Stailey, Special Projects Coordinator; Tony Augsburger, Supervisor of Reprints and Bluelines; Leslie Popplewell, Media Archive Coordinator

Dummies Packaging and Book Design: Patti Crane, Packaging Specialist; Lance Kayser, Packaging Assistant; Kavish + Kavish, Cover Design

♦

The publisher would like to give special thanks to Patrick J. McGovern, without whom this book would not have been possible.

♦

Contents at a Glance

Cartoons at a Glance

By Rich Tennant

"I DON'T GET IT. WE'VE MADE IT SMALLER, FASTER, AND LESS EXPENSIVE, AND IT STILL DOESN'T SELL! JEEZ, BOBBY, DON'T LEAN ON THE MOUSE LIKE THAT."

page 77

"OK, I'VE GOT THIS INTRANET THING DOWN. LIKE HERE— MY REPORT ON INVENTORY MANAGEMENT WILL INCLUDE A VIDEO CLIP FROM www.rottingmeat.com."

page 9

The name is bond.com, JAMES bond.com.

page 219

"OH, I'LL GET US IN — I USED TO RUN TECH SUPPORT AT AN INTERNET ACCESS COMPANY."

page 169

SEVERAL HOURS PASSED BEFORE WAYNE DISCOVERED THAT HE WAS LOOKING AT HIS SCREEN SAVER AND NOT OUT THE SUBMARINE'S PORTHOLE

"IT'S INCREDIBLE! I'M SEEING LIFE FORMS NEVER BEFORE IMAGINED!! BIZARRE, COLORFUL, ALMOST WHIMSICAL!!!"

page 313

"I think the cursor's not moving, Mr. Dunt, because you've got your hand on the chalk-board eraser and not the mouse."

page 105

"IT'S ANOTHER DEEP-SPACE PROBE FROM EARTH, SEEKING CONTACT FROM EXTRATERRESTRIALS. I WISH THEY'D JUST INCLUDE AN E-MAIL ADDRESS."

page 143

"Can someone please tell me how long 'Larry's Lunch Truck' has had his own page on the intranet?"

page 27

Fax: 508-546-7747 • *E-mail:* the5wave@tiac.net

Table of Contents

Part VI: Coding Active Server Pages 169

Chapter 12: Delving into Active Server Pages 171

Chapter 13: Activating Your Pages with ADO 183

Introduction

*W*elcome to the world of intranet and Web database publishing! The idea behind database publishing is simple: Information-hungry users want to be able to use a standard Web browser to view Web pages that draw data from databases such as Microsoft Access and SQL Server.

The problem has been that until recently, linking your databases to an intranet or the Internet was just too hard. If your eyes glaze over at the sound of words like CGI, Perl, and UNIX, fear not. Intranet and Web database publishing no longer require you to master these very *techie* technologies.

In this book, you find out how you can use standard and inexpensive Windows software to easily publish your data on either the World Wide Web or your corporate intranet. In the process, I try to keep the assumptions and buzzwords to a minimum, but I don't insulate you so much that you can't get any real work done.

Where and when it makes sense, this book concentrates on making the most of timesaving wizards that are part of Access 97, SQL Server, and Visual InterDev. This book doesn't stop where the wizards end, however. I also delve into the source code the wizards produce, showing you how to customize and extend the results.

About This Book

Think of this book as a friendly, approachable guide to taking data stored in databases and publishing it on the Web or your corporate intranet. This book concentrates on publishing using free or inexpensive software from Microsoft running on standard Windows-based personal computers. The book focuses on the following products:

- **Operating systems:** Windows 95 or Windows NT
- **Databases:** Microsoft Access 97 and Microsoft SQL Server
- **Web servers:** Microsoft Internet Information Server (for Windows NT Server), Peer Web Services (for Windows NT Workstation), and Personal Web Server (for Windows 95)
- **Web development tools:** Microsoft Visual InterDev
- **Web server technologies:** Internet Database Connector (IDC), Active Server Pages (ASP), and ActiveX Data Objects (ADO)

Fear not. You don't have to buy into the whole package hook, line, and sinker! For example, if your Web server is UNIX-based, you can still use the static HTML pages that the Access 97 and SQL Server Web publishing wizards produce. I cover all that in Part II. And much of the discussion in later parts of the book applies to any database for which you have an ODBC driver, so you're not limited to using Access or SQL Server. Finally, you don't have to own a copy of Visual InterDev to take advantage of many of the book's chapters.

This book isn't a survey, though, so you don't find a chapter on every possible way to publish data on the Web. You don't find coverage of non-Windows operating systems such as UNIX, OS/2, or the Macintosh. This book focuses primarily on the use of Microsoft products and technologies such as Access 97, SQL Server, Visual InterDev, IDC, and ASP.

I'm not saying that alternatives to the tools and databases presented in this book are necessarily bad choices. Many of these alternative products, such as Allaire's Cold Fusion, Borland's IntraBuilder, NetDynamic's NetDynamics, Visual Café for Java, and Netscape's LiveWire provide excellent Web database publishing solutions.

I chose to focus on primarily Microsoft-based solutions for several reasons. First, Windows 95 and Windows NT are very popular operating systems. More likely than not, you're using one of these operating systems rather than UNIX or a Macintosh. Second, you probably already own a copy of Access 97 because it's the world's most popular database. Third, the Microsoft Web browser and Web servers are free for the asking. And finally, SQL Server and Visual InterDev, although not free, are very competitively priced and rich in features. When you add it all up, Microsoft offers a compelling arsenal of products for database-based Web development at a very competitive price.

Conventions Used in This Book

This book includes code samples in the VBA, VBScript, JavaScipt, HTML, and IDC languages. All the code samples use the same basic convention: I have italicized the text wherever I have included placeholders for text you need to type. For example, in the following VBScript code sample, the recordset, source, activeconnection, cursortype, locktype, and options are placeholders for several arguments that you need to type:

```
recordset.Open source, activeconnection,
cursortype, locktype, options
```

I also use an arrow to indicate when you should choose menu commands consecutively. For example, when you see the command File⇨Save As, you should choose the File menu and then choose Save As from the menu that appears. The underlines in each command are hot keys — simply press Ctrl+F simultaneously, release, and then press Ctrl+A, and you've found a quick way to accomplish the same task.

Foolish Assumptions

To make this book a reasonable size, I had to make several assumptions about you, the esteemed reader. Besides being the most attractive person in the world, you:

✔ Use and are fairly comfortable with Windows 95 or Windows NT.

✔ Know how to use a Web browser.

✔ Have access to a company intranet or the World Wide Web.

✔ Have access to a Web server or are willing to install one on your desktop machine.

✔ Have some experience creating and querying databases in Microsoft Access or SQL Server, or some other SQL database, and have access to the data stored in one of these database products.

✔ Don't faint at the site of raw HTML or are at least willing to consult your handy HTML reference (such as *HTML For Dummies,* 3rd Edition, by Ed Tittel and Steve James, published by IDG Books Worldwide, Inc.) when you face an unfamiliar tag.

✔ Brush twice a day and floss regularly.

Note that you won't learn hypertext markup language (HTML) or how to use your database in this book. If you don't have at least a passing knowledge of HTML, go out and buy *HTML For Dummies,* by Ed Tittel and Steve James, published by IDG Books Worldwide, Inc. You also need to know how to create at least basic database objects such as tables and queries in Microsoft Access or your favorite server database. If you don't, you may want to pick up a book such as *Access 97 For Windows For Dummies,* by John Kaufeld, or *SQL Server 6.5 Secrets,* by David K. Rensin and Andrew M. Fedorchek. (Both books are published by IDG Books Worldwide, Inc.)

In addition, this book doesn't cover Internet commerce. Although I discuss how to publish a catalog, for example, I don't include coverage of how to bill credit cards or perform secure purchasing transactions.

Chapter 18 lists some alternatives to the software I cover in this book, along with contact information. I also list several commerce software solutions in that chapter.

How This Book Is Organized

I organized this book into eight parts, each of which comprises two or more chapters. There's no requirement that you read the book in chapter order. As much as possible, I've tried to make each chapter self-contained. However, the complexity of the text does, for the most part, increase as the page numbers increase, so readers with little experience in database publishing may want to read the book in chapter order. Those readers with experience in Web page design or database publishing can feel free to skip around, though. Anytime a chapter topic builds on earlier material, I include a cross-reference to the earlier information so that you can jump back to that section if you feel you're suddenly in over your head.

Without further ado, here's a brief description of the eight parts.

Part I: Building Better Intranets and Web Sites

This part begins with an overview of the Internet, intranets, HTML, and Web technologies. Part I also explains the difference between server-side and client-side processing and outlines common extensions to HTML, such as CGI, Java, IDC, ASP, and ActiveX. Finally, this part discusses how to choose a Web server and how to acquire and configure a Microsoft Web server.

Part II: And You Thought Web Publishing Was Hard

Part II proves that Web database publishing is quite easy, thanks to the Web publishing wizard built into Microsoft Access 97. In the chapters in this part, you discover how to use the Access Publish to the Web Wizard to publish Access tables, queries, and reports to the static HTML format. You also figure out how to modify the HTML produced by the wizard, how to post your pages to a Web server, and how to automate the publishing process.

Part III: What About SQL Server Data?

Not to be outdone by Access 97, SQL Server 6.5 also ships with a Web publishing wizard of its own called the SQL Server Web Assistant. This part introduces you to the SQL Server Web Publishing Assistant and shows you how to generate Web pages from SQL Server tables, views, and stored procedures. You also explore using the advanced scheduling capabilities built into the Web Assistant to publish Web pages at either a regular interval or when data in the underlying SQL Server tables changes.

Part IV: Getting Dynamic with the Internet Database Connector

In Part IV, you create dynamic Web pages using the Internet Database Connector (IDC). Using IDC technology, you can create pages linked to live Access and SQL Server databases. This part starts out showing you how to create IDC-enabled pages using the Access Publish to the Web Wizard. You also create IDC-enabled pages, by hand, that query and update data stored in Access and SQL Server databases.

Part V: The Future Is Here: Active Server Pages

As good as the IDC technology is, it can only take you so far. The newest Microsoft server-side technology, Active Server Pages (ASP), lets you build even more powerful and full-featured Web sites. In this part's chapters, you find out how to publish Access tables and queries to the ASP format. You also discover how to use the Access Publish to the Web Wizard to publish forms that can update records in Access databases.

Part VI: Coding Active Server Pages

The chapters in this part dispense with the Access wizard and show you how to create Active Server Pages by hand. In these chapters, you find out how ASP and the interrelated ActiveX Data Objects (ADO) work. In addition, you explore using VBScript (and a little JavaScript) to create dynamic, server-side scripts that read and write records to your Access, SQL Server, and other Open Database Connectivity (ODBC) compliant databases.

Part VII: A Virtual Web Publishing Studio: Visual InterDev

In Part VII, I introduce an amazing Web publishing tool, Visual InterDev. Using Visual InterDev and its wizards, you create live database forms with more functionality than the forms produced by the Access Publish to the

Web Wizard. This part also explores using the Visual InterDev Query Designer and design-time ActiveX controls. The final chapter in this part shows you how to use Active Server objects to store Web application-wide data, interact with HTML forms, read and write cookies, and execute ActiveX Automation servers.

Part VIII: The Part of Tens

All *...For Dummies* books conclude with several short chapters that each include a list of ten items. This book is no exception. The lists in this Part of Tens tackle subjects such as the ten things to consider when choosing the right mix of publishing software (including a discussion of alternatives to the software discussed in the book), the ten most common things that can go wrong with dynamic database publishing and how to fix them, and the ten most frequently asked questions about Visual InterDev.

Icons Used in this Book

Here and there in the text you may run into some icons. No, I'm not talking about little pieces of religious art — these icons are little, goofy-looking pictures that I've inserted to help keep the non-coffee drinkers awake. Here are some of the icons you may run across:

You find this icon next to a part of a chapter that may be especially technical. Less battle-tested readers may want to skip over these sections on the first reading. On the other hand, those readers who love the gory details may want to home in on this cute little icon.

This icon signifies a special tidbit of information that may just save you a ton of time. Then again, you may already know the tip.

You find this icon next to a piece of advice to which I want you to pay close attention. So slow down a second when you see this icon.

This icon marks things to watch out for that can cause great harm to your code, computer, or love life.

This icon alerts you to an example or some delectable software program that you can find on the CD that accompanies this book. So grab that CD and toss it gently into your CD-ROM drive when you see this icon.

What's On the CD?

The CD that comes with this book contains all the examples you find in the book plus several other goodies. Here's a sampling:

- ✔ The sample Meals databases in two flavors: Access 97 and SQL Server 6.5

- ✔ Internet Explorer 4.0, the latest version of Microsoft's popular Web browser

- ✔ The Microsoft Access Upsizing Tools, an Access 97 add-in for moving your data to SQL Server

- ✔ A sample ActiveX server written in Visual Basic 5.0 for making mortgage payment calculations, complete with source code

See the About the CD appendix for more details and information on how to install the software found on the CD.

Where to Go from Here

Intranet & Web Databases For Dummies can only get you started. You have to load the software discussed in these pages and get your feet wet. If you want, you can start with the examples you find in the book, but by all means don't stop there. And don't be afraid to make some mistakes. As the saying goes, practice makes perfect, but also be aware that the Internet can be a big *time-sink*. (That's technospeak for something that can eat up a lot of your time without your knowing it.) So don't forget to come up for air every so often.

For those who are looking to go even further, you can find some leads in Chapter 18. Don't forget, too, that the Internet itself is a great source of additional information on the Internet and intranets. So fire up your favorite Web browser, point it to your favorite search engine, and query away. And remember that Internet search engines are really just huge and powerful databases.

Have fun!

Part I
Building Better Intranets and Web Sites

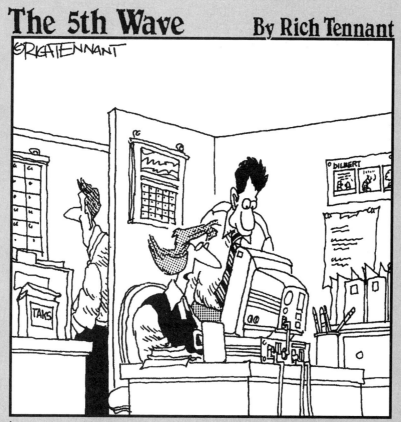

The 5th Wave — By Rich Tennant

"OK, I'VE GOT THIS INTRANET THING DOWN. LIKE HERE— MY REPORT ON INVENTORY MANAGEMENT WILL INCLUDE A VIDEO CLIP FROM www.rottingmeat.com."

In this part . . .

Corporate intranet sites and the World Wide Web are full of mostly static Web pages that display dead information. These dead pages require considerable work to keep up-to-date. At the same time, corporate databases are full of underutilized information waiting to be made available to the masses. What if you could generate Web pages from all that untapped data, killing two birds with one, so to speak, stone? You can, thanks to a proverbial stone called *database publishing*.

Chapter 1 starts the database publishing ball rolling with a look at the issues. The chapter begins with a brief definition of terms followed by a discussion of the differences between static and dynamic content. Chapter 2 focuses on a key piece to any intranet or Web publishing solution: the Web server. Here, you find information on the various Web servers out there, with an emphasis on how to acquire and set up one of the free Web servers from Microsoft.

Chapter 1

Clients, Servers, and Browsers in All Their Glory

In This Chapter

▶ Understanding how the Web works

▶ Using database publishing to help create Web pages

▶ Exploring server-side extensions to HTML

*T*he World Wide Web and private, intranet-based Webs consist of millions of Web pages. Many of these pages, however, are out of date because of the labor needed to update the content. Even if the pages are current, many of these same pages, while perhaps visually appealing (after all, you know where most of the time and money go), have marginal value.

At the same time, many corporations are sitting on megabytes or gigabytes of useful information that remain inaccessible to many potential information consumers (users).

Database publishing may solve both problems because it can help you create information-rich Web pages that are accessible to any user equipped with a Web browser. Corporations can take this useful but inaccessible information and turn it into Web pages that users can easily search, navigate, view, and, in some cases, even update from their familiar Web browsers.

In this chapter, I lay the groundwork for the rest of the book, beginning with a brief explanation of how HTML and the Web work. I also discuss the common extensions to HTML and where database publishing fits into this puzzle. If you're already familiar with these basics, feel free to skip this chapter.

How the Web Works

The World Wide Web and private intranet-based Webs are *client/server systems.* This means that tasks are divided between a *client application* (a Web browser) and a *server application* (a Web server). An *Internet or intranet connection* links the client and server applications, which speak a common language and use standard protocols. (A protocol is just an agreed upon set of conventions for communicating.)

Terminology Primer

The world of the Internet and intranets contains a lot of fairly new terms. Here's a primer for those readers who may be a little behind the current terminology. Feel free, of course, to skip those terms that you already know.

- **Internet:** The Internet is a public global network of millions of computers tied together using the Transmission Control Protocol/Internet Protocol (TCP/IP) and related protocols. Unlike most private networks, no company owns or controls the Internet. The Internet consists of lots of parts, with each part using a different set of protocols to communicate. These parts include e-mail, gopher sites, ftp sites, Usenet newsgroups, and relay chats. The most exciting and popular part of the Internet, however, is the World Wide Web.

- **World Wide Web:** The World Wide Web (or simply the Web) is the graphical, multimedia side of the Internet that you can explore by using a Web browser.

- **Intranet:** An intranet is a private, corporate network that uses Internet protocols, conventions, and software, but which is not directly accessible from the Internet. Many corporations have gateways that connect private intranets to the public Internet through firewalls that attempt to prevent unwelcome users from gaining access to the private intranet content. Although the World Wide Web is a part of the public Internet, most intranets have private Web sites that users can access using Web browsers.

- **Extranet:** An extranet is a collaborative network that links multiple intranets. For example, an extranet may link the intranets of a producer and a supplier. The intranets may link across the Internet (using a security protocol) or through privately owned or leased lines.

- **HTML:** Hypertext markup language (HTML) is the language of the Web. Web pages are created using this simple language that consists of text and tags that Web page designers use to control the formatting, placement, and behavior of the text.

- **HTTP:** Hypertext transfer protocol (HTTP) is the high-level protocol (sitting on top of the low-level TCP/IP protocol) that Web browsers and servers use to pass Web pages between them.

- **Web browser:** The Web browser sits on the client machine sending HTTP requests for Web pages to the Web server over the network and displaying the requested HTML pages when received. The Web browser can also work in a client-only mode to display local HTML documents stored on the client.

✔ **Web server:** The Web server is responsible for processing HTTP requests for HTML pages. When the Web server receives a request for a page, it locates the page on the server and then passes the page back to the client again using the HTTP protocol.

Internet Web servers — especially those servers serving popular Web sites — must be ready to process a potentially large number of simultaneous requests. Intranet Web servers, on the other hand, usually serve far fewer requests for Web pages. Web servers run on a variety of operating systems, including UNIX, Windows NT, Windows 95, OS/2, and the Macintosh operating system.

How the parts work together

When you enter a *uniform resource locator* (*URL*) address into the address box of your browser or click a hyperlink, the following sequence of steps, shown in Figure 1-1, occurs:

1. **The Web browser sends an HTTP request over the Internet (or intranet) to the Web server named in the first part of the URL.**

   For example, if the URL is `http://anysite.com/anypage.html`, the server name is anysite.com.

2. **The Web server reads the specific HTML page named in the second part of the URL.**

   The specific page for the example in Step 1 is anypage.html.

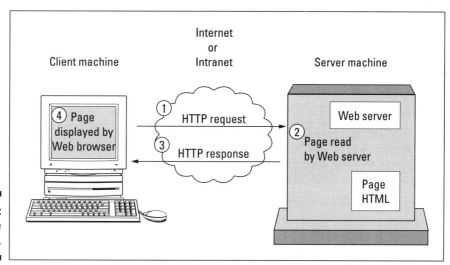

Figure 1-1:
How the
Web works.

3. **The Web server sends the requested HTML page across the network using the HTTP protocol to the Web browser client machine.**

4. **The Web browser displays the received HTML page to the user.**

Static versus Dynamic Web Pages

The sequence of steps from the preceding section describes how the Web works when the content involves only *static* HTML. The content is static because all the content of these Web pages gets determined at page design time, and that content never changes until the people who created the pages change them. With *dynamic* content, a customized page of HTML is created on demand using a template or script that is run when the page is requested.

Static content

Today, the majority of Web pages are static. Static HTML is easy to create because the language, HTML, is universal and simple. The Web server has little trouble serving up static Web pages quickly and efficiently. In addition, you can easily transfer Web pages created on one platform to a different platform. For example, a page created on a Windows 95 desktop machine moves to a Sun Microsystems server running the UNIX operating system without a problem.

Sound familiar?

Interestingly, the Web sounds remarkably similar to what happens in a classic client/ server database system when you click the next record button in many client applications.

1. **The client application interprets the button click as a request for a specific record and sends the request as a Structured Query Language (SQL) string across a local area network to the server database engine.**

2. **The database server executes the SQL on the server.**

3. **The database server returns the resulting records over the network to the client.**

4. **The client displays those records to the user.**

Perhaps the world of the Web isn't so new after all.

The major problem with static content is the need to keep it up to date and relevant. Fortunately, database publishing can help ease the burden of generating the static Web pages. The publishing wizards that ship with Access 97 and SQL Server 6.5 make it easy for you to generate and regenerate static Web pages based on database queries and reports. Figure 1-2 shows a Web page produced with the Access Publish to the Web Wizard, which has converted an Access report into an HTML page. For more detail on this form of static publishing, take a look at Parts II and III of this book.

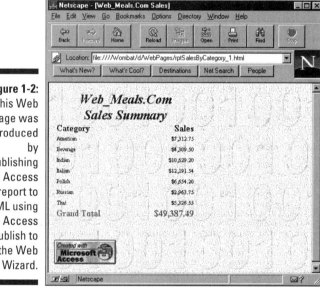

Figure 1-2: This Web page was produced by publishing an Access report to HTML using the Access Publish to the Web Wizard.

Dynamic content

Being able to generate Web pages from database records by using static technology is great, but dynamic content comes out ahead in multiple ways:

- ✔ The Web page is linked to the database and created automatically by a database query at the time the page is requested by the user.

- ✔ Users get to request customized pages that return just the records they want rather than having to scan through lots of irrelevant static pages in the hopes of coming across the records they were searching for.

- ✔ Users can update the data using their Web browser.

Dynamic content comes in two flavors: server-side and client-side extensions.

Server-side extensions

You can find two general types of server-side programs: Common Gateway Interface (CGI) programs and proprietary application programming interface (API) programs.

- ✔ **CGI applications:** Most Web servers support the ability to call CGI programs from a Web page. The CGI specification allows parameters to pass back and forth between the Web server and a script or program that runs on the server. While CGI support is widespread, CGI applications tend to run slowly and are not well integrated with Web servers.

- ✔ **ISAPI applications:** Microsoft and other vendors have come out with programming interfaces that integrate more tightly with their Web servers. In this book, you explore several Internet Server Application Programming Interface (ISAPI) programs that work with Microsoft Internet Information Server and other Microsoft Web servers.

  In Part IV, you take a look at the first ISAPI application: the Internet Database Connector (IDC). The IDC does one thing and does it well: The IDC enables you to link your Web pages to databases supporting the Open Database Connectivity (ODBC) standard (see Figure 1-3).

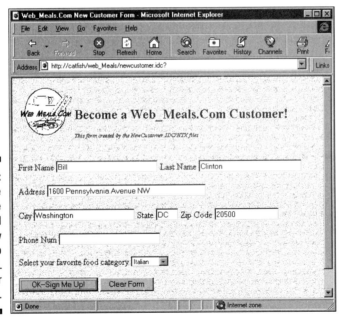

Figure 1-3:
This page uses the IDC to add new records to an SQL Server table.

In Parts V through VII, you explore another ISAPI application: Active
Server Pages (ASP). Although more difficult to create than IDC pages,
ASP pages support complex database processing, as well as interaction
with nondatabase programs. In Part V, you find out how to use the
Access Publish to the Web Wizard to create ASP forms you can use
to view and update data stored in Access databases (see Figure 1-4).
In Parts VII and VIII, you discover how to use an exciting new develop-
ment tool, Visual InterDev, to create more advanced, full-featured
ASP pages (see Figure 1-5).

Figure 1-4:
The Access
Publish to
the Web
Wizard
produced
this ASP
Web page
that you
can use to
browse and
update
records
in an
Access 97
database.

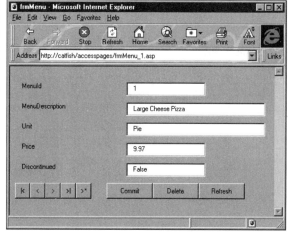

Figure 1-5:
The Visual
InterDev
Data Form
Wizard
produced
this ASP
Web page
that you can
use to
browse and
update
records in
an SQL
Server
database.

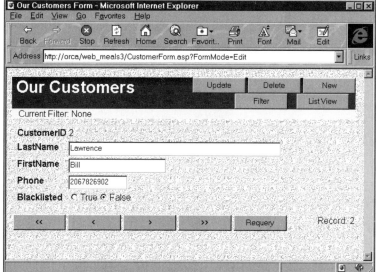

In most cases, the Web pages that server-side programs produce are pure HTML and therefore can be displayed using any Web browser. This flexibility is possible because all the database processing, or other processing, occurs completely on the server. Exception: The forms produced by the Access Publish to the Web Wizard can be used only with Internet Explorer because of their use of the HTML Layout Control and client-side VBScript code.

Client-side extensions

The HTML passed back to your Web browser may contain more than HTML. Some examples of client-side HTML extensions include Java applets, ActiveX controls, Dynamic HTML, and scripting languages such as JavaScript and VBScript.

While client-side HTML extensions don't work with all browsers, they can make for more exciting and interactive pages. For example, a client-side ActiveX control may play background music or a Java applet may produce dazzling special effects. Because people do most database publishing on the server side, however, this book doesn't cover client-side processing in great detail.

Chapter 2

Setting Up Your Microsoft Web Server

● ●

In This Chapter

▶ Downloading Microsoft Web servers for free

▶ Understanding the differences between the various Microsoft Web servers

▶ Creating virtual Web directories

▶ Assigning the right security settings

● ●

*O*ne of the first tasks you need to do when developing Web database applications is to select, install, and configure a Web server. This book focuses on the use of Microsoft technologies, so don't be surprised that this chapter concentrates on Microsoft Web servers. In this chapter, you find out how to select the right Microsoft Web server and how to configure it for database publishing. This chapter also offers a discussion of non-Microsoft alternatives.

Choosing a Microsoft Web Server

Using a Microsoft Web server is a lot like a good news/bad news joke. The good news is that all the servers are free. The bad news is that you have so many servers to choose from that deciding on the best one for you may be hard. Don't worry — the next few sections help you decide.

Why are Microsoft Web servers different?

Besides being free, the major distinction between Microsoft Web servers and other Web servers is the Microsoft servers' support for the Internet Server Application Programming Interface (ISAPI). This low-level programming interface allows for the creation of programs that integrate tightly with the Web server, creating dynamic applications that are both feature-rich and efficient.

Both Microsoft technologies for creating dynamic Web pages — the Internet Database Connector (IDC) and Active Server Pages (ASP) — are ISAPI applications. (See Chapter 1 for more details on ISAPI, IDC, and ASP.)

So many servers, so little time

Microsoft has created numerous versions of Web servers (also known as *Internet servers*) for several different platforms, including Windows 95, Windows NT Workstation, Windows NT Server, and the Macintosh.

All the different Web servers, however, boil down to two basic classes:

✔ Internet class servers

✔ Intranet class servers

A summary of the various Microsoft Web server products appears in Table 2-1.

Table 2-1	Microsoft Internet Servers		
Server Class	*Operating System*	*Product Name*	*Product Versions*
Internet	Windows NT Server 4.0	Internet Information Server	1.0, 2.0, 3.0, and 4.0
Intranet	Windows NT Workstation 4.0	Peer Web Services/Personal Web Server*	2.0, 3.0, 4.0
Intranet	Windows 95	Personal Web Server	1.0, 4.0
Intranet	Macintosh OS	Personal Web Server	1.0, 4.0

*Microsoft renamed Peer Web Services for Windows NT Workstation to Personal Web Server for Version 4.0.

Which one is right for me?

Which Microsoft Web server you choose revolves around one central question, "Which class of server do you need?" The answer to this question revolves around the Web site traffic that you expect.

✔ If you host your Web site on an intranet with a low level of traffic (ten or fewer simultaneous connections), you have several choices. You can use Peer Web Services or Personal Web Server running on Windows NT Workstation, Windows 95, or a Macintosh.

✔ If you plan to host your Web site on the Internet or on a moderately busy intranet (more than ten simultaneous connections), then you need to use Internet Information Server (IIS). IIS runs only on Windows NT Server.

The decision is that simple.

The Microsoft licenses for Peer Web Services and Personal Web Server specify no more than ten simultaneous connections.

How about the Web server version?

The later the product's version number, the more features it supports. You can host Web sites made up of only static Web content with any of the Web server versions listed in Table 2-1.

If you want to host Web sites using dynamic content, keep in mind the following:

✔ If you want Internet Database Connector (IDC) support, you can't use IIS Version 1.0. Any other version of Web server will do, however.

✔ If you want Active Server Pages (ASP) support, you need IIS Version 3.0 or greater, Peer Web Services 3.0, or Personal Web Server 1.0 or greater. (If you use Personal Web Server 1.0, however, you need to separately download and install ASP support because the Personal Web Server 1.0 setup files don't include ASP support.)

What about Microsoft Commerce Server?

Microsoft Commerce Server is a component of the Enterprise Edition of Microsoft Site Server that was developed for the deployment of Internet stores. An Internet store (or commerce Web site) is a Web site that must handle online purchasing of goods using secure credit card transactions.

As you may guess, *this* Microsoft Web server package doesn't come free. Microsoft Site Server 2.0, Enterprise Edition costs $4,999 for the first domain (distinct Web site) and $499 for each additional domain. Wow — that's quite a bit different than the price of the other Microsoft Web servers.

Implementing Your Microsoft Web Server

Acquiring, installing and configuring a Microsoft Web server is pretty painless. The next few sections discuss the details.

Acquiring Microsoft Web servers

You can wrestle yourself up a copy of one of the Microsoft Web server products in a few different ways. Some of the possibilities include

- ✔ Microsoft NT Workstation 4.0 comes with Peer Web Services 2.0.
- ✔ Microsoft NT Server 4.0 comes with Internet Information Server 2.0.
- ✔ The CD-ROM versions of NT Service Packs 2 and 3 both come with Peer Web Services 3.0 and Internet Information Server 3.0. Later service packs may ship with Personal Web Server 4.0 and IIS 4.0.
- ✔ All the current versions of the Web servers are available for download from the Microsoft download site at `www.microsoft.com/msdownload`.

All the preceding Web servers are free, with no strings attached.

Installing Microsoft Web servers

To install a Microsoft Web server, run the appropriate install program that comes with the Web server. Each version of each product has a slightly different install program, but locating and running the program shouldn't be a problem.

Setting up virtual directories

Before you can host Web pages on your Web server, you have to have a place to put them. Web pages go into Web directories, also known as *virtual directories*.

Creating a Web directory entails different steps for each of the various versions of Microsoft Web servers. However, I list the general steps here (for Windows platforms):

1. **Using Windows 95 or Windows NT Explorer, create a new physical directory (also called a folder) on your Web server machine.**

   Create the new directory below the `\InetPub\wwwroot` directory of your server.

2. **Using your Web server's management program, create a new virtual directory that points to the physical directory you created in Step 1.**

Most versions of Microsoft Web servers include a management program called Internet Service Manager that you can use to create the virtual directory. For example, in Figure 2-1, you can see how to create a new Web virtual directory using Version 3.0 of the IIS Internet Service Manager program. IIS 4.0 includes a wizard that walks you through the virtual-directory-creation process (see Figure 2-2).

On some versions of Personal Web Server, however, the main Web server management program is called Personal Web Manager. In these cases, you must create a new virtual directory using the Personal Web Server Version 4.0 Personal Web Manager program, as shown in Figure 2-3.

When creating a new virtual Web directory, you must set the access permissions to the settings appropriate for your application. Take a look at the section "Setting permissions" later in this chapter.

If you're using Visual InterDev to manage your Web site, you don't need to perform any of these steps. Instead, use the Web Project Wizard to create a new Web project. The wizard creates the virtual Web directory for you and even sets the appropriate permissions on the directory. Cool!

Figure 2-1:
Creating a new virtual Web directory using Internet Service Manager Version 3.0.

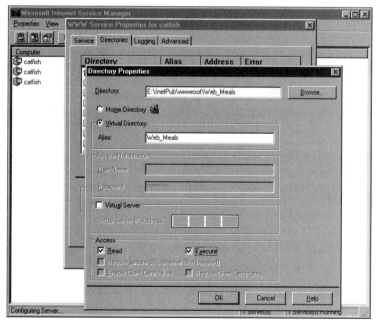

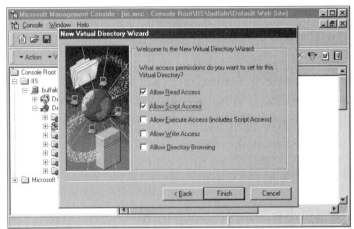

Figure 2-2:
Creating a
new virtual
Web
directory
using the
New Virtual
Directory
Wizard
that's part
of Internet
Service
Manager
Version 4.0.

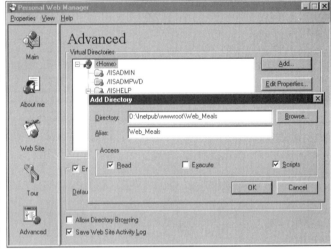

Figure 2-3:
Creating a
new virtual
Web
directory
using
Personal
Web
Manager
Version 4.0.

Setting permissions

Setting the correct level of access permissions for your virtual directories is critical to running a secure yet functional Web server. To minimize security problems, always set the security level to the minimum level needed to run your applications, never higher.

You can set several virtual directory access permissions for the anonymous Web user using your Web server management program. You can set all these permissions to either true (checked) or false (unchecked):

✔ **Read:** Enables Web clients to read or download files.

✔ **Script:** Enables Web clients to execute scripts using a script engine such as ASP or IDC. (This permission is not available on some versions of Microsoft Web servers; in these cases, you must use the Execute permission instead.)

✔ **Execute:** Enables Web clients to execute any application, including script engines and .DLL and .EXE files.

✔ **Write:** Enables Web clients to upload files or to modify files.

In the vast majority of cases, you don't ever want to assign the Write permission for the anonymous Web user. If you assign this permission to the anonymous Web user, hackers can bring down your Web site or steal your intellectual property. Assigning the Write permission is kind of like handing a lit match to visitors of your gun powder factory.

The appropriate security settings you choose for a virtual directory depend on the nature of the content that the directory may hold. Take a look at the following guidelines:

✔ If the virtual directory holds nothing but static content, assign Read access, and nothing more.

✔ If the virtual directory holds IDC or ASP files, assign Read and Script access. (In some versions of Microsoft Web servers, there is no Script access; in these cases, you must instead assign Execute access for the directory.)

✔ If the virtual directory holds executable files that your application needs to run, assign Read and Execute access.

In addition to the access permissions you can assign to virtual directories using your Web management program, you can assign permissions to individual Web directory files if the files are located on a Windows NT File System (NTFS) disk drive. If you need this additional level of security, you can assign these permissions to the anonymous user account created by your Web server installation using Windows NT Explorer. By default, this account is named IUSR_*computername*. For example, if your server name is Catfish, then the anonymous account is IUSR_Catfish.

Other Web Servers

Although this book focuses on Microsoft servers, primarily because they are free and work best with Microsoft's Web development tools, you do have other options.

IIS-compatible servers

At least two vendors produce Web servers or Web server add-ons that are compatible with Microsoft Web servers.

WebSite Professional 2.0, a Web server from O'Reilly and Associates, includes support for Active Server Pages and other ISAPI applications. You can find out more information about WebSite Professional at www.ora.com.

ChiliSoft sells an ASP clone called Chili!ASP that works with Netscape Web servers running under Windows NT and Lotus Go Web server. O'Reilly, IBM, and Oracle Web Server versions, as well as UNIX versions, were under development as this book went to press. Versions for these servers may be available now. In addition, Chili!ASP works with Visual InterDev. For more information, set your Web browser to www.chilisoft.net.

If you're wondering what Microsoft thinks of this ASP clone, I can tell you this much: Microsoft includes a link to the Chili!ASP Web page from its Site Builder Network Downloads page.

Noncompatible servers

For one reason or another, you may want (or are required) to use a non-Microsoft server that doesn't support ISAPI. If this is the case, you can still use any of the *static* pages that the Access Publish to the Web Wizard or the SQL Server Web Assistant produces, but you cannot use any of the *dynamic* content produced by the Access wizard or Visual InterDev. Sorry.

Part II
And You Thought Web Publishing Was Hard

The 5th Wave   By Rich Tennant

"Can someone please tell me how long 'Larry's Lunch Truck' has had his own page on the intranet?"

In this part . . .

*W*ith the introduction of Access 97, publishing data to a corporate intranet or the World Wide Web has gotten a heck of a lot easier. In Chapter 3, you find out how to use the Publish to the Web Wizard to convert data from your Access tables and queries into static HTML pages. Chapter 4 shows you how to spiff up things a bit by publishing formatted reports and using HTML templates. Finally, in Chapter 5, you discover how to use publication profiles, the Web Publishing Wizard, file-transfer protocol, and a little VBA code to automate the publishing process.

Chapter 3

A Wizard after Your Own Heart

*W*hen Microsoft released Microsoft Access 1.0 back in 1992, it created a new type of programming aid that the company affectionately called a "wizard." Back then, the Access wizards created pretty rudimentary forms and reports, and — I don't want to have to say it, but I'll be frank — were basically for neophytes. Since that time, however, wizards have matured into fairly sophisticated pieces of software. In addition, you no longer have to wear a disguise while using one for fear of being labeled a programming patsy.

Arguably, the most sophisticated and useful wizard in Access's long and distinguished history is that masterpiece, the Access Publish to the Web Wizard. This baby takes your familiar Access data — stored in the ever-popular MDB format — and converts it into living, breathing Web pages that are ready for hosting on your intranet or Internet Web server. Wow! In this chapter, I introduce you to this vast and wonderful wizard. (And you thought you had to be a rocket scientist to publish databases on the Web.)

Creating Your Web Page

Before you can hope to create Web pages using the Access Publish to the Web Wizard, you need to have open an Access 97 database that contains at least one table. After all, you can't publish data on the Web if you don't have any data. (That reminds me: What did the baby computer say when it got hurt? Answer: I want my *da-ta!*)

The Access Publish to the Web Wizard comes only with Access 97. If you are using an earlier version of Access, you need to upgrade to Access 97 before you can use this wizard.

Wizards 101

Microsoft wizards, with a few exceptions, pretty much all work the same way. Each wizard consists of a series of pages — sort of like an electronic book. You work your way through the pages by answering questions on the page and then clicking the Next button at the bottom of each page. When you reach the end of the wizard, you click the Finish button and the wizard goes off and does whatever it was meant to do. For example, the Access Publish to the Web Wizard creates Web pages based on data in your database.

You can always stop the wizard by clicking the Cancel button. The wizard quits, dropping you off where you began.

In the early pages of the wizard, the wizard disables the Finish button — this means that at least one mandatory page remains. When the Finish button is enabled, however, you can click it to complete the wizard, skipping any remaining but optional pages. At any time (after the first page), you can back up by clicking the Back button. Occasionally, a page also has an Advanced button — click this button to jump to a side page for viewing or entering advanced information.

To use the Access Publish to the Web Wizard, fire up Access and follow these steps:

1. **Open an Access database.**

   If you don't want to risk messing up one of your databases, then copy the Meals.Mdb database from the CD-ROM, which you can find in the back of this book, onto your hard disk. (It's also the database you see in the figures in this chapter.) The premise of the Meals database is simple: You're running a meal-delivery service for which you currently take orders over the phone. You'd like to add the ability to take orders over the Internet.

2. **Choose File⇨Save As HTML to start the wizard.**

   Because it's a wizard, you were probably thinking that you start the Access Publish to the Web Wizard by selecting Tools⇨Add-Ins from the menu. Good guess, but Microsoft thought it'd be more fun to hide the wizard under the File menu.

   Access responds by displaying the introductory page of the Publish to the Web Wizard, shown in Figure 3-1. On this page, the wizard introduces itself, explaining briefly what it does. You also get to view a neat graphic of a giant, reddish puzzle piece asteroid floating above planet Earth as seen from the moon. (And you thought this wasn't going to be fun.) Toward the bottom of the page, you see something about publication profiles that are likely grayed out. Don't worry about this part of the page for now — I cover it in Chapter 4.

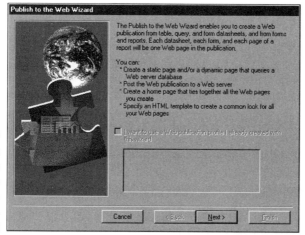

Figure 3-1:
Meet the
Publish to
the Web
Wizard.

3. **Click the Next button.**

   Page 2 appears, where you get to select one or more objects from the database to publish (see Figure 3-2).

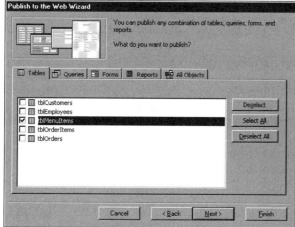

Figure 3-2:
On the
second
page of the
Publish to
the Web
Wizard, you
get to
select the
objects that
you'd like to
publish.

4. **Choose the item that you want to publish by clicking the check box next to its name.**

   If you want to start simple, choose any table. For this step, I chose a table from Meals.Mdb called tblMenuItems, which contains a list of menu items that I'd like to publish on the Web.

5. Click the Next button.

On the third page, you can optionally select an existing HTML document to serve as a template for the Web pages that the wizard creates (see Figure 3-3). You use a template to control how your pages look. For example, using a template, you can place a background image behind your published data. (I explain templates in more detail in Chapter 4.)

6. Click the Browse button to select one of the templates that are installed with Access and then click Select to return to page 3.

For the example, I selected the Gray.htm template file (see Figure 3-4).

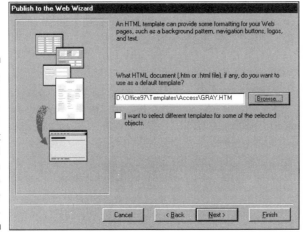

Figure 3-3:
On the third page of the wizard, you can select an optional publication template to spruce things up.

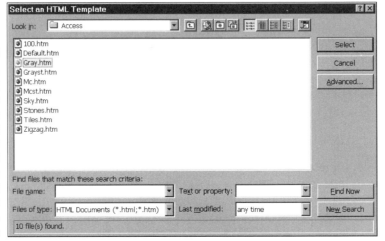

Figure 3-4.
When you hit the Browse button on page 3, you get a list of template files from which to choose.

7. Click Next.

On page 4 of the wizard, you face an important decision, namely, how the wizard publishes your data. You can choose from one of the following options (see Figure 3-5):

- **Static HTML:** This option has one major advantage over the other two formats — the pages that this format produces work with any Web server and any Web browser. You don't even need a Web server to take advantage of static HTML!

- **Dynamic Internet Database Connector (IDC) format:** This option creates Web pages that are linked to your Access database, but it requires you to use a Microsoft Web server. I discuss this option in Chapter 8.

- **Dynamic Active Server Pages (ASP) format:** This option also creates Web pages that are linked to your database, but includes the added capability of allowing you to update the database from the Web page. I discuss this option in Chapters 10 and 11.

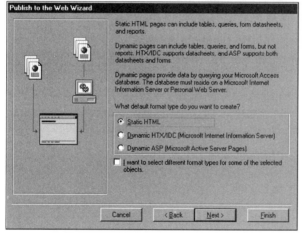

Figure 3-5: On this page of the wizard, you get to choose the Web publishing format for your pages.

8. Select Static HTML and click Next.

The Publish to Web Wizard is rather polite. Rather than putting the generated pages anywhere it feels like, the wizard asks you to specify a location on page 5. Initially, the wizard suggests that great Microsoft dumping ground on your hard drive, C:\My Documents. (On Windows NT systems, the wizard suggests a different but analogous folder.) Using C:\My Documents isn't a good idea because your Web pages get mixed in with anything else that happens to be lying around in the My Documents folder. (For those of you who aren't totally comfortable with the Windows 95/NT 4.0 technospeak, a *folder* is what used to be called a *subdirectory* in earlier versions of Windows.) You can redirect the well-meaning wizard anywhere you'd like. You can even tell the wizard to use the File Transfer Protocol (FTP) to send your pages to a remote Web server. (Chapter 5 discusses this option.)

I suggest creating a new folder and placing all your Web pages in this new folder. The wizard doesn't create the folder for you, so you need to start up Windows Explorer and create the new folder before you can select it from the wizard.

9. Enter the name of the folder into the folder text box, as shown in Figure 3-6.

For example, I specified the folder WebPages. (You can also click the Browse button to navigate to the folder.)

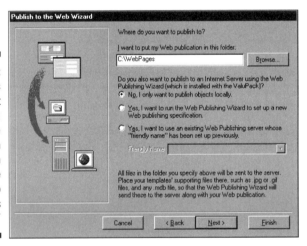

Figure 3-6:
Get this page right and you won't have to sing, "Oh where, oh where have my Web pages gone . . . ?"

You can skip the question about the Web Publishing Wizard. The default response, "No, I only want to publish objects locally" is just peachy.

10. Click Next.

On page 6, the wizard offers to create a home page that links to each of the pages you ask it to produce, as shown in Figure 3-7. In general, generating a home page with these links is a good idea for at least two reasons. First, the page name that the wizard chooses is based on the published object names, which may be long and cryptic. Second, when you publish to one of the dynamic formats, getting the hyperlink right can be tricky.

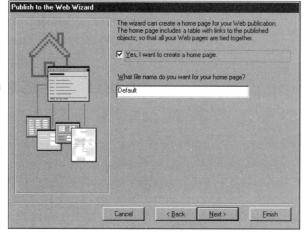

Figure 3-7:
Producing a
home page
makes it
easy to
hyperlink to
your Web
pages.

11. Click the Yes, I want to create a home page check box and then enter a name for the home page in the text box.

For now, the default name, Default, should be just fine.

12. Click the Next button to move to the final wizard page.

On this page, you can choose to save your answers to a Web publication profile (see Figure 3-8). I cover the profile stuff in detail in Chapter 4. For now, simply proceed to Step 13.

13. Click the Finish button.

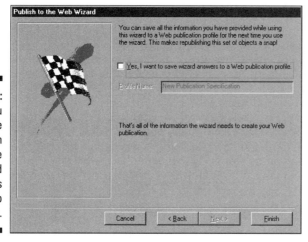

Figure 3-8:
When you
click the
Finish
button, the
wizard
creates
your Web
pages.

After clicking the Finish button, the wizard disappears and the cursor changes to an hourglass while the pages generate. Unless you've asked to create numerous Web pages or publish objects with lots of rows, the wizard creates them fairly quickly. Unlike some other wizards, the Publish to the Web Wizard doesn't confirm the generation of pages with a dialog box. The only way you know that it's done generating your pages is that the cursor changes to a regular selection cursor again. Once this happens, you're ready to try out the new pages.

Testing Your Page

After you run the Access Publish to the Web Wizard, you end up with one or more files in the folder you designated for saving Web pages. The number of files that you have depends on which options you chose while running the Wizard.

For example, I ended up with two files — Default.html and tblMenuItems_1.html — in my WebPages folder. My first file is the home page I opted for back on page 6 of the wizard. The second file is the actual page generated from the records in the tblMenuItems table of Meals.Mdb. As you can see, the wizard names the Web page by appending _1 to the end of the object name and giving it an extension of .html.

No matter how many files you end up with, you still need to do a few other things before you can view your Web pages using your browser.

One more thing . . .

If you chose to use a template back on page 3 of the wizard, you have to perform one additional step. (If you didn't, you can skip to the next section.) You need to copy any GIF or JPG files referenced in the template. If you don't copy the files, the background and Access logo don't appear on the page — hardly a fatal mistake, but you may as well go for the full effect.

You need to copy the files from the Access templates folder to the folder that contains your published Web pages. (The exact name of the Access templates folder varies, depending on where you installed Office. For example, if you installed Office in the C:\MSOffice folder, then you can find the files in the C:\MSOffice\Templates\Access folder.) "Which files?" you ask. Well, that depends on the chosen template. All the built-in templates require the Access JPG file (msaccess.jpg). In addition, for each template, there's a JPG file with the same root name as the template. For example, because I chose the gray.html template file, I need to copy the gray.jpg file. Thus, for the Web pages I generated, I need to copy these two files to my WebPages folder:

- ✔ gray.jpg
- ✔ msaccess.jpg

Preview time

It's time to relax and preview the results of your grueling session with the Access Publish to the Web Wizard. If you published your pages to the static HTML format, you can view the pages with any Web browser, whether or not you have a Web server handy. To bring up the wizard-produced home page, start your browser — any browser — and type the following into the Address or Location text box of the browser:

```
drive:\path\homepage.html
```

For example, if you told the wizard to place your Web pages in the C:\WebPages folder and requested a home page named default.html, you would enter the following:

```
C:\WebPages\default.html
```

If you use Microsoft Internet Explorer 4.0, your browser looks something like that shown in Figure 3-9.

Figure 3-9: This wizard-produced home page isn't anything to write home about, but click the hyperlink, and get whisked away to your dream page.

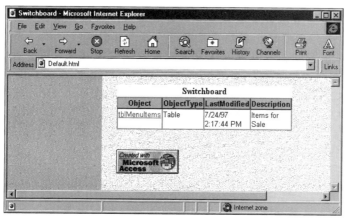

Now click the hyperlink on this page (in most browsers, the link appears underlined and in blue) and the published page appears in your browser. If you use IE 4.0, your screen looks similar to Figure 3-10. If you use IE 3.0, your screen matches Figure 3-11. If you prefer Netscape Navigator 3.0, your screen looks like the one shown in Figure 3-12.

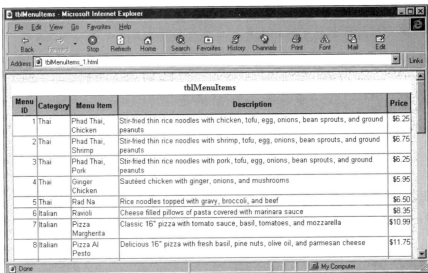

Figure 3-10: The product of your grueling session with the Publish to the Web Wizard as shown in version 4.0 of Microsoft Internet Explorer.

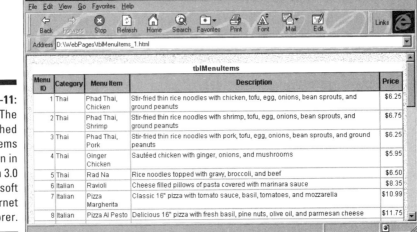

Figure 3-11: The published menu items as shown in version 3.0 of Microsoft Internet Explorer.

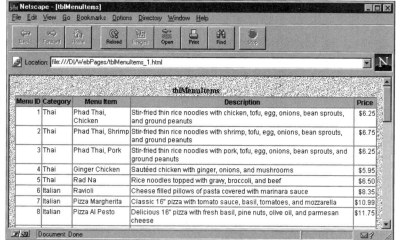

Figure 3-12:
The
published
menu items
as shown in
version 3.0
of Netscape
Navigator.

Digging into the Static HTML Pages Produced by the Wizard

When you choose to publish to the static HTML format, the wizard works pretty much like this: After noting your responses to its questions, the wizard reads the data from the table, query, form, or report you chose to publish, surrounds it with a bunch of HTML tags, and plugs it into an HTML document file. The HTML file the wizard produces is just regular old HTML.

Viewing the source

To view the source of the published data page, simply open the HTML file with Windows Notepad (or another editor). If you use Windows Notepad, the source HTML looks something like Figure 3-13.

Most browsers have a View Source menu command that you can use to view the HTML source code for any Web page. In Internet Explorer, choose View⇨Source. In Netscape Navigator, choose View⇨Document Source.

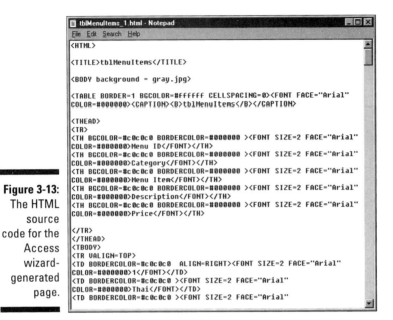

Figure 3-13:
The HTML
source
code for the
Access
wizard-
generated
page.

If you look at the HTML in Figure 3-13, you may be surprised at how volumi-
nous it is and how difficult it is to read. The size is the result of a couple of
factors. First, the wizard uses an HTML table to display the data. HTML
tables are, by their very nature, difficult to create and read. Second, the
wizard includes tags for coloring and font in each and every cell of the table.
The good news, however, is that once you exclude the formatting tags, the
remaining HTML is really quite simple.

Here's the first part of my example Web page (with color, alignment, and font
tags removed for clarity's sake only). This HTML creates the column head-
ings for the HTML table:

```
<THEAD>
<TR>
<TH>Menu ID</TH>
<TH>Category</TH>
<TH>Menu Item</TH>
<TH>Description</TH>
<TH>Price</TH>
</TR>
</THEAD>
```

And here's a row of data (again, with color, alignment, and font tags removed) for my example Web page:

```
<TR>
<TD>11</TD>
<TD>Polish</TD>
<TD>Bigos</TD>
<TD>A steaming bowl of Polish hunters stew made with cab-
        bage, several different kinds of meats and
        sausage, sauerkraut, and lots of other goodies
        </TD>
<TD>$5.95</TD>
```

Modifying the HTML

You can easily modify the HTML that the Access Publish to the Web Wizard produces. Simply open the pages using any text or HTML editor and have at it.

For example, if you look at the HTML that the wizard produces, you may be bothered by the use of your Access object name in the title of the page as well as the HTML table caption. That's not very user-friendly! Fortunately, the remedy to this is easy. Follow these steps:

1. **Start by opening the HTML file that the wizard created in your favorite text or HTML editor.**

   The name of the published object appears in two places in the HTML file produced by the Access wizard:

   - The title of the page
   - The caption of the table

2. **Change the title to something more friendly.**

   The wizard sets the title of the page to the name of the published Access object. You can find the title on or around the third line of the file (the title may appear on a different line for some templates) surrounded by the <TITLE> and </TITLE> tags. In the tblMenuItems example, it looks like this:

   ```
   <TITLE>tblMenuItems</TITLE>
   ```

   Most browsers place the title text in the caption of the title bar of the browser (see Figures 3-10, 3-11, and 3-12).

For example, I changed my title text in the title bar to:

```
<TITLE>Welcome to Web_Meals.Com</TITLE>
```

HTML jockeys may notice that the Microsoft templates don't include <HEAD> and </HEAD> tags. Fortunately, most Web browsers work just fine without these tags, but Microsoft should have been more careful.

3. Change the caption of the table to something more descriptive.

The wizard also uses the name of the published object as the caption for the HTML table. You can find the caption on or around the eighth line of the generated HTML (the caption may appear on a different line for some templates). In my example, the table caption line looks like this:

```
COLOR=#000000><CAPTION><B>tblMenuItems</B></CAPTION>
```

I changed the caption to something more descriptive:

```
COLOR=#000000><CAPTION><B>Our Menu</B></CAPTION>
```

Viewing your changes

After you save your changes to the file, pull it up in your browser to see your edited page. If you had your browser open when you were editing the page, you need to tell your browser to reread the page from your hard disk before the changes appear. If you use Internet Explorer or Netscape Navigator, choose View⇔Refresh. The modified version of my page is shown in Figure 3-14.

Figure 3-14:
My edited
Web page,
as shown in
version 4.0
of Microsoft
Internet
Explorer.

Menu ID	Category	Menu Item	Description	Price
			Our menu	
1	Thai	Phad Thai, Chicken	Stir-fried thin rice noodles with chicken, tofu, egg, onions, bean sprouts, and ground peanuts	$6.25
2	Thai	Phad Thai, Shrimp	Stir-fried thin rice noodles with shrimp, tofu, egg, onions, bean sprouts, and ground peanuts	$6.75
3	Thai	Phad Thai, Pork	Stir-fried thin rice noodles with pork, tofu, egg, onions, bean sprouts, and ground peanuts	$6.25
4	Thai	Ginger Chicken	Sautéed chicken with ginger, onions, and mushrooms	$5.95
5	Thai	Rad Na	Rice noodles topped with gravy, broccoli, and beef	$6.50
6	Italian	Ravioli	Cheese filled pillows of pasta covered with marinara sauce	$8.35
7	Italian	Pizza Margherita	Classic 16" pizza with tomato sauce, basil, tomatoes, and mozzarella	$10.99
8	Italian	Pizza Al Pesto	Delicious 16" pizza with fresh basil, pine nuts, olive oil, and parmesan cheese	$11.75

Chapter 4

Spiffing Up Your Pages

In This Chapter

▶ Understanding which objects the Access Publish to the Web Wizard publishes

▶ Publishing an Access report

▶ Using and creating your own publishing templates

*T*he Access Publish to the Web Wizard is adept at publishing a variety of Access objects, not the least of which is the formatted Access report. And if publishing a report doesn't give you enough control over formatting, you can create custom publishing templates to spiff up things even more. In this chapter, you discover how easy it is to create nicely formatted HTML pages by publishing Access reports. In addition, you find out how to create custom publishing templates.

What Other Kinds of Objects Can I Publish?

The Access Publish to the Web Wizard publishes more than just tables. Table 4-1 details which objects you can publish when choosing the static HTML format.

Table 4-1	Objects Published to Static HTML	
Access Object	*Publishable?*	*What's Published?*
Tables	Yes	Datasheet
Queries	Yes	Datasheet
Forms	Yes	Record source is published as a datasheet
Reports	Yes	HTML look-alike of formatted report
Macros	No	N/A
Modules	No	N/A

Table 4-1 concerns publishing Access database objects to the *static HTML* format only. You can also publish Access objects to one of the *dynamic* formats: Internet Database Connector (IDC) and Active Server Pages (ASP). The IDC format supports publishing tables and queries. The ASP format supports publishing tables, queries, and forms. You can use the ASP-published forms to update records in your Access database. The IDC and ASP formats are the subjects of Parts IV and V of this book, respectively.

As shown in Table 4-1, you can publish queries, which in many cases is a big improvement over tables. By publishing queries, you can explicitly control the specific fields and rows you include in the published Web page.

Notice that the wizard does *not* publish facsimiles of your forms when you choose the static HTML output option. Instead, the wizard merely publishes the record source of the form in a format that is similar to how tables and queries get published. Oh, well.

Unlike tables, queries, and forms, when you publish an Access report using the static HTML format, the wizard creates an HTML facsimile of the formatted Access report. In the next section of this chapter, you can look at an example of publishing a report to the static HTML format.

Publishing Access Reports

Publishing Access reports has several advantages over publishing tables. When you publish an Access report, you can

- Include and exclude fields
- Incorporate data from multiple tables
- Include calculations
- Sort the rows
- Filter the rows (in the underlying query)
- Group the data and publish totals and subtotals

In addition, when publishing reports using the Publish to the Web Wizard, the wizard preserves your formatting selections for text boxes and labels. Thus, your published reports retain the fonts, font sizes, font colors, and font styles from the report. In other words, your published reports don't look as boring as your other published objects.

Running the wizard

Follow these steps to use the Publish to the Web Wizard to publish a report to the static HTML format:

1. **Choose File⇨Save As HTML to start the Publish to the Web Wizard.**

   Page 1 of the wizard appears.

2. **Click Next to skip over page 1.**

3. **Click the Reports tab, on page 2, to view the list of reports in your database.**

4. **Click the checkbox to the left of the report that you want to publish, as shown in Figure 4-1.**

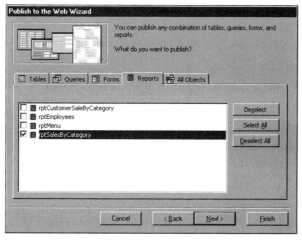

Figure 4-1: On the second page of the wizard, you select the objects you want to publish.

For example, I chose the report rptSalesByCategory, in the Meals.Mdb sample database on the CD. This report summarizes product sales by the category of food. If you preview this report in Access, note that the report uses several different size fonts, font colors, and font styles. In addition, the report (shown in Print Preview view in Figure 4-2) contains a total price at the bottom.

5. **Click Next to proceed to page 3.**

Figure 4-2:
The
rptSalesBy
Category
summarizes
sales
by food
category.

6. **If you want, select a template to use on page 3 of the wizard.**

7. **Click Next to proceed to the next page of the wizard.**

8. **Select Static HTML as the publishing format on page 4 of the wizard and click Next.**

   You can only publish reports to the static HTML format, so you must choose this format.

9. **Enter the name of the folder where you want the wizard to place the generated Web pages and click Next.**

10. **Specify the name of an optional home page on page 6 by clicking the Yes, I Want to Create a Home Page check box and entering the name; click the Next button to proceed to the seventh and final page of the wizard.**

11. **Click Finish to skip the optional page 7 and publish the report.**

    The wizard immediately publishes your report.

When you click Finish, the wizard generates the Web pages and places them in the publishing folder.

The wizard does not, however, copy any image files referenced in the template to the publishing folder. You must do this yourself. (See Chapter 3 for more details.)

Time to take a look

Start up your favorite browser so you can take a gander at the Web page version of your report. With your browser loaded, enter the following into the Address or Locations text box of the browser:

```
C:\WebPages\report1.html
```

If you used a different publishing folder, enter that folder instead of C:\WebPages. In place of report, enter the name of your Access report.

Click the hyperlink containing the name of your report, and your browser loads the published report, as shown in Figure 4-3 (again in Internet Explorer 4.0). Notice that the font formatting is preserved. In case you're wondering if the formatting shows up only by using the Microsoft browser, fear not. The report looks just as good in most other browsers, such as Netscape Navigator 3.0 (shown in Figure 4-4).

Figure 4-3:
The Web page version of the rptSalesBy Category report from the Meals database retains most of the formatting of the original report.

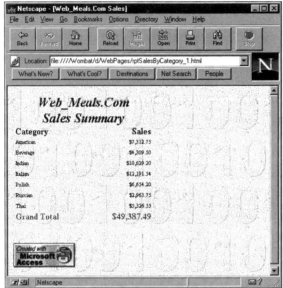

Figure 4-4:
The Web
page
version
of the
rptSalesBy
Category
report as
shown in
Netscape
Navigator 3.0.

What the wizard publishes

In general, the Access Publish to the Web Wizard does a nice job in converting the report's formatting into the HTML equivalent. The wizard publishes
the following report elements:

- ✔ Font attributes, including font name, font size, font color, and font style
- ✔ Data formatting and justification
- ✔ Subreports
- ✔ Horizontal and vertical spacing

What the wizard doesn't publish

On the other hand, the wizard isn't perfect. Who is? The Publish to the Web
Wizard doesn't publish the following report elements:

- ✔ Lines
- ✔ Rectangles
- ✔ Shading
- ✔ Image, object frame, and graph controls
- ✔ Custom controls

In addition, the wizard may have difficulty publishing reports with small fonts and tight spacing. Hey, it ain't perfect! The wizard does the best it can, but sometimes the results aren't up to snuff. HTML just doesn't give you the fine control that the Access report writer gives you.

Generally, the wizard does an admirable job converting Access reports into the equivalent static HTML Web pages.

Publishing a Multipage Access Report

When you publish reports made up of multiple pages, the wizard dutifully creates an HTML page for each page of the Access report. If you use one of the built-in templates, however, when you publish your multipage report, the wizard fails to link the pages together (see example in Figure 4-5). You can remedy this situation in a couple of ways:

- ✔ Don't use a template.
- ✔ Use a custom template containing navigation hyperlinks.

I discuss these options in more detail in the following sections.

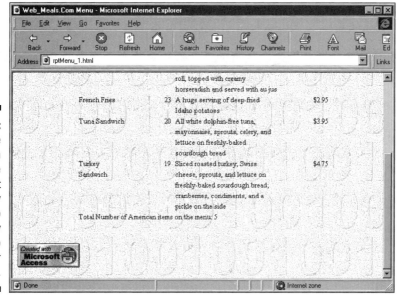

Figure 4-5: An example of a multipage report that lacks any way to easily navigate to the other pages.

No template

If you don't select a template and you choose to publish a report, the Publish to the Web Wizard is smart enough to insert navigational hyperlinks into each published page.

You can try this solution by republishing the report using the wizard. When you get to the third page, opt for no template file by leaving the default template text box blank. When you leave the box blank, you end up with a published report that includes navigational hyperlinks at the bottom of each page, as shown in Figure 4-6.

You don't have to give up using templates just to get the ability to hyperlink from one page of the report to another. Instead, you can create a custom template file that includes the necessary navigation hyperlinks.

Using a custom template

Another way to get navigational hyperlinks onto your published reports is to use a custom template that includes these links. I created a custom template that you can use, named Web_MealsRpt.htm. (To create your own template, see the following section, "Creating Custom Templates.")

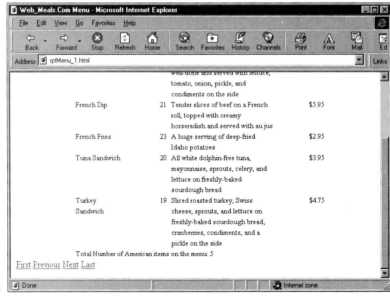

Figure 4-6: The bottom of the first page of my republished rptMenu report (published without any template) contains navigational hyperlinks.

To use a custom template when publishing a report, follow these steps:

1. **Republish your report one more time using the wizard.**

   If you want to follow along with my example (but you don't have to), you need to copy the web_meals.htm template from the CD that comes with this book to your templates folder. The location of the templates folder varies, depending on where you installed Office. For example, if you installed Office in the C:\MSOffice folder, then you can find the files in the C:\MSOffice\Templates\Access folder. You also need to copy six image files (first.gif, next.gif, previous.gif, last.gif, web_meals.gif, and gray.jpg) from the CD to your WebPages folder.

2. **When you get to the third page, click the Browse button.**

3. **Select the template file in the dialog box, as shown in Figure 4-7, and then click the Select button.**

4. **Finish publishing your report as you normally would.**

Figure 4-7: The Web_MealsRpt.htm template includes navigational buttons and a logo.

To see your new masterpiece, fire up your browser. In my example, shown in Figure 4-8, the page has navigational buttons. (If you followed along with my example and the button images don't show up in your browser, you probably forgot to copy them from the CD to your WebPages folder.)

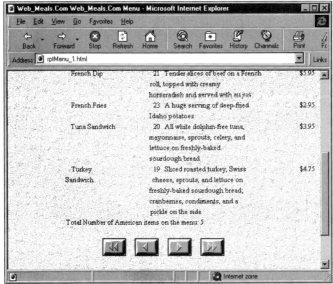

Figure 4-8:
The bottom
of the first
page of the
rptMenu
report
(published
using the
Web_Meals
Rpt.htm
template)
contains
buttons for
navigating
to the other
pages of
the report.

Creating Custom Templates

The Access Publish to the Web Wizard supports the use of HTML templates to guide the wizard as it generates your Web pages. You can use template files to

- ✔ Set a background color or image
- ✔ Include a logo or other images
- ✔ Set the title of the page
- ✔ Control alignment of elements
- ✔ Insert navigational hyperlinks to connect multiple report pages
- ✔ Insert a page number

Anatomy of a template

The Access Publish to the Web Wizard template files are made up of nothing more than HTML. Within the template, you use special comments, or *tokens,* to indicate where you want the wizard to place various elements of the published object. Table 4-1 offers a summary of these tokens. When the wizard generates a page, it replaces the tokens with the Access elements listed in Table 4-1.

Table 4-1	Wizard Template Tokens
HTML Template Token	**Replaced With**
`<!-AccessTemplate_Title-->`	Name of published object
`<!-AccessTemplate_Body-->`	Published detail
`<!-AccessTemplate_FirstPage-->`	Hyperlink to the first published page (reports)
`<!-AccessTemplate_PreviousPage-->`	Hyperlink to the previous published page (reports)
`<!-AccessTemplate_NextPage-->`	Hyperlink to the next published page (reports)
`<!-AccessTemplate_LastPage-->`	Hyperlink to the last published page (reports)
`<!-AccessTemplate_PageNumber-->`	Page number of current page

Because the Publish to the Web Wizard creates multiple HTML files for reports only, the last five tokens in Table 4-1 aren't useful except when publishing reports. Nothing can prevent you from using these tokens with other published objects, but the hyperlinks don't go anywhere and the page number is always 1.

Following is the HTML behind the Web_MealsRpt.htm sample template file on the CD.

```
<HTML>
<HEAD>
<TITLE>Web_Meals.Com <!-ACCESSTEMPLATE_TITLE--></TITLE>
</HEAD>
<BODY background = gray.jpg>
<IMG SRC="web_meals.gif" ALT="web_meals.com logo">
<BR>
<!-ACCESSTEMPLATE_BODY-->
<BR>
<CENTER>
<A HREF=<!-AccessTemplate_FirstPage-->>
<IMG SRC="first.gif" ALT="[|<First]"></A>
  
<A HREF=<!-AccessTemplate_PreviousPage-->>
<IMG SRC="prev.gif" ALT="[<Prior]"></A>
  
```

(continued)

(continued)

```
<A HREF=<!—AccessTemplate_NextPage-->>
<IMG SRC="next.gif" ALT="[Next>]"></A>
  
<A HREF=<!—AccessTemplate_LastPage-->>
<IMG SRC="last.gif" ALT="[Last>|]"></A>
<BR><BR>
Page <!—AccessTemplate_PageNumber-->
</CENTER>
<BR>
<IMG SRC = "msaccess.jpg">
</BODY>
</HTML>
```

In this template, I use a background image (gray.jpg) and another image (web_meals.gif) for the logo. I also reference four other images (first.gif, prev.gif, next.gif, last.gif) to provide the navigation buttons. Throughout this template file, I use the Access Publish to the Web Wizard tokens from Table 4-1 to indicate to the wizard where I want to place the published element as it merges the published report with the custom template file.

If you open the Web_MealsRpt.htm template file directly in your browser, you see something similar to the screen shown in Figure 4-9. If you open this file directly in your browser, you can get some idea of the complete page. Yes, I admit it — the logo is pretty lame, but hey, I'm not an artist!

Figure 4-9:
The HTML template file, complete with a background, a rather lame-looking logo, navigational buttons, and a placeholder for the page number.

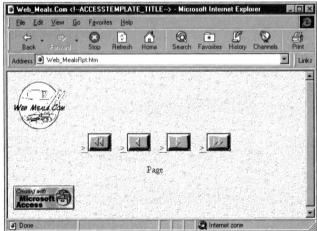

Not just for reports

You can create and use custom templates with all published database objects, not just reports. The navigational buttons and page number tokens, however, don't make any sense if you use them with other objects.

You may want to create two sets of templates: one set for use with multipage reports and another set for use with all other database objects.

I created another template file that you can find on the CD at the back of this book. The template file, Web_Meals.Htm, is identical to the Web_MealsRpt.htm template file except that it doesn't contain the navigation button and page number tokens. Use this sort of template with all database objects other than multipage reports.

The HTML behind this version of the template is much simpler than for the report-version of the template:

```
<HTML>
<HEAD>
<TITLE>Web_Meals.Com <!—ACCESSTEMPLATE_TITLE--></TITLE>
</HEAD>
<BODY background = gray.jpg>
<IMG SRC="web_meals.gif" ALT="web_meals.com logo">
<BR>
<!—ACCESSTEMPLATE_BODY-->
<BR>
<IMG SRC = "msaccess.jpg">
</BODY>
</HTML>
```

Again, I use the gray.jpg background image and the same lame-looking logo as the other template file. In this version of the template, I use two tokens: `<!—ACCESSTEMPLATE_TITLE—>` tells the wizard where to place the name of the published object and `<!—ACCESSTEMPLATE_BODY—>` tells the wizard where to replace the published object.

If you want more practice, try publishing the qryCustomerAndCategory query from the Meals.Mdb sample database using the Web_Meals.Htm template file. The resulting Web page looks like the one shown in Figure 4-10.

Figure 4-10:
The
qryCustomer
AndCategory
query
published
to static
HTML using
the Web_
Meals.Htm
template.

Chapter 5

Posting and Republishing Pages

• •

In This Chapter

▶ Integrating your Web pages into your Web site

▶ Moving your Web pages to your Web server

▶ Creating and using Web-publishing profiles

▶ Publishing static HTML pages on a regular schedule using VBA

• •

*A*fter you create your content using the Access Publish to the Web Wizard, you need to integrate it into your Web site by, among other steps, moving it to your Web server and linking it to your other Web pages. You may also want to reduce the tedium by automating the Web page-generation process using publication profiles and VBA code. In this chapter, you explore how to move your published pages to your Web server, how to integrate your pages into your Web site, and how to automate the database publishing process.

Integrating Your Pages into Your Web Site

Using your browser to view data is fun, but you probably want to include your published pages as part of a Web site. After all, the point of publishing your data is to make it available to users either within your company intranet or out on the great World Wide Web. Your Web pages need to be hosted on a Web server.

Before you can move your published pages to your Web server, you must integrate the pages into your Web site. If you're fairly comfortable with HTML and Web page design (or employ someone who is), this process isn't particularly difficult. You need to

✔ Create your home page and other nondata pages

✔ Create links to your data pages from your nondata pages

✔ Create links from your data pages back to your nondata pages

If you have an existing Web site in place, then you merely cross-link the existing Web pages to your newly published data pages. Here's where a good Web site management program such as FrontPage or Visual InterDev may come in handy.

Obviously, I leave out a lot of little details here. When building a Web site, do some organizational planning. If you plan to create a complex site, you may need to assemble a team of experts to help create the HTML and artwork and manage the hardware and Web server software. Of course, you can tap into a lot of good books to help you build a Web site. Take a look at *Creating Web Pages For Dummies,* 2nd Edition, by Bud Smith and Arthur Bebak, and *Setting Up An Internet Site For Dummies,* 2nd Edition, by Jason Coombs and Ted Coombs. You may also want to take a look at *FrontPage For Dummies* by Asha Dornfest. (IDG Books Worldwide, Inc., publishes all three of these books.)

Figure 5-1 shows an example of a home page I created for the fictitious Web_Meals.com Web site. This very basic home page connects a bunch of the published data pages generated in Chapters 3 and 4. Not terribly useful, but it's a start.

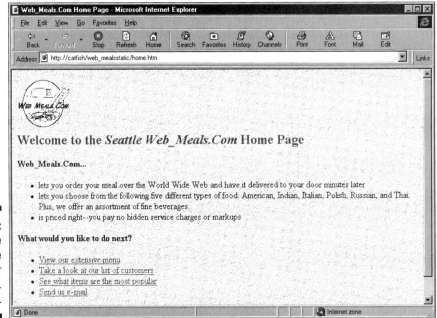

Figure 5-1:
A sample
home page
for
Web_Meals.
com.

The Postman Always Rings Twice

How you post your Web site to your Web server depends on your setup. Possible setups include

- ✔ Your Web server and publishing workstation are one and the same or connected via a local area network (LAN). (See the section "When the server's just around the corner," later in this chapter.)
- ✔ A machine on your company intranet hosts your Web server. (See the section "When the server's across town" later in this chapter.)
- ✔ An Internet Service Provider (ISP) hosts your Web server. You connect to the ISP over a dial-up line or router. (See the section "When the server's across town" later in this chapter.)

In the next few sections, you explore publishing under each of the preceding scenarios.

When the server's just around the corner

If your workstation doubles as your Web server, or if you connect to your Web server across a LAN, you shouldn't have any trouble posting your files to your server.

On page 5 of the Access Publish to the Web Wizard, simply enter the folder on the server where you want the wizard to deposit the files. You can use either a relative path (for example, `f:\webpages`) or a Universal Naming Convention (UNC) path (for example, `\\bubba\c\webpages`). A UNC path is usually a better bet because a relative path changes as you add or remove local or network drives whereas a UNC won't break in these cases.

For example, I can find my local Web server on a Windows NT Server machine named

```
catfish
```

If I want to post my files to the following `catfish` share (I like using UNC paths),

```
\e\inetpub\wwwroot\web_meals
```

I simply enter the following code into the publishing folder text box:

```
\\catfish\e\inetpub\wwwroot\web_meals
```

It's that simple: actually even simpler, if your Web server is the same machine as your publishing workstation.

When the server's across town

Life, unfortunately, isn't always that simple. Sometimes you have to post your files to a server that's not on your LAN. In these cases, you can use a nifty wizard called the Web Publishing Wizard.

The Publish to the Web Wizard and Web Publishing Wizard have very similar names — they sure do, but what would life be without a little confusion?

Where do you get this nifty wizard with a name that sounds a lot like the Publish to the Web Wizard? I'm glad you asked. The Web Publishing Wizard ships with several Microsoft products, including Office 97 and Internet Explorer 4.0.

If you can't find a copy of the wizard, you can download it from www.microsoft.com/windows/software/webpost.

As I write this, two versions of the Web Publishing Wizard are available: Version 1.1 and 1.5. If CompuServe or Hyperware hosts your Web server, use Version 1.1. Otherwise, Version 1.5 is the better choice. (Later versions of the wizard may support CompuServe and Hyperware servers — check www.microsoft.com for more details.)

Using the Web Publishing Wizard

Even though the Web Publishing Wizard may not sound like it does much, this wizard can navigate a vast array of different protocols and configurations to move your precious pages to your Web server.

Before you fire up the Web Publishing Wizard, you need to make sure that you have write access to the Web server's folders. In addition, if you're using a dial-up line, you need to install dial-up networking and possibly create a script to connect to the ISP. Check with your ISP or the Web Publishing Wizard help file for more details.

You also need to get the following information ready before you begin:

- ✔ **The main URL of your Web server.** For example, http://www.mywebsite.com.
- ✔ **The URL of your Web site within the Web server.** For example, http://www.mywebsite.com/web_meals.
- ✔ **The protocol you use to send files to the Web server.** For many servers, the protocol is ftp.
- ✔ **The folder or directory under your site where you want to post your files.** For example, www/htdocs.

> ✔ **The name you must give to your home page.** On Microsoft servers, this name is, by default, default.htm. (You can also use default.html.) On most other servers (including UNIX-based servers), this name is index.htm. (You can also use index.html.)

On UNIX-based servers, addresses are case-sensitive. The easiest way to succeed in this environment is to make all filenames and addresses lower-case.

Posting Web pages to a server for the first time

After you have the necessary information in hand, follow these steps to post your Web pages to your Web server:

1. **Fire up the Web Publishing Wizard.**

   The easiest way to fire up the wizard is to just directly run the wizard. You also can launch it from the Access Publish to the Web Wizard by selecting the second radio button on page 5 of that wizard (shown in Figure 5-2).

   The Web Publishing Wizard displays its opening page, which explains what the wizard does.

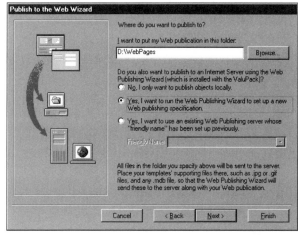

Figure 5-2: Launching the Web Publishing Wizard from the Access Publish to the Web Wizard.

2. **Click Next to continue.**

3. **On page 2 of the wizard, enter the name of a file to publish or, more typically, an entire folder to publish, (see Figure 5-3) and then click Next.**

If you ran the Web Publishing Wizard from the Publish to the Web Wizard, the suggested folder is the folder you entered on page 5 of that Publish to the Web Wizard.

Figure 5-3:
On page 2 of the Web Publishing Wizard, you enter the location of the Web pages that you want to post to a Web server.

4. **Name the Web server on page 3 if this is the first time you're running the wizard and then click Next.**

   The wizard isn't asking for the actual URL of the server. Rather, the wizard asks you to create a specification or *friendly* name that you can recall later for additional postings to the same server. If you've run the wizard before, you can select the server from a combo box containing the list of specification names.

   For the example, I use the name `web_meals` (shown in Figure 5-4).

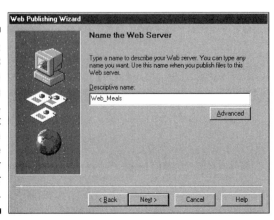

Figure 5-4:
On page 3 of the Web Publishing Wizard, you must supply a descriptive name for this server specification.

5. On page 4 of the wizard, supply the complete URL of your Web site.

This URL is the same URL you use to hyperlink to your Web site using your browser.

For the example, I use `www.mywebsite.com/web_meals` (shown in Figure 5-5). Check with your ISP if you're unsure of the address. On this page, the wizard also asks you to confirm the name of the local folder that contains your Web files. This folder name should be the same name you entered on page 2 of the wizard.

Figure 5-5:
On page 4
of the Web
Publishing
Wizard, you
enter the
URL of your
Web site.

6. Click Next.

At this point, the wizard attempts to log on to your Web server. If the wizard detects that you use a dial-up line, the wizard attempts to connect you by using your default dial-up connection. However, if you connect to your ISP through a router, the connection is made using the router instead. At this point, the wizard displays the Enter Network Password dialog box.

7. Enter the user name and password you use to log on to your ISP and then click OK to login.

After your click Next, the wizard attempts to automatically detect your service provider's protocol for posting Web pages and then figure out all the remaining details for you. If the wizard succeeds, you can skip the remaining steps.

If the wizard fails in its attempts, you see a fifth page (shown in Figure 5-6) informing you of your rotten luck. Fear not, however; you may still be able to get things working without an angry e-mail message to your Webmaster.

Figure 5-6:
You get this
message
when the
wizard has
failed to
automatically
connect
you to
the ISP.

8. Click Next after reading page 5.

When you click Next, you advance to page 6.

9. Select a service provider from the drop-down list and click Next.

On page 6, you must tell the wizard what service provider or transfer protocol to use. At this point, the correct protocol is likely FTP, so you may as well give FTP a whirl (see Figure 5-7).

Figure 5-7:
Time to tell
the wizard
what
protocol to
use: FTP is
a likely
candidate.

10. Enter the name of the FTP server into the first text box of page 7.

Page 7 varies based on the protocol you select on page 6. If you selected the FTP protocol, you should see a page similar to that shown in Figure 5-8. If you get this page right, you are home free.

For example, if your Web server is named `www.mywebsite.com`, then it's more than likely that the name of your FTP server is `ftp.mywebsite.com`.

11. Enter the name of the subfolder where you'd like to place your Web files into the second text box on page 7.

Recall that on page 4 of the wizard, you entered the URL of your Web site. Do not enter any portion of that URL here. This subfolder is a folder *below* that URL. (Does this sound like the voice of experience talking?) The URL you entered back on page 4, incidentally, appears for you in the third text box of this page for informational purposes only.

For example, if your Web files need to be placed into the `www.mywebsite.com/web_meals/www/htdocs` folder on your Web server, enter only the `www/htdocs` portion of the address here (shown in Figure 5-8).

Figure 5-8:
The subfolder name you entered into the second text box should include any part of the URL displayed in the third text box.

12. Click Next.

The (hopefully) final page of the wizard should now appear, as shown in Figure 5-9.

13. Click the Finish button and cross your fingers as the Web Publishing Wizard attempts to post your files to your Web server.

Posting your files just may work if you typed the correct addresses into page 7 (and prior pages), if you have write access to the needed folders on your server, if your Web server is up and running, and if your communications link works.

Figure 5-9:
Click the
Finish
button, and
who knows,
it just may
work this
time.

If all goes well, the Publishing Files dialog box appears with a progress report of the posting efforts (shown in Figure 5-10). Finally, when the wizard is done, you see a success dialog box. If you're not so lucky, you may need to talk with your ISP or fiddle around with the answers you provided to the wizard. Keep trying!

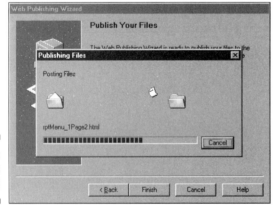

Figure 5-10:
Yes, it's
working!

That's about it. After you post your pages, you may as well fire up your browser and point it to your new Web site. Isn't the smell of success sweet?

Republishing to a Web server using the wizard

After you get the Web Publishing Wizard working the first time, you should have no problem getting the wizard to repost to a saved specification name (also known as *a Web Publishing Wizard friendly name*) for additional uploads to the same Web site. Select the name of your saved specification on page 3, click Next, and then click Finish on page 4 of the wizard.

If you're running the Web Publishing Wizard from the Publish to the Web Wizard, reposting your pages is even easier. Just choose the existing friendly name, as shown in Figure 5-11.

Figure 5-11: After you set up a server specification using the Web Publishing Wizard, you only need specify its name on page 5 of the Publish to the Web Wizard.

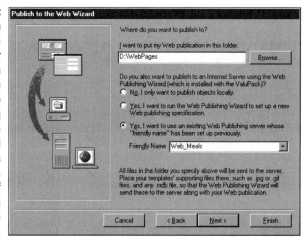

Don't Reinvent: Use Publication Profiles

If you don't want to keep working your way through every page of the Publish to the Web Wizard, you don't have to. (For those of you who may be confused by the similar names, I'm no longer talking about the Web Publishing Wizard. Instead, I've switched back to talking about the wizard that's part of Access 97 — you know, the one that takes your tables, queries, and reports and spits them out as HTML.) Fortunately, this wizard lets you save your answers to a publication profile.

Creating a publication profile

The last page of the Publish to the Web Wizard (page 7) allows you to save your answers to a Web publication profile, as shown in Figure 5-12. You simply need to click the check box next to Yes, I want to save wizard answers to a Web publication profile and then type the profile name. When you create a publication profile, Access stores away every answer you make to every wizard question. If you need to recall your answers later, you're just a couple of mouse clicks away.

You can create as many publication profiles as you like — the database stores the profiles as hidden properties. This has two implications: First you can copy a database to another computer and its publication profile goes with it. Second, you can't reuse a publication profile with multiple databases.

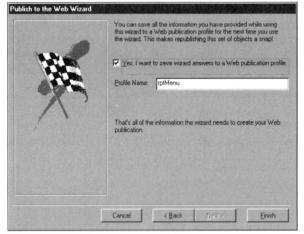

Figure 5-12:
If you save your wizard answers to a publication profile, you never have to face these questions again.

Recalling a publication profile

Recalling a saved publication profile is pretty darn easy:

1. **Start the Publish to the Web Wizard.**

   Page 1 of the wizard appears.

2. **Click the check box next to I want to use a Web publication profile I already created with this wizard.**

3. **Select the desired profile from the list (see Figure 5-13).**

4. **Click Finish.**

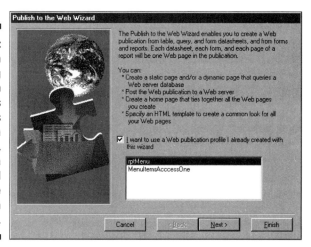

Figure 5-13:
Using an existing publication profile is as easy as clicking a check box, selecting a profile, and clicking the Finish button.

That's all there is to it. The wizard republishes your pages using the answers you specified when you created the publication profile.

Sloughing Off with VBA

Using saved Web publication profiles can save you quite a bit of work, but you or your users still need to interact with the wizard. Sometimes you may want to slough off even more and automate the whole process so that you can, for example, press a single button on a form, causing Access to publish the pages for you. Well, I have news for you: The Access VBA language includes direct support for this sort of shortcut.

You probably think that this shortcut involves some wildly complex series of commands that work only if you're standing on your head, pointing towards Redmond, and whistling the theme song to *Green Acres*. Well, it turns out that the process is a bit easier than that. In fact, you can perform the whole process by using a single line of VBA code!

Using frmPublish

Before I get into the details, take a look at an example of how you can use the final product of your coding efforts. Open frmPublish in the Meals.Mdb database, enter an output file name, and click Publish, as shown in Figure 5-14. When you do this, the VBA code attached to the command button publishes the report as static HTML using a Web publication profile that I had previously saved to the database. And it works even if you're not whistling the *Green Acres* theme song!

Figure 5-14:
When you click the Publish button, VBA code publishes the rptMenu report to the specified file.

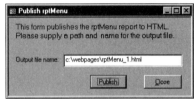

frmPublish Uncovered

And now for the code behind frmPublish's Publish button:

```
DoCmd.OutputTo acOutputReport, "rptMenu", _
acFormatHTML, Me!txtFile, False, _
"C:\MSOffice\Templates\Access\Web_MealsRpt.HTM"
```

You need to, of course, replace the italicized text with your own arguments. Replace rptMenu with the name of the object you want to publish. Replace Me!txtFile with the name of a control that contains the output file name. Replace C:\MSOffice\Templates\Access\Web_MealsRpt.HTM with the name of a publishing template (see Table 5-1 for more details on each of the OutputTo arguments).

No kidding — that's it!

For those who prefer to use macros, you can use the equivalent OutputTo macro.

Take a look at all the arguments to the OutputTo method. I summarize the arguments in Table 5-1.

Table 5-1	Arguments to the OutputTo method
Argument	*Description*
ObjectType	The type of object to publish; indicated with one of these constants: acOutputForm, acOutputModule, acOutputQuery, acOutputReport, or acOutputTable
ObjectName	The name of the object

Argument	Description
OutputFormat	The output format (OutputTo can publish to a number of formats in addition to HTML); indicated with one of these constants: acFormatASP, acFormatHTML, acFormatIIS, acFormatRTF, acFormatTXT, or acFormatXLS
OutputFile	The path and name of the output file
AutoStart	Whether the application associated with the output format should automatically start after the object has been published; True or False
TemplateFile	The name of the template file

If you take another look at the DoCmd.OutputTo statement behind frmPublishMenu, you see that the arguments indicate the following:

- ✔ ObjectType = acOutputReport indicates that you want to publish a report.

- ✔ ObjectName = "rptMenu" is the specific report that you want to publish.

- ✔ OutputFormat = acFormatHTML indicates that you want to publish to the static HTML format. As you can see from the other constants listed in Table 5-1, you can also use OutputTo to output various objects to Excel, Rich Text Format, Text, and several other file formats.

- ✔ OutputFile = Me!txtFile passes to the OutputTo method the value stored in the txtFile text box on the form.

- ✔ AutoStart = False indicates that you don't want to automatically launch the application associated with the output format after publishing the object. If set to True, the published file loads into your browser as soon as the file publishes.

- ✔ TemplateFile = "C:\MSOffice\Templates\Access\Web_MealsRpt.HTM" tells the OutputTo method to use this HTML template when publishing the object. The exact path that you use here may vary depending on where you installed Office 97.

A possible hitch

I know of one major shortcoming of using the VBA OutputTo method to publish an Access object. OutputTo doesn't use a Web publication profile so it doesn't run the Web Publishing Wizard to post your files to a remote server. OutputTo can post your files to another computer attached to yours via a LAN, but it can't post files to a remote server.

One way around this problem, however, is to use the Windows 95/NT ftp command and an ftp script file to upload your files to the remote server using the FTP protocol.

Say that you want to upload all the files from a folder to a remote server based on the following:

- ✔ Source folder: the `c:\webpages` folder
- ✔ Target directory: the `www\htdocs` folder
- ✔ ftp server: `ftp.mywebsite.com`
- ✔ Username: `mary`
- ✔ Password: `fishlips`

To do so, create the following ftp script file using a text editor and save it to the `\ftp` folder of your C drive as `ftp1.txt`:

```
open ftp.mywebsite.com
mary
fishlips
binary
prompt
cd www/htdocs
mput c:\webpages\*.*
quit
```

For those who care, the script works like this: The first line opens a connection with the Web server, which prompts you for a user name and password. That information takes care of the second and third lines. (If you don't need to specify a user name and password, delete these two lines.) Line 4 sets the transfer mode to binary, which is necessary if you're uploading anything other than pure text files. Line 5 toggles prompt mode off — this turns off the confirmation of file transfers that `mput` would normally ask for. On line 6, the script requests that the remote host change the directory to `www/htdocs`. Line 7 performs the actual transfer of files. Finally, the eighth line logs off the server and exits the script.

Then add the following VBA statement to the event procedure attached to the `Publish` command button:

```
Shell "ftp -s:c:\ftp\ftp1.txt"
```

The preceding code tells VBA to launch the ftp program using the `c:\ftp\ftp1.txt` script file.

Putting it all together, the `cmdPublish` event procedure looks like this:

```
Private Sub cmdPublish_Click()
 DoCmd.OutputTo acOutputReport, "rptMenu", _
  acFormatHTML, Me!txtFile, False, "rptMenu"

 Shell "ftp -s:c:\ftp\ftp1.txt"
End Sub
```

Not too shabby! Note that you needn't use the shell statement if you're attached to the Web server across a LAN. In these cases, just directly specify the target folder using the `OutputFile` argument of the `OutputTo` method.

Like Clockwork

Using a simple Access form, the Access Publish to the Web Wizard, and code attached to a form's Timer event, you can publish HTML pages on a regular schedule without user intervention.

The timer event

A form's `Timer` event in Access triggers every time the `TimerInterval` elapses. By default, however, the `TimerInterval` property of a form is set to 0. You can change this default by setting the `TimerInterval` property on the form's property sheet, as shown in Figure 5-15.

Figure 5-15:
The
TimerInterval
property for
this form is
set to 60,000
milliseconds
or 1 minute.

To publish HTML pages on a regular schedule using the Publish to the Web Wizard, follow these general steps:

1. **Attach code that uses the** `OutputTo` **method to publish pages using the Access Publish to the Web Wizard to the form's Timer event property.**

   How to do this was discussed in the earlier section "Sloughing Off with VBA."

2. **Set the TimerInterval property of the form to a non-zero value to enable the Timer event.**

   If you'd like the Timer event procedure to execute once a minute, you need to set TimerInterval to a value of 60,000 because TimerInterval measures its time in milliseconds.

An example

I created an example of a form, frmPublishTimer, that regularly publishes a report every minute using the `OutputTo` method and the Timer event (as shown in Figure 5-16).

Figure 5-16:
This form publishes the rptMenu report every minute (or the time interval of your choosing).

Timer Publishing Form

This form publishes the rptMenu report to HTML once every minute using the following output file

Output file name: c:\webpages\rptMenu_1.html

Interval (minutes): 1   Close

The code behind frmPublishTimer is shown here:

```
Option Compare Database
Option Explicit
' This module-level global variable is
' used to track the last time the object
' was published
Private mdtmLastPublished As Date
Private Sub cmdClose_Click()
```

```
 DoCmd.Close
End Sub
Private Sub Form_Load()
 ' Initialize mdtmLastPublished to the current time
 mdtmLastPublished = Now()
End Sub
Private Sub Form_Timer()
 ' This boolean variable is used to prevent the
 ' code from re-executing before it is done.
 ' Because the publishing process might take
 ' longer than the interval setting,
 ' we must prevent the code from re-executing
Static fAlreadyExecuting As Boolean

If fAlreadyExecuting = True Then
Exit Sub
End If

 ' We've gotten this far in the code, so
 ' set the fAlreadyExecuting flag. Think of it
 ' as a VBA-version of a "do not disturb" sign
fAlreadyExecuting = True

 ' If the number of minutes between now and
 ' the last time the code ran exceeds the interval
 ' go ahead and publish now
If (Now() - mdtmLastPublished) * 1440 >= _
CLng(Me!txtInterval) Then
 ' Change the mdtmLastPublished time to now
mdtmLastPublished = Now()
 ' Change the last argument to point to the
 ' correct path to the template file on your machine
DoCmd.OutputTo acOutputReport, "rptMenu", _
acFormatHTML, Me!txtFile, False, _
"C:\MSOffice\Templates\Access\Web_MealsRpt.HTM"
 ' We're leaving now, so let's take
 ' the "do not disturb" sign down
fAlreadyExecuting = False
End If

End Sub
```

If you're not real comfortable with VBA code, you can just ignore this code for now. For most purposes, the only line of code you really need to modify is the one that begins with `DoCmd.OutputTo`.

Part III
What about SQL Server Data?

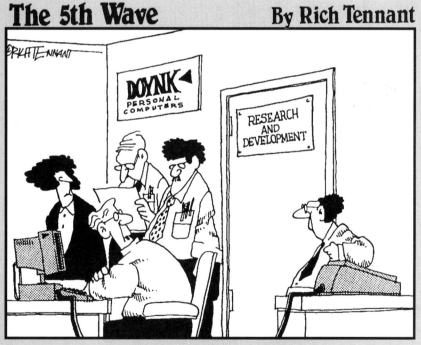

In this part . . .

SQL Server 6.5 includes a dandy wizard of its own called the SQL Server Web Assistant. Using the Web Assistant, you can convert SQL Server data into static HTML pages. In Chapter 6, you find out how to use the Web Assistant to produce HTML pages from tables, views, free-form SQL, and stored procedures. In Chapter 7, you master the Web Assistant's varied scheduling options. Among the options, you can publish and republish HTML pages on a regular schedule or when data in the underlying tables change. Also in Chapter 7, you discover how to use Web Assistant templates, as well as a bit about how the Assistant works.

Chapter 6

A Wizard That Speaks SQL

In This Chapter

▶ Understanding the server advantage

▶ Running the SQL Server Web Assistant

▶ Publishing tables, views, SQL, and stored procedures

*N*ot to be totally outdone by its little desktop database brother Access 97, the Microsoft server database SQL Server 6.5 also includes a wizard that generates HTML pages from database records: the SQL Server Web Assistant.

In this chapter, you find out how to use the SQL Server Web Assistant to generate HTML pages. You also explore using the Web Assistant to publish the data from SQL Server tables, views, SQL statements, and stored procedures.

If you don't own a copy of SQL Server 6.5 (or later), you can skip this chapter and the next one, too.

The Server Advantage

Access 97 is a great desktop database that you can use to manage vast amounts of information in an accessible and friendly, yet powerful environment. As you discover in Part II, Access 97 comes with a great wizard for publishing data to your corporate intranet or the World Wide Web.

SQL Server (as well as other server databases), however, offers several advantages over desktop databases such as Access. Namely, SQL Server:

✔ Can manage much larger databases exceeding a gigabyte in size.

✔ Is much more scalable. This means that SQL Server allows you to add many more users than desktop databases such as Access without a corresponding drop in performance.

✔ Can support many different front-end applications.

✔ Offers a more robust, more secure database engine that is less suscep-
tible to downtime and corruption than desktop databases such as
Access.

✔ Supports true client/server access unlike desktop databases, such as
Access, that operate using a file-server paradigm. This means (among
other things) that queries in SQL Server generate less network traffic
because the query executes on the server and only the result passes
back to the client. (When you use desktop databases such as Access to
manage the data, all the work is done on the client machine.)

These are just some of the reasons that many corporations store larger and
more critical databases on database servers such as SQL Server.

If you work in a large corporation, the decision as to where to store the data
likely has already been made for you. If so, the preceding information is
pretty much moot; on the other hand, it's always nice to know.

Getting Started

To use the SQL Server Web Assistant, you must be using Microsoft SQL
Server Version 6.5 or later. The Web Assistant is not a part of earlier versions of the product, nor is it a part of versions of SQL Server from Sybase.

When you install SQL Server 6.5 or the client utilities, the setup program
creates a shortcut to the SQL Server Web Assistant and adds the shortcut to
the SQL Server 6.5 start menu group.

After you launch the SQL Server Web Assistant, the first page of the SQL
Server Web Assistant appears, as shown in Figure 6-1. Follow these steps to
create the Web Assistant to publish an SQL Server table:

1. **Enter the name of the server (or** `local` **if you're running the Assistant on the server computer) and a login name and password; click
Next to move to page 2.**

2. **On page 2 of the Assistant — the query page — choose from one of
three options for building your query, as shown in Figure 6-2.**

   Keep this step simple and stick with the first option: Build a query from
   a database hierarchy. Translated into English, this option means that
   you want to publish a table or saved view. If you want to choose a
   different option, see the section "Query Options" later in this chapter.

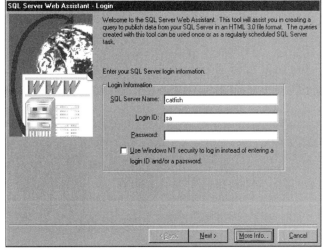

Figure 6-1:
The first page of the SQL Server Web Assistant requires you to log in.

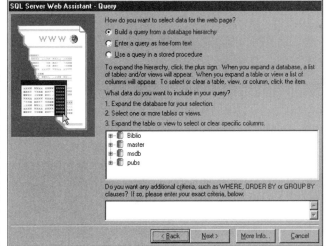

Figure 6-2:
On the query page, you specify how you want to select data from the SQL Server database.

3. Select the columns that you want to display.

In the tiny list box on the query page, you must drill down to the columns you wish to display in a series of steps. (Is it just me, or could this page have been designed with less useless text and more space for selecting objects?) To drill down:

• Click the plus sign to the left of your pubs database to expand the list of tables in the pubs database.

• Scroll down until you see the table you want. For example, I'm
  choosing dbo.titles. Click the plus sign to the left of the table to
  expand the list of columns in the table.

• Single-click the funny-looking box to the left of the columns you
  want to display. The box-like objects turn green when selected
  (see Figure 6-3).

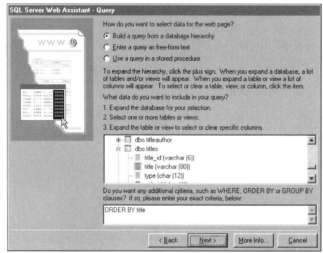

Figure 6-3:
It's a tight
squeeze,
but
selecting
the columns
requires
only a few
mouse
clicks.

4. If you want, enter an optional WHERE **or** ORDER BY **clause in the text
box below the object selection list box.**

For example, if you want to sort the records by title, you could enter
the following ORDER BY clause:

```
ORDER BY title
```

5. Click Next to continue to page 3.

On page 3 of the Assistant, you can choose from several different
scheduling options, as shown in Figure 6-4. I go over these options in
detail in Chapter 7.

**6. Choose Now to immediately generate the Web page, and then click
Next to advance to page 4.**

On page 4, you get to specify a bunch of things, not all of which have to
do with files, as you may expect from the title of the page.

What's up with the dbo prefix?

Ever wonder why SQL Server prefaces table names with dbo.? Me, too. When you find out why, please let me know . . . just kidding.

Anyway, to make a long story short, the dbo. prefix is supposed to let you know that the database owner created this table as opposed to some other user. Is this useful? I doubt it — perhaps in some future version, this cute little useless prefix will disappear. One can always hope.

7. Specify the name of the HTML output file.

With very little originality (or smarts), the wizard — er, Assistant — suggests saving the output to the root folder of your server's C drive as WEB.HTML. Unlike the Access Publish to the Web Wizard, no effort is made to make the filename tied to the published table, view, query, or stored procedure that you have chosen to publish. You come in at this point. I suggest that you direct the output to a more descriptive filename in a less generic location. For example, I saved my filename to the following folder:

```
c:\webpages\titles.html
```

By default, the SQL Server Web Assistant saves its output to a file location on the server machine. This is true even if you're executing the Web Assistant from a workstation that's not the same as the server.

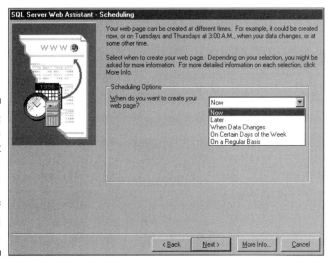

Figure 6-4: The Web Assistant lets you choose from a variety of scheduling options.

You get an error if you attempt to save the HTML to a nonexistent folder.

8. Indicate where the Web page formatting information should come from.

You can choose to have the formatting information come from an HTML template file, or you can opt to specify several formatting options on this page and the next. I discuss template files in Chapter 7, so for now select the second option, The following information.

9. If you chose the second option in Step 8, enter two titles.

You insert the first title into the page using the <TITLE> tag and becomes the caption of the browser window. Insert the second title at the top of the page. For example, I entered SQL Server Pubs Database into the first text box and Publication Titles into the second, as shown in Figure 6-5.

The final question on page 4 has to do with URL links.

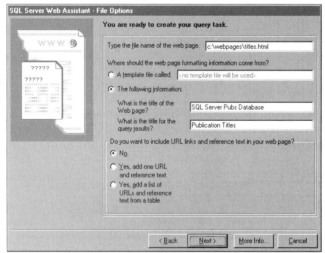

Figure 6-5:
You get to specify the name of the output file on this page as well as several formatting options.

10. Leave the default setting at No and click Next to advance to page 5.

Again, I defer discussion of URL links to Chapter 7.

On the final page of the Assistant — the formatting page — you get to specify a few more options that pertain to formatting. These options appear in Figure 6-6.

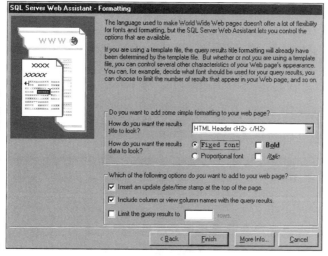

11. **Select a heading tag for the results title you entered on page 4 (the entry for which I entered** Publication Titles**).**

    Using a combo box control, you can choose any ⟨H⟩ tag from ⟨H1⟩ to ⟨H6⟩ where a tag of ⟨H1⟩ makes the title very large and a tag of ⟨H6⟩ makes the title quite small.

    The default of ⟨H2⟩ makes a reasonable choice.

    The results title combo box disables if you selected a template file on page 4.

12. **Set a few font formatting preferences for the results.**

    These settings affect the formatting of the data records. You can select either a fixed font (the results look like a typewriter) or a proportional font (the results look like the text in this book). In addition, you can opt that the results appear using bold or italics (or both).

    Choose whatever settings you'd like. (Am I fun or what?)

    At the bottom of the formatting page, the Assistant lists three additional options:

    • Insert an update date/time stamp at the top of the page.

    • Include column or view column names with the query results.

    • Limit the query results to some specified number of rows.

A date/time stamp is nice to have on the page. The stamp gives users browsing your page an idea of the timeliness (or staleness) of the data.

In most cases, you want to include column names, which make it easier for users to know what they're looking at.

Finally, you may wish to limit the number of records that the query returns. This option is especially useful when you're unsure of the number of records your query may return.

13. **When you finish with the formatting page, go ahead and click Finish.**

After a short delay, you see a beautiful checkered flag image and some congratulatory words, as shown in Figure 6-7.

Figure 6-7:
This cheery little page notifies you that you've successfully made it through the Web Assistant without reformatting your hard drive, bringing down the server, or launching any nuclear missiles.

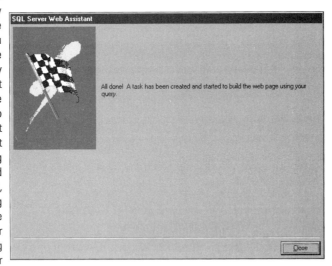

After that laborious session with the SQL Server Web Assistant, what do you have to show? An HTML page — what else? What's more, you get an HTML page that works with any Web browser. For example, Figure 6-8 shows my sample Web page as seen in Netscape Navigator 3.0.

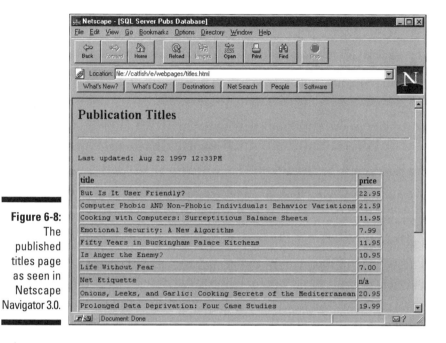

Figure 6-8:
The
published
titles page
as seen in
Netscape
Navigator 3.0.

Query Options

On the query page (page 2) of the SQL Server Web Assistant, you get to select from one of three query options:

- ✔ Build a query from a database hierarchy
- ✔ Enter a query as free-form text
- ✔ Use a query in a stored procedure

In order to follow along with the remaining examples in this chapter, you need to run the meals.sql script on the CD-ROM at the back of this book. The meals.sql script creates the SQL Server version of the meals database on your SQL Server machine. If you decide to follow along with my example (although you don't need to), make sure that you have at least 5MB of free space on your server before running the script. In addition, if you want to place the Meals device somewhere other than C:\MSSQL\DATA\MEALS.DAT, you must edit the script prior to executing it. See the comments at the beginning of the meals.sql for more details on how to edit the script.

A page with a view

If you completed the steps in the "Getting Started" section on the query page earlier in this chapter, you probably selected the first option (Build a query from a database hierarchy) and then proceeded to build a query from an existing table. You can also use the database hierarchy option with a saved view.

Free-form like a bird

When you select the second query option on the query page (Enter a query as free-form text), you essentially ask for a blank slate. You can enter any valid Transact-SQL statement you like that generates one or more rows of data.

The second query option makes sense only for those users who are quite comfortable with Transact-SQL (SQL Server dialect of the structured query language).

Using the free-form text query option, you can pull data from multiple tables, apply WHERE and ORDER BY clauses, or summarize data using a GROUP BY clause.

For example, say that you want to publish a GROUP BY query that summarizes total sales for each employee from the SQL Server version of the Meals database. The SQL for the query, which joins together four tables (tblEmployees, tblOrders, tblOrderItems, and tblMenuItems), follows:

```
SELECT SubString(LastName + ", " + FirstName,1,30)
AS Employee,
Sum(Quantity*Price) AS Sales
FROM tblMenuItems INNER JOIN ((tblEmployees
INNER JOIN tblOrders ON tblEmployees.EmployeeID =
tblOrders.EmployeeID)
INNER JOIN tblOrderItems ON tblOrders.OrderID =
tblOrderItems.OrderID)
ON tblMenuItems.MenuID = tblOrderItems.MenuID
WHERE Delivered = 1
GROUP BY SubString(LastName + ", " + FirstName,1,30)
```

If you enter this SQL statement into the large text box of the query page (after selecting the free-form text option and the Meals database), your screen looks something like that shown in Figure 6-9.

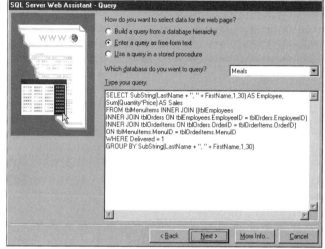

Figure 6-9:
Boy, that's
a long
query! I
wonder if it
actually
works?

SQL Server checks the syntax of your query when you click Next. If a syntax error appears, the Web Assistant lets you know with a not-very-helpful error message, shown in Figure 6-10.

Figure 6-10:
This
message
does a lot to
help you
find your
mistake.
Yeah, right!

If you get an error message like the one shown in Figure 6-10, but you can't locate your mistake, follow these steps:

1. **Copy your SQL statement to the clipboard.**

2. **Start up the SQL Query Tool (select Tools⇨SQL Query Tool from SQL Enterprise Manager).**

3. **Paste the SQL into the SQL Query Tool window and attempt to execute the query there.**

   You may still get a somewhat cryptic error message, but it's likely to help you more than the brain-dead error message you get from the Web Assistant.

The HTML page generated by the Web Assistant for my four-table SQL statement is shown in Figure 6-11.

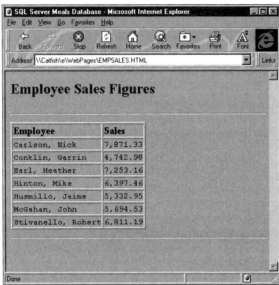

You can save yourself a load of time by always pretesting your free-form SQL. Use the SQL Enterprise Manager Query Tool, ISQL/W, or some other query tool before entering it into the Web Assistant query page.

Stored procedure, anyone?

You can also use a stored procedure to generate a Web page. Just select the Use a query in a stored procedure query option on the query page of the Wizard, select the database from the first combo box, and select the stored procedure from the second combo box (see Figure 6-12). After you select the stored procedure, the Web Assistant displays the text of the stored procedure, as shown in Figure 6-12. (In the figure, the stored procedure shown in the example is a saved version of the four-table GROUP BY query used in the last section.)

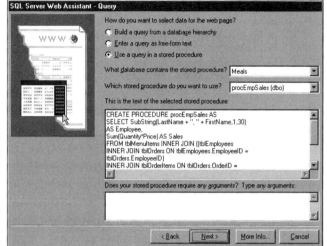

Figure 6-12:
Publishing a
SQL Server
stored
procedure
is easy.

If the stored procedure has input parameters, you can enter them into the text box at the bottom of the page. Unfortunately, the SQL Server Web Assistant provides no mechanism for entering parameters on the fly when the user is browsing the Web page. (The Access Publish to the Web Wizard *can* do this, as I discuss in Chapter 8 and 10.)

No matter which query option you choose — table, view, SQL statement, or stored procedure — once you click Next on the query page of the Web Assistant, the remaining pages of the SQL Server Web Assistant are identical. (Chapter 7 goes into some of these remaining pages in more detail.)

Chapter 7

Keeping Your Pages Fresh

. . . .

In This Chapter

▶ Republishing Web pages when data changes

▶ Publishing Web pages on a regular schedule

▶ Publishing templates

▶ Understanding how the SQL Server Web Assistant works

. . . .

*T*he SQL Server Web Assistant includes a scheduling component that the Access Publish to the Web Wizard lacks. This component lets you choose from several different scheduling options, including a provision that regenerates the HTML whenever the data in the underlying tables changes. In this chapter, you find out how to master the various scheduling options that the Assistant offers and how to use a template to guide the publishing process. You also gain a little insight into how the Assistant works.

Scheduling Options

Although the SQL Server Web Assistant doesn't support any options for generating dynamic pages using the dynamic protocols, the Assistant does provide several options that allow you to regenerate Web pages on some scheduled basis. On page three of the wizard, you can choose from one of the following scheduling options:

- ✔ Now (see Chapter 6)
- ✔ Later (see the section "You can pay me now or pay me later," later in this chapter)
- ✔ When Data Changes (see the section "Ch-ch-changes," later in this chapter)
- ✔ On Certain Days of the Week (see the section "Like clockwork," later in this chapter)
- ✔ On a Regular Basis (see the section "Like clockwork," later in this chapter)

Ultimately, you must decide which scheduling option works best for your situation. (See the section "Which option is best?" later in this chapter.)

The wizard doesn't provide any mechanism for posting your published HTML pages to a remote Web server. You can, however, always use the SQL Executive to create additional CMDExec tasks, which executes the Windows NT FTP program (see Chapter 5).

You can pay me now or pay me later

The Later option isn't too exciting. When you select this option, the SQL Server Web Assistant prompts you for a date and time at which it can generate the Web page (once). If the Web page involves an especially long query, the Later option may make sense. Otherwise, you haven't gained much. An example of using this option appears in Figure 7-1.

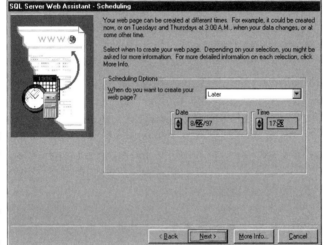

Figure 7-1: Deferring page generation to a later time.

Ch-ch-changes

The When Data Changes option is undoubtedly the most exciting of the lot and is what really sets the SQL Server Web Assistant apart from the Access Publish to the Web Wizard. When you choose this option, the wizard writes triggers that regenerate the HTML page whenever rows in any selected tables change. Wow!

When you choose the When Data Changes option on the scheduling page (page 3) of the Web Assistant, you need to select the table or tables to which you wish to tie the regeneration of the HTML pages (see Figure 7-2). These tables don't have to be the same as the names of the published objects, but obviously the two should be related in some way. Click the little box to the left of the table name to select that table.

You can also choose to create triggers that operate at the *column* level. To do so, click the + to the left of any of the tables in the list and select the names of the specific columns for which you want to tie page regeneration. When you do so, the update and insert triggers created by the Assistant fire off only if you make a change to the selected columns. (The delete trigger still fires if you delete a row. A delete isn't a column-specific action.)

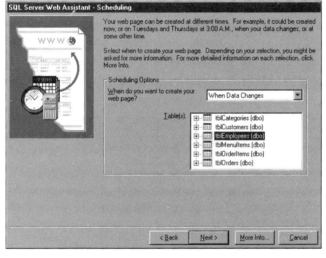

Figure 7-2:
You can easily tie page regeneration to database changes on a table or column basis.

If, in a previous lifetime, you've already created triggers for the tables, the polite little Assistant warns you that it has to modify your existing triggers by displaying a dialog box (see Figure 7-3). In this case, you get to say yea or nay to the modifications before the Web Assistant alters the triggers.

When you select the When Data Changes option, the Web Assistant doesn't create an HTML page until data in one of the selected tables actually changes.

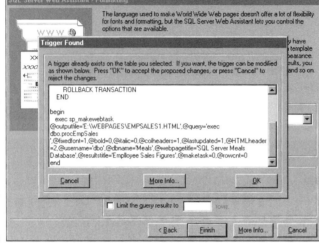

Figure 7-3:
If the Assistant discovers an existing trigger, it lets you know.

Like clockwork

When you choose the option On Certain Days of the Week on the scheduling page of the Web Assistant (page 3), the Web Assistant displays several additional controls on the wizard page. You can select one or more days of the week and a time at which to publish your page, as shown in Figure 7-4. Click once to select a day and twice to deselect a day.

You also can choose On a Regular Basis, in which case the Web Assistant lets you select an interval, as shown in Figure 7-5.

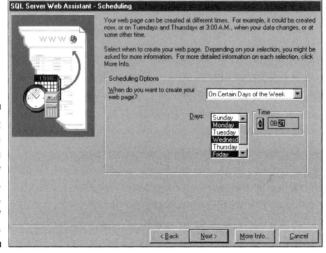

Figure 7-4:
This page republishes every Monday, Wednesday, and Friday at 8:21 a.m.

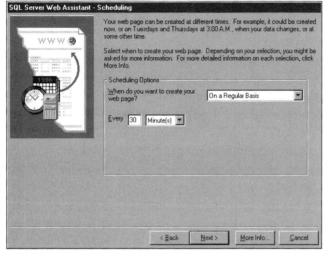

Figure 7-5:
This page
republishes
every 30
minutes.

Regardless of which of these two options you choose (On Certain Days of the Week or On a Regular Basis), the Web Assistant complies by creating a scheduled task that the SQL Server Executive service manages.

You can view, modify, and delete the scheduled tasks that the Web Assistant creates. Do so by choosing Server⇔Scheduled Tasks from the SQL Server Enterprise Manager, which displays the Manage Scheduled Tasks dialog box, shown in Figure 7-6.

If you want to see additional information about a task listed in this dialog box, double-click the selected task to display the Edit Task dialog box (see Figure 7-7). Here, you can disable the task, modify its schedule, or view a history log of the task.

Even though you may have a list of tasks displayed in the Manage Scheduled Tasks dialog box, they will never run unless you started the SQL Executive service. You can manually start and stop this process by choosing Server⇔SQL Executive from the SQL Enterprise Manager. In addition, if you choose Server⇔SQL Server⇔Configure, you can opt to automatically start the SQL Executive service at server boot time — which ain't such a bad idea.

Which option is best?

The scheduling option you choose depends on your particular situation. You must balance the timeliness of Web pages against the potential increased load on the server.

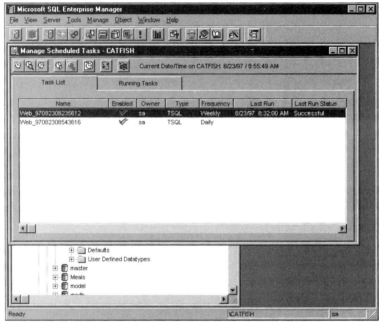

Figure 7-6:
You can view the tasks created by the Web Assistant in the Manage Scheduled Tasks dialog box of the SQL Enterprise Manager.

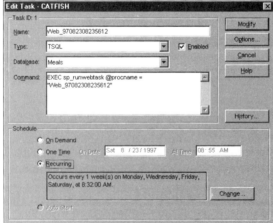

Figure 7-7:
You can edit the schedule of a task, disable it, or view its history using the Edit Task dialog box.

For example, say that you want your data to be very timely. If the database gets updated quite frequently (perhaps even several times a minute), choose the On a Regular Basis option with a short time interval (say, every 15 or 30 minutes). That option, rather than the When Data Changes option, makes more sense because you reduce the number of times the page is regenerated. After all, constant page-generation can impact the performance of your server.

On the other hand, if the data changes quite infrequently, the more sensible option is When Data Changes.

Using a Template

On the File Options page of the SQL Server Web Assistant (page 4), you can specify a template that the Web Assistant can use when publishing your Web page. Unlike the Access Publish to the Web Wizard template, the SQL Server Web Assistant template allows for only a single tag:

```
<%insert_data_here%>
```

You use the preceding tag to indicate (what else?) where the Assistant can insert the rows of data.

When you select a template, most of the other formatting options on the File Options page (as well as one of the options on the Formatting page) become disabled, as shown in Figure 7-8. The Web Assistant does this to indicate that it will derive those settings from your template file.

Figure 7-8: Choosing a template file disables most formatting options on the File Options page.

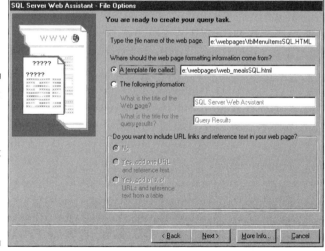

The following is a sample template file I created for the fictional Web_Meals.Com business:

```
<HTML>
<HEAD>
<TITLE>Web_Meals.Com</TITLE>
</HEAD>
<BODY background = gray.jpg>
<IMG SRC="web_meals.gif" ALT="web_meals.com logo">
<BR>
<H2>Our Menu</H2>
<%insert_data_here%>
<BR>
<H6><I>Produced by the SQL Server Web Assistant</I></H6>
</BODY>
</HTML>
```

When you use a template, you can have the Assistant generate Web pages that have a consistent look and feel without having to do a lot of post-Assistant processing.

For example, the page produced by publishing the tblMenuItems table using the Web_MealsSQL.HTML template appears in Figure 7-9 in Internet Explorer 4.0.

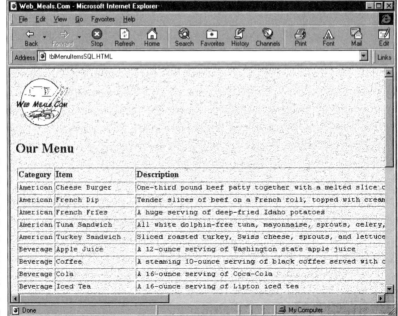

Figure 7-9: This Web page looks a little less barren than pages generated without a template.

URLs Are Us

When you don't use a template, the SQL Server Web Assistant lets you add a single URL reference or a list of URL references to the bottom of the generated page. I guess the logic is that if you're using a template, you put in your own links. (A URL is the *Uniform Resource Locator* — an Internet/intranet address.) Nothing too earth-shattering here. Just a little convenience.

If you select Yes, add one URL and reference text, the Web Assistant requests a URL and a label from you, as shown in Figure 7-10. To add a URL, simply type your URL in the text box next to the option.

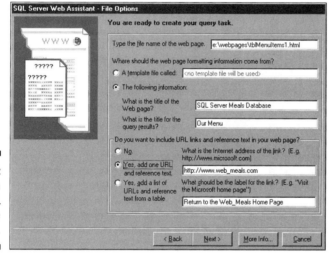

Figure 7-10:
Adding a
single URL
to the
Web page.

You also can choose to grab a bunch of URL addresses from a table, as shown in Figure 7-11. For example, I chose tblURLs, a table in the Meals sample database. When you select this option, you must enter a SQL statement that returns two columns of data. The first column should contain the actual URL address (in the form `http://youscratchmyitchiscratchyours.com`). The second column should contain a label you wish to display on the page for the link (in the form Click Me!). A sample Web page generated by using a list of URL addresses from tblURLs appears in Figure 7-12.

How Does It Work?

After the SQL Server Web Assistant gathers all the answers you have graciously provided, the Assistant does all its magic by executing a system-stored procedure, `sp_makewebtask`.

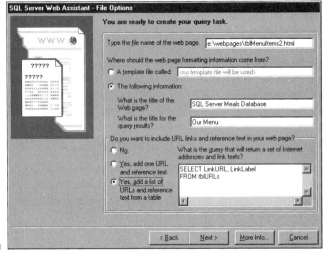

Figure 7-11:
Adding a list of URLs from the tblURLs table.

Figure 7-12:
A SQL Server Web Assistant-generated Web page complete with a list of URL addresses.

Nothing prevents you from calling `sp_makewebtask` yourself without going through the wizard. If you schedule a Web page to generate when data changes, you can see that the trigger the Web Assistant wrote calls — you guessed it — `sp_makewebtask`, as shown in Figure 7-13.

Figure 7-13:
This trigger
calls a
system
procedure
to generate
a Web page
whenever
you insert a
new row
into the
table.

An easy way to figure out the correct calling convention for any system-stored procedure is to use the `sp_helpsql system` procedure. For example, to obtain some help text for the `sp_makewebtask` procedure, run a query with the following Transact SQL: `sp_helpsql sp_makewebtask`.

The `sp_makewebtask` system procedure doesn't actually generate the Web pages. It calls an extended stored procedure (an *extended stored procedure* is a stored procedure written in a compiled programming language such as C++ and lives inside a DLL file) named `xp_makewebtask` to do the actual page operation.

Is That All There Is to the Assistant?

If you're disappointed that the SQL Server Web Assistant doesn't support dynamic querying or updating of data, don't fret. In later parts of the book, I show you how to use Visual InterDev, the Internet Database Connector (IDC) and Active Server Pages (ASP) to create truly dynamic Web pages that draw their data from SQL Server.

Part IV
Getting Dynamic with the Internet Database Connector

The 5th Wave · By Rich Tennant

"I think the cursor's not moving, Mr. Dunt, because you've got your hand on the chalk-board eraser and not the mouse."

In this part . . .

The Access 97 Publish to the Web Wizard can produce two types of Web pages: static and dynamic. Although any Web server can host static HTML pages, these pages are only as current as the last time you generated them. Fortunately, the Access Publish to the Web Wizard also supports dynamic publishing.

This part covers the first type of dynamic publishing supported by the wizard: the Internet Database Connector (IDC). In Chapter 8, you find out how to generate the IDC pages using the Access Publish to the Web Wizard. In Chapter 9, you find out how to code IDC pages without the benefit of the wizard. You can use these hand-tuned pages to read and write data to Access and SQL Server tables.

Chapter 8

Generating Dynamic Web Pages with the Access Wizard

. . . .

. . . .

*T*he difference between static HTML and dynamic IDC pages comes down to the difference between pushing and pulling. When you use the Access Publish to the Web Wizard to generate static HTML pages from database records, you *push* the pages out to your server based on some schedule that you — the publisher — must determine. The data is only as fresh as the last time you pushed the pages out to the server. On the other hand, when you use the Access Publish to the Web Wizard to publish database records to the Internet Database Connector (IDC) format, you merely create a specification that allows users to *pull* the latest database records to them *at the moment they link to the IDC Web page.*

In the static pull world, the onus is on you, as the publisher, to ensure your pages are as timely as possible. In the dynamic pull world, you no longer need to worry about when to republish the pages because users always get the most up-to-date data at the moment they request the IDC page.

In this chapter, I show you how to use the Access Publish to the Web Wizard together with the Internet Database Connector (IDC) format to create dynamic *pull* Web pages. You explore how to create the IDC pages from Access tables and queries, including parameter queries, and how to link to these pages from any browser.

Publishing to the IDC Format

Publishing to the Internet Database Connector (IDC) format using the Access Publish to the Web Wizard is only slightly more involved than publishing to the static HTML format.

Say that a database changes fairly frequently and you'd like to create a dynamic version that is always current. Although you can create such a page using static HTML, you have to regenerate the page every time the database changes. With the IDC format, you need to create the page only once. Actually, you don't create an IDC Web page. Instead, you create a specification that the Web server uses at run time to create the page on the fly.

All the examples I use in this chapter come from the Meals.MDB database on the CD-ROM at the back of this book.

The IDC format pages work only with the following Microsoft Internet servers:

- ✔ Internet Information Server (for Windows NT Server), Version 2.0 or later
- ✔ Peer Web Services or Personal Web Services (for Windows NT Workstation)
- ✔ Personal Web Server (for Windows 95)

If you use a different Web server, you can't use the IDC format. On the other hand, the Microsoft servers are free. The servers cost nothing, nada! Thus, even if you use a different Web server, you may want to install one of the Microsoft Web servers on a test machine where you can experiment with the IDC pages. Check out Chapter 2 for information on obtaining and configuring the Microsoft Web servers.

After you install one of the Microsoft Web servers, you must decide where the IDC pages can reside on your server. Unlike pure HTML files, IDC pages must reside in a Web directory to which you've assigned both Read and Script rights. (Head over to Chapter 2 for information on how to create Web directories and set the correct access permissions.)

For the examples in this chapter, I created a Web directory (following the steps from Chapter 2) with the following name:

```
\inetpub\wwwroot\web_meals
```

and the following alias name:

```
/web_meals
```

Make sure that you assign both Read and Script access rights to your Web directory (see Chapter 2).

How you publish

To use the Publish to the Web Wizard to publish an Access database object to the IDC format, follow these steps:

1. **Choose <u>F</u>ile⇨Save As <u>H</u>TML to start the Access Publish to the Web Wizard.**

   The wizard starts, displaying the first page.

2. **Click <u>N</u>ext to proceed to page 2.**

   You don't need to do anything on page 1 unless you want to retrieve an existing saved profile (see Chapter 5).

3. **On page 2, select an object to publish and click <u>N</u>ext.**

   If you want an example to follow along with, use the qryMenuItemsSorted query from the Meals.MDB database. This query sorts the menu items by category and item, which should make for a nice menu.

4. **On page 3, select the template you want to use to publish to the IDC format, if any, and click <u>N</u>ext.**

   For example, I chose the Web_Meals.htm template fill, which you can find on the CD-ROM.

5. **On page 4, select Dynamic HTX/IDC (Microsoft Internet Information Server), as shown in Figure 8-1, and click <u>N</u>ext.**

   Choosing this object tells the wizard that — you guessed it — you want to publish the selected object to the IDC format.

   When you publish to the IDC format, you need to enter an additional page of information that isn't necessary when you publish to the static HTML format (see Figure 8-2).

   Remember that because the IDC format is a *dynamic* format, the IDC pages produced by the wizard need to establish a link to your Access database to create the HTML file on the fly at the moment the user requests the IDC page.

6. **Type your name for the Open Database Connectivity (ODBC) data source into the first text box on page 5 of the wizard.**

   For example, I typed WebMeals as my data source name.

   Don't worry that you haven't yet created the ODBC data source — you can do that later after you're finished using the wizard.

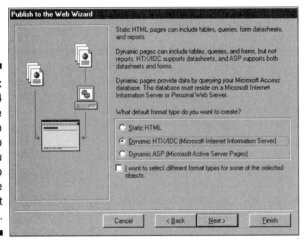

Figure 8-1:
On page 4
of the
Publish to
the Web
Wizard, you
get to
choose the
output
format.

Figure 8-2:
You use this
page to
identify the
data source
that
connects
the IDC files
to the
Access
database.

7. If your database is protected by Access security, enter a user name and password for the data source in the second and third text boxes on the wizard page, and click Next.

Because the Meals database I'm working with isn't secured, I left these text boxes blank (see Figure 8-2).

The last two text boxes on the wizard page apply only to Active Server Pages, so you can leave them blank.

The way the IDC format works, all users log on by using the same user name and password. This doesn't make for a terribly flexible (or secure) system because users browsing your Web site can easily read the IDC file. However, you still can protect your data adequately from any potentially malicious activity. Create an account specifically for Web access and limit the account's access rights to read-only access for the tables in the database you're publishing.

The remaining pages of the wizard are the same as when you publish to the static HTML format.

See Chapter 3 for more details on completing these pages.

When you click Finish, the wizard quits and creates the IDC files.

What you get

When you use the Publish to the Web Wizard to publish an Access database object to the IDC format, you end up with the following two files:

- **An Internet Database Connector specification file with the .IDC extension.** This file specifies the source for the data. The data this file retrieves is merged by the Internet Database Connector with the HTX file to produce an HTML page, which gets sent back to the client. In my example, this file has the name qryMenuItemsSorted_1.IDC.

- **An HTML Extension file with the .HTX extension.** This file specifies the layout for the data retrieved by the Internet Database Connector using the IDC file. In my example, this file has the name qryMenuItemsSorted_1.HTX.

If you want details on the internals of these files, head over to Chapter 9. For now, I just cover how to get the files working on your system.

Making the IDC files work

The server is meant to execute the IDC and HTX files. But you need to take several additional steps before the server can execute the files: You must copy the files to your Web server and create an ODBC System data source that points to the Access database where the data gets stored.

Unlike the static HTML files produced by the wizard, you *can't view* the data retrieved by the IDC and HTX files without involving a Web server. If you open the IDC or HTX file directly in your browser, your browser employs the file protocol to directly read the file instead of routing the page through the server.

Copying the files to your server

Before you can execute the IDC files, you need to copy the files to your server. Copy the published HTX, IDC, and HTML files (along with any .GIF or .JPG files) from the wizard output folder (in the example, C:\WebPages) to an executable Web directory (folder) on your Web server (in the example, \inetpub\wwwroot\web_meals).

You also need to copy the Access database to a folder that your Web server can access. The location of this folder can be on another machine on the network, but you get the best performance if you place the file on your Web server machine. For the example, I copied the Meals.mdb file to the same folder to which I copied the IDC and HTX files, \inetpub\wwwroot\web_meals.

Creating the ODBC data source

On the Web server machine, you must create an ODBC system data source that points to the Access 97 database from which the Internet Database Connector reads records. You use the ODBC Data Source Administrator program to create and manage data sources.

Follow these steps to create a data source:

1. **From the Windows Control Panel, fire up the ODBC Control Panel applet and click the System DSN tab to display existing system data sources.**

   Creating a system data source is important because user data sources are not accessible to Web users. After clicking the System DSN tab, your screen should look something like Figure 8-3.

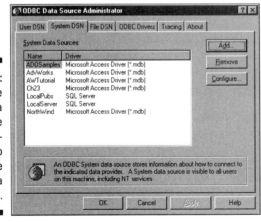

Figure 8-3: You use the ODBC Data Source Administrator to manage ODBC data sources.

2. Click the A_d_d button to create a new data source.

The Create New Data Source dialog box appears.

3. Select Microsoft Access Driver (*.mdb) and click _F_inish.

Despite the button's caption, the only thing you finish at this point is selecting the driver you want to use. When you click Finish, the ODBC Microsoft Access 97 Setup dialog box, shown in Figure 8-4, appears.

Figure 8-4:
In this dialog box, you get to name your data source and specify which database it should point to.

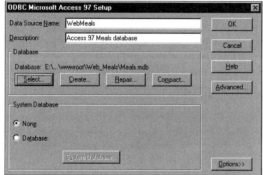

4. Type a name for the new data source.

For example, I typed WebMeals in the Data Source Name text box to match the name of the data source I referenced in the wizard.

5. Type whatever you want in the _D_escription text box and click _S_elect to select the database.

The Select Database dialog box appears.

6. Point to the database you want and click OK to select it.

For the example database, I located Meals.mdb in the server's \inetpub\wwwroot\web_meals folder.

You return to the ODBC Microsoft Access 97 Setup dialog box.

7. Click OK to exit the ODBC Data Source Administrator.

Remember that you must create a *system* data source, not a user data source, on the Web server machine. If you create a system or file data source by mistake, make sure that you delete it before creating a system data source with the same name.

Previewing the results

Now you're ready to preview your published IDC Web page. The exact address you link to, however, depends on whether you use an intranet or the Internet, and your server or domain name.

- **Intranet:** If your Web server connects to your machine across a LAN or intranet, you need to know the name of the Web server and the virtual Web directory where the files are located. Enter a URL in the following format:

  ```
  http://server_name/virtual_directory/page.idc?
  ```

  where *server_name* is the machine name of the Web server, *virtual_directory* is the Web folder that hosts the Web page, and *page.idc* is the name of the IDC page that the Access wizard generates.

  For example, if your local Web server has the name *catfish* and the files are located in the \inetpub\wwwroot\web_meals directory, type the following address into your browser:

  ```
  http://catfish/web_meals/qryMenuItemsSorted_1.idc?
  ```

- **Internet:** If you post your Web files to an Internet server, you need to enter a URL in this format:

  ```
  http://www.site_name/virtual_directory/page.idc?
  ```

  where *site_name* is the domain name of the Web server, *server_folder* is the Web folder that hosts the Web page, and *page.idc* is the name of the IDC page that the Access wizard generates. For example, if your site name is Web_Meals.Com and it's located in the server's root directory, you enter the following address into your browser:

  ```
  http://www.web_meals.com/qryMenuItemsSorted_1.idc?
  ```

When you link to an IDC page, you must append a question mark to the end of the address.

The results of the IDC query

The results of executing the example IDC query appear in Figure 8-5. IDC queries execute entirely on the server. Only the results of the query in the form of standard HTML get sent back to the browser. Thus, IDC pages are not tied to Microsoft Internet Explorer as Figure 8-5 shows you.

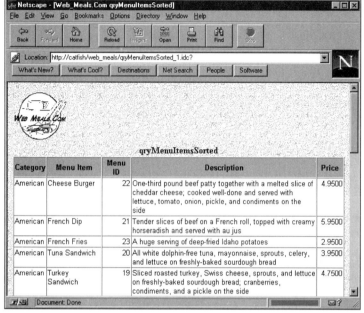

Figure 8-5:
The results
of the IDC
query
shown in
Netscape
Navigator.

My users won't type that!

You have no need to lose any sleep over the fact that users have to link to your IDC pages using a weird syntax like this:

```
http://www.mysite.com/page.idc?
```

Although the actual IDC hyperlink must be in this form, your users do not need to type this address. Have your users link to a home page made of standard HTML. And on this home page, place the actual link to the IDC file. Thus, the odd hyperlink becomes completely transparent to your browser-happy users. And if you ask the wizard to create a home page for you (see Chapter 3 for more details), you then get an example of how to set up the hyperlink to your IDC page.

What Else Can You Publish?

You're not limited to publishing queries to the IDC format. Table 8-1 lists the types of objects you can publish to this format.

Table 8-1		Access Objects You Can Publish to the IDC Format
Access Object	*Publishable?*	*Comments*
Table	Yes	
Query	Yes	Select and Totals queries only. Supports parameters.
Form	Yes	Publishes underlying datasheet for form.
Report	No	
Macro	No	
Module	No	

When you publish a form to the IDC format, the wizard publishes the data sheet for the form's record source, not a facsimile of the form.

Probably the most exciting thing about the IDC format is the ability to publish parameter queries (see the following section). When you do so, the wizard creates an extra HTML page that prompts the user for one or more parameters and passes that information along to the IDC query.

Publishing Parameter Queries

Publishing a parameter query to the IDC format is not that much more involved than publishing a regular query (without parameters). Most of the extra work you need to perform comes up front in making sure that the query is set up correctly before invoking the Publish to the Web Wizard.

Creating a parameter query in Access boils down to these four essential steps:

1. **Create a regular select query.**

2. **Enter each parameter surrounded by brackets in the criteria section of the query grid.**

3. **Declare each parameter and its data type by choosing Query⇨Parameters.**

   This displays the Query Parameters dialog box. In Figure 8-6, I have defined three query parameters.

4. **Click OK to save the parameters.**

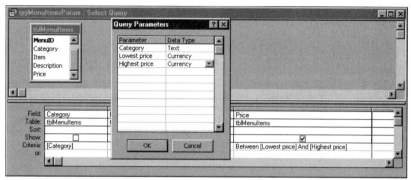

Figure 8-6:
You must
declare
your
parameters
before you
publish the
query.

The problem is that many users don't perform Step 3, but Access — the
astute and helpful program it is — can still run the query because it normally guesses the parameter data types for you. Well, it turns out that the
Access Publish to the Web Wizard needs the parameter declarations in
order to correctly publish parameter queries. Thus, before you publish a
parameter query, you need to ensure that all the query's parameters
declare.

Follow these steps to publish the query:

1. **Create a parameter query using the Access query tool.**

   Make sure that you declare each and every parameter.

2. **Start up the Access Publish to the Web Wizard and choose to publish
   the parameter query in the IDC format.**

   See the section "How you publish" earlier in this chapter for details on
   how to publish a query. After choosing the IDC format on page 4 of the
   wizard, click the Next button.

3. **On page 5 of the wizard, enter the name of a data source and click
   Finish.**

   When you click Finish, the wizard prompts for each parameter as it
   generates the IDC files. The prompt is a side effect of the wizard's need
   to open the parameter query to publish it.

4. **Click OK for each parameter without entering any data.**

   The data you supply for these parameter prompts has no bearing on
   the published pages.

5. **The wizard generates the published Web pages for your query.**

The trouble with wild cards

Many Access queries include criteria that combine a parameter with a wild-card character to make for a very flexible query. For example, the criteria for the LastName field of the qryLastNameLikeParam query in the Meals database look like this:

```
Like [First few letters of last
   name] & "*"
```

If you publish this query, however, you find that when you enter criteria of one or more letters into the text box, your Web browser displays an unwanted page that looks similar to the one shown in the accompanying figure.

A bug in the wizard creates a bogus SQL string when publishing this sort of query. The solution is pretty simple, however, requiring you to edit the WHERE clause of the SQL statement in the IDC file. Replace the following WHERE clause:

```
WHERE (((tblCustomers.LastName)
   Like '%First few letters of
   last name%' & '%%'));
```

with this WHERE clause:

```
WHERE (((tblCustomers.LastName)
   Like '%First few letters of
   last name%%'));
```

The only difference between these two WHERE clauses is that in the second WHERE clause I deleted five characters between the parameter and the wildcard character (an apostrophe, space, ampersand, space, and an apostrophe).

When you make this fix and save the IDC file, the query runs without a hitch.

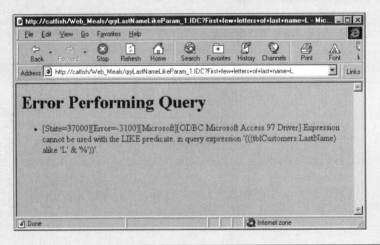

When publishing a parameter query to the IDC format, the wizard creates three files:

- ✔ **An Internet Database Connector (IDC) file.** When I published the qryMenuitemsParam query, the wizard named the IDC file for this query qryMenuItemsParam_1.IDC.

- ✔ **An HTML Extension (HTX) file.** In the same example, the wizard named this file qryMenuItemsParam_1.HTX.

- ✔ **An HTML page that collects the parameters and submits them to the IDC file.** In my example, the wizard has named this file qryMenuItemsParam_1.HTML.

After you copy the published files (and any .GIF and .JPG files needed for the pages) to your Web server, you're ready to test your published parameter query.

Once again, you need to force the server to process your pages. You need to add an `http://` prefix to the address to force the server to execute your query. This time, however, you want to link to the HTML page that collects the parameters rather than the IDC page itself. Again, the exact address you enter depends on your configuration.

For example, if an intranet server named `catfish` hosts the Web pages, and the files are located in the virtual directory, you enter the following address:

```
http://catfish/web_meals/qryMenuItemsParam_1.html
```

If instead, you use an Internet server named Web_Meals.Com, and you place the Web pages in the server's root directory, then you enter the following address:

```
http://www.web_meals.com/qryMenuItemsParam_1.html
```

If you're publishing a parameter query from a database for which you've never set up an ODBC data source, don't forget to create the data source. Take a look at the section called "Making the IDC files work," earlier in this chapter.

When you link to your file, the Web page prompts you for the parameters, as shown in Figure 8-7. When you enter values into the parameter text boxes and click the Run Query button, your browser passes the parameters to the IDC page on the server. The IDC page then requests that the server execute the IDC query, returning to your browser a page like the one shown in Figure 8-8.

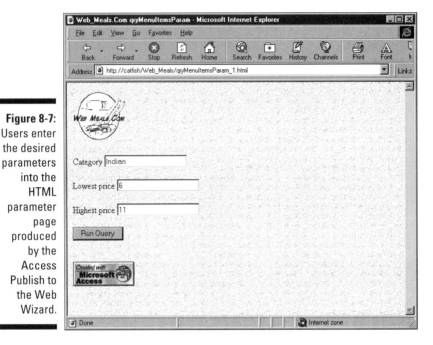

Figure 8-7:
Users enter
the desired
parameters
into the
HTML
parameter
page
produced
by the
Access
Publish to
the Web
Wizard.

Figure 8-8:
This IDC
parameter
query
displays
only the
records
meeting the
parameter
criteria.

Chapter 9

Exploring the Innards of IDC

*A*lthough the Access 97 Publish to the Web Wizard gives you a great start in generating IDC files (see Chapter 8), the wizard takes you only so far. The Access wizard can't help you in two areas in particular: using the IDC to update data and using the IDC with server data. This chapter tackles both these areas and more.

How the IDC Works

The Internet Database Connector is a special application that runs on Microsoft Internet servers, acting as a go-between for your Web pages and databases.

The IDC is an Internet Server Application Programming Interface (ISAPI) application. See Chapters 1 and 2 for more information on ISAPI and how it compares to the Common Gateway Interface (CGI) standard.

To create an IDC query, you must create two files: the IDC and the HTX file.

> ✔ **IDC file:** In the IDC file, you specify a data source and an SQL statement that the IDC uses to read or write records to an Open Database Connectivity (ODBC) database. You also specify here the name of the corresponding HTX file. IDC files use the file extension .IDC.

✔ **HTX file:** In the HTML Extension (HTX) file, you specify how the data retrieved using the IDC file is to appear to the user. The HTX file consists of standard HTML, along with special IDC tags, that tell the IDC where to place the data as it merges with the HTX file. HTX files use the file extension .HTX. What a surprise!

Note the distinction between the IDC (the technology) and the IDC file (the specification file with the .DIC extension that you must create to use the IDC). Yes, it can be a little confusing!

When you hyperlink to an IDC file, the following sequence of steps occurs:

1. **The Web server recognizes that the IDC file you requested requires special processing, so it passes along the IDC file to the IDC dynamic link library (DLL).**

2. **The IDC DLL reads the IDC file, passing the SQL statement and the name of the data source to the Open Database Connectivity (ODBC) Administrator program.**

3. **The ODBC Administrator program passes the SQL statement to the appropriate ODBC driver, which then passes the SQL statement along to the database.**

4. **The database runs the query and returns any rows to the IDC DLL via ODBC.**

5. **The IDC DLL merges the returned rows with the HTX file, producing a standard HTML file, which it passes along to the Web server.**

6. **Finally, the Web server passes the HTML file back to the browser over the Internet or intranet connection.**

Because the result of the IDC request is a standard HTML file, you can use any browser with the IDC. On the other hand, the server that hosts the IDC pages must support ISAPI and the IDC, which means that you have to use a Microsoft Web or compatible server (see Chapter 2 for details about compatible servers).

Constructing the IDC and HTX files is pretty easy because both are fairly simple files. The only requirements you need are a working knowledge of SQL and HMTL.

The IDC file

You use the IDC file to identify the ODBC data source and SQL statement you want to send to the data source. The IDC file consists of a series of statements in the following format:

```
field: value
```

Only three statements are necessary; several additional statements are optional. The required statements are

- ✔ Datasource: You use this statement to specify the name of the ODBC system data source.

- ✔ Template: You use this statement to specify the name of the HTX file that guides the formatting of the output. To make things simple, I recommend you always use a name that's the same as the root name (the part of the file without the extension) of the IDC file but with the HTX extension.

- ✔ SQLStatement: You use this statement to specify the SQL statement that retrieves the data from the data source. The SQL dialect needs to be plain vanilla ODBC SQL. If you need to use more than one line for the SQL statement, start continuation lines with a plus character (+). You may reference parameters passed to the IDC page by surrounding them with percent signs. You may include multiple SQLStatement statements.

Here's the syntax of an IDC file:

```
Datasource: odbc_system_data_source
Template: htx_file_name
SQLStatement: sql_statement
```

For example, say that you want to create a simple IDC Web page that contains the categories from the tblCategories table of the Access Meals database. (This example presumes that you've already created an ODBC data source named WebMeals that points to the Meals.mdb file. Check out Chapter 8 for more details on creating an ODBC data source.) I created an IDC file named categories.idc that looks like this:

```
Datasource: WebMeals
Template: categories.htx
SQLStatement: SELECT Category
+ FROM tblCategories;
```

This file doesn't do anything until you also create an accompanying HTX file.

The HTX file

You use the HTX file to indicate how you want the output that the IDC query generates laid out on your Web page. The HTX file is a mixture of standard HTML- and IDC-specific tags.

You indicate where the data records go by using the `<%begindetail%>` and `<%enddetail%>` tags. Repeat everything between these two tags for each row that the IDC query returns.

Between the `<%begindetail%>` and `<%enddetail%>` tags, you indicate where the values of fields (that the IDC query returns) go with field tags in the form `<%field_name%>`.

Here's the basic shell of an HTX file that displays a single field in a list:

```
<HTML>
<HEAD>
<TITLE>title</TITLE>
</HEAD>
<BODY>
heading<BR>
<%begindetail%>
  <%field_name%><BR>
<%enddetail%>
</BODY>
</HTML>
```

For example, here's the HTX file that corresponds to the categories.idc file (categories.htx) from the section "The IDC file" earlier in this chapter:

```
<HTML>
<HEAD>
<TITLE>Web_Meals.Com</TITLE>
</HEAD>
<BODY>
<H2>The Web_Meals.Com Food Categories</H2>
<B>Category</B><BR>
<%begindetail%>
   <%category%><BR>
<%enddetail%>
</BODY>
</HTML>
```

When a user links to your IDC page, the IDC query executes on the server, the results become merged with the HTX file, and the resulting HTML gets sent back to your browser. For example, if you link to the categories.idc example file, your screen should resemble the page shown in Figure 9-1 (assuming that you're using Internet Explorer 4.0).

You need to link to an IDC file using the HTTP protocol. Also, don't forget to append a question mark to the right side of the URL. See Chapter 8 for more details.

Figure 9-1:
The
categories.idc
Web page,
as shown in
Internet
Explorer 4.0.

Beyond Read-Only Queries

In addition to creating read-only select queries, you can use the IDC to update data. When designing a page that you use to update data using the IDC, you need to consider two issues:

    ✔ Collecting the data

    ✔ Using the collected data to update data in the database

Although the IDC helps you with making the update, it can't help you with collecting data. You need to somehow collect the necessary data from the user by using an HTML form.

If you're unfamiliar with HTML forms, you may want to pull out an HTML reference before continuing with this section. One such reference is *HTML For Dummies,* 3rd Edition, by Ed Tittel and Stephen N. James (IDG Books Worldwide, Inc.).

In the following example, I create a Web page that customers can use to add their names and addresses to the customer list stored in the tblCustomers table in the SQL Server version of the Meals database. The example, which you can find on the CD-ROM at the back of this book, involves three files:

    ✔ **AddCustomer.HTML:** This HTML page uses an HTML form to collect the information needed to insert a new row into the Meals database.

    ✔ **AddCustomer.IDC:** This IDC file inserts the new row into the Meals database.

    ✔ **AddCustomer.HTX:** This HTX file provides feedback that the insert indeed worked.

I explain these three files in detail in the following sections and show you how they work.

If you want to try the example out at home, you must create an ODBC data source named WebMealsSQL that points to the SQL Server version of the Meals database. If you need more information on how to do this or on how to create the SQL Server version of the Meals database, head over to Chapters 6 and 8. Chapter 6 discusses creating the Meals database, and Chapter 8 shows you how to create ODBC data sources.

If you're creating your own files, you must create an ODBC system data source that points to the database that you want to use. You can use any database as long as you have an ODBC driver for the database. Databases you may use include desktop databases, such as Access, FoxPro, or Paradox, as well as server databases, such as SQL Server, Oracle, or DB2.

The AddCustomer.HTML file

This standard HTML file requires an HTML form to collect the information from the user and pass the information along to the IDC file. Following is what the HTML looks like:

```
<HTML>
<HEAD>
<TITLE>Web_Meals.Com New Customer Form</TITLE>
</HEAD>
<BODY background = gray.jpg>
<IMG SRC="web_meals.gif" ALT="web_meals.com logo"
ALIGN=left>
<FONT COLOR="0000FF">
<BR><BR><H2>Become a Web_Meals.Com Customer!</H2>
</FONT><BR CLEAR=ALL>
<FORM METHOD="GET" ACTION="AddCustomer.IDC">
First Name <INPUT TYPE="Text" NAME="FirstName" SIZE=25>
Last Name <INPUT TYPE="Text" NAME="LastName" SIZE=25><P>
Address <INPUT TYPE="Text" NAME="Address" SIZE=40><P>
City <INPUT TYPE="Text" NAME="City" SIZE=25>
State <INPUT TYPE="Text" NAME="State" SIZE=4>
Zip Code <INPUT TYPE="Text" NAME="ZipCode" SIZE=15><P>
Phone Num <INPUT TYPE="Text" NAME="Phone" SIZE=25><P>
Special information we should know about you
<INPUT TYPE="Text" NAME="Notes" SIZE=50><P>
<INPUT TYPE="Submit" VALUE="OK-Sign Me Up!">
<INPUT TYPE="Reset" VALUE="Clear Form">
```

```
<P><A HREF=default.html>On second thought,
I don't want to become a customer</A>
</FORM>
</BODY>
</HTML>
```

The preceding code is just standard HTML form code. A bunch of input text controls collects the data. The FORM tag points the results to the AddCustomer.IDC file when the user clicks the submit button.

The AddCustomer.IDC file

Following is the IDC file that adds the record to the database:

```
Datasource: WebMealsSQL
Template: AddCustomer.HTX
SQLStatement: INSERT INTO tblCustomers
+ (FirstName, LastName,
+ Address, City, State,
+ ZipCode, Phone, Notes)
+ VALUES ('%FirstName%', '%LastName%',
+ '%Address%', '%City%', '%State%',
+ '%ZipCode%', '%Phone%', '%Notes%')
Username: WebUser
Password:
```

This IDC file differs in three ways from the read-only example found in the section "How the IDC Works," earlier in this chapter:

- ✔ Uses an SQL Server data source, WebMealsSQL.

- ✔ Includes the Username and Password statements that you must use with server databases like SQL Server that require a logon.

- ✔ Uses an action query SQL statement (the INSERT statement) to add rows to a table.

When linking to a server database, security becomes an issue because most server databases require some sort of logon. In this example, I create a WebUser login for SQL Server (by choosing Manage⇨Logins from SQL Enterprise Manager) and assign the appropriate permissions to the Meals database objects for this account (by choosing Object⇨Permissions).

You can use any standard SQL statement with the Internet Database Connector. The IDC, however, doesn't support nonstandard SQL extensions such as the Access TRANSFORM or DISTINCTROW keywords. Some of the statements you can use with the IDC include

- ✔ SELECT: Returns a list of existing rows
- ✔ INSERT: Adds new rows to a table
- ✔ DELETE: Deletes rows from a table
- ✔ UPDATE: Modifies values in existing rows

The AddCustomer.HTX file

When you create an IDC file that performs an action that returns no rows, you normally use the HTX file to confirm that the action occurred. You must have an HTX file because the IDC requires it to know what to do when the query is done. In the AddCustomer example, I create a very simple HTX file that confirms the addition of the new customer and lets the user continue with some other activity.

The following HTX file doesn't contain any special IDC tags — just straight HTML:

```
<HTML>
<HEAD>
<TITLE>Web_Meals.Com New Customer</TITLE>
</HEAD>
<BODY>
<H3>Thanks for becoming a new customer!</H3>
<P><A HREF=default.html>Continue...</A>
</BODY>
</HTML>
```

Testing the example

The AddCustomer.HTML form appears in Figure 9-2, as seen in Netscape Navigator. To use it, a customer enters his or her name and address and then clicks the OK — Sign Me Up! Button. This action submits the form and all the values in its controls to the AddCustomer.IDC page.

If the INSERT statement succeeds, the HTX file merges with the IDC output and gets sent back to the user as HTML, as shown in Figure 9-3. (In this example, no data is merged with the HTX file because an INSERT statement doesn't return any rows.)

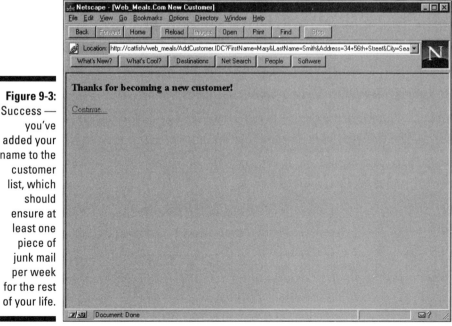

Figure 9-2:
Entering
data
into the
AddCustomer
HTML file
as shown in
Netscape
Navigator
3.0.

Figure 9-3:
Success —
you've
added your
name to the
customer
list, which
should
ensure at
least one
piece of
junk mail
per week
for the rest
of your life.

Troubleshooting errors

If the IDC query can't perform its assigned duties because of some problem with the SQL statement, the ODBC driver, security, or the server, the query returns an error message to the user.

For example, the first time I attempted to run the AddCustomer.IDC query (after I worked the other bugs out), I received the error message shown in Figure 9-4. At that point, I hit myself in the head and, when I had recovered from the trauma, instantly realized that I had forgotten to assign the Insert permission to the WebUser account.

Other errors that may occur include

- **Data source name not found:** This means that either you never created the data source on the server or you forgot to make it a system data source. If you get this error, make sure that you first delete the user data source (using the ODBC Data Source Administrator program) before creating a system data source with the same name.

- **Access forbidden:** This error, shown in Figure 9-5, occurs when you've placed the IDC files in a Web directory that lacks the Script (Execute in some version of Microsoft Web servers) permission. While normal static HTML files don't need the Script/Execute permission, IDC and ASP files do. Chapter 2 has information on how to create Web directories with the necessary permissions.

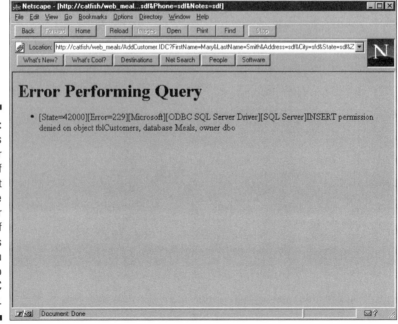

Figure 9-4: You get this sort of error message if you don't have the proper set of permissions when you attempt to run an IDC query.

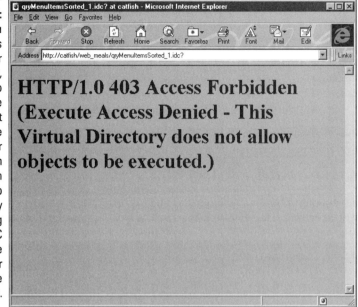

✔ **Other:** Database errors may occur because the IDC query would break rules, cause a referential integrity error, or attempt to perform some other illegal situation.

Making the IDC Dance

You can do lots more with the Internet Database Connector. In this section, I share with you various tips and tricks that can help you to get the most out of the IDC.

Limiting the records

Web pages containing more than a few hundred records eat up valuable network bandwidth and are pretty useless for the user, who must then scroll through too much data. Usually, such Web pages are a sign that the data was not filtered properly. You can avoid pages with an excessive number of returned records by using the `MaxRecords` statement to limit the number of rows a query can return.

For example, the following IDC file (orders10.htx) never returns more than ten records:

```
Datasource: WebMealsSQL
Template: orders10.htx
SQLStatement: SELECT OrderId, OrderTime FROM tblOrders;
MaxRecords: 10
Username: webuser
Password:
```

The IDC and delimiters

The string delimiter for IDC queries is a single-quote character ('). For example, the following WHERE clause works with either SQL Server or Access data:

```
WHERE LastName = 'Jones'
```

As you may know, Access normally allows you to delimit strings with either a single quote or a double quote. Well, in IDC land, you can't use the double quote character (") in criteria. If you do, the query will generate an error.

For dates, the correct delimiter to use depends on which database you use. When querying SQL Server databases with the IDC, you need to treat dates the same as strings. (This is consistent with how SQL Server handles dates internally.) For example, the following works with SQL Server:

```
WHERE OrderDate = '03/01/97'
```

On the other hand, when querying Access databases using the IDC, you can't use the normal data delimiters, the pound sign (#) or a single quote. Both characters cause an error. Instead, treat the date as if it were a number — that is, don't use any delimiter. For example, the following code works with Access:

```
WHERE OrderDate = 03/01/97
```

Wildcard characters

You may need to use query criteria that return records based on a wildcard match. Different databases support different wildcard characters, however. In IDC land, you have to use the ANSI standard SQL wildcard characters, which I summarize in Table 9-1. You must use these wildcard characters even if the data source — for example, Access — internally supports a different set of wildcard characters.

Table 9-1	ANSI and Access Wildcard Characters	
ANSI Character	*Returns Values Where*	*Equivalent Access Character*
%	One or more characters	*
_	Exactly one character	?

However, there's a twist: The IDC protocol uses the percent sign character (%) to delimit fields. Thus, anytime you need to use % in an IDC SQL statement as a wildcard character you must double it up, using %% instead.

For example, the following IDC file (l_customers.idc), which selects records from an Access database (Meals.mdb), returns all records where LastName begins with an L:

```
Datasource: WebMeals
Template: l_customers.htx
SQLStatement: SELECT FirstName, LastName
+ FROM tblCustomers
+ WHERE LastName LIKE 'L%%';
```

Following is the sample HTX file (l_customers.htx) in which I used a table to present the records in a neat and tidy fashion:

```
<HTML>
<HEAD>
<TITLE>Web_Meals.Com</TITLE>
</HEAD>
<BODY>
<H2>'L' Customers</H2>
<TABLE BORDER=2>
<TR><B><TD>Firstname</TD><TD>Lastname</TD></B></TR>
<%begindetail%>
  <TR><TD><%firstname%></TD><TD><%lastname%></TD></TR>
<%enddetail%>
</TABLE>
</BODY>
</HTML>
```

The results of this query appear in Internet Explorer 3.0 in Figure 9-6.

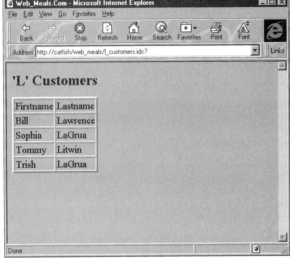

Figure 9-6:
This query returns all customers with a last name beginning with the letter L.

Formatting

Normally, the records that an IDC query returns are formatted in a fairly unappealing manner, as the results of a query shown in Figure 9-7 demonstrate. (The IDC files are on the CD-ROM as format1.idc and format1.htx.) Notice how the date and currency fields are formatted — not exactly what most people would like to see.

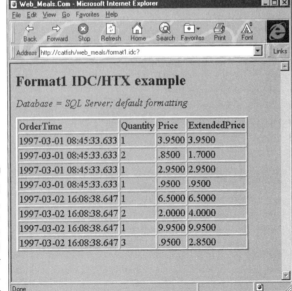

Figure 9-7:
By default, three fields are formatted rather poorly.

You may think that you can fix the formatting in the HTX file. I made the same guess, but am sorry to say it's wrong. The HTX specification includes no provision for controlling the formatting of fields. The only way to format the data differently is to use your database's conversion and formatting functions to massage the data into a more appealing format before it merges with the HTX file.

The solution differs for each database you use. For example, with SQL Server, you need to use a combination of the Convert and Round functions to get the desired effect.

Following is the SQL statement from the format1.idc file that produced the poorly-formatted page shown in Figure 9-7:

```
SQLStatement:
+ SELECT OrderTime, Quantity, Price,
+ Price*Quantity AS ExtendedPrice
+ FROM tblOrders INNER JOIN tblOrderItems
+ ON tblOrders.OrderId = tblOrderItems.OrderId
+ INNER JOIN tblMenuItems
+ ON tblOrderItems.MenuId = tblMenuItems.MenuId
+ WHERE tblOrders.OrderId <= 2;
```

Following is the fixed-up SQL statement after using the Convert and Round functions to fix up the formatting:

```
SQLStatement:
+ SELECT Convert(Char(8), OrderTime, 1)
+ AS OrderDate, Quantity,
+ '$' + Convert(Char(8), Round(Price,2)) AS ItemPrice,
+ '$' + Convert(Char(8), Round(Price*Quantity,2))
+ AS ExtendedPrice
+ FROM tblOrders INNER JOIN tblOrderItems
+ ON tblOrders.OrderId = tblOrderItems.OrderId
+ INNER JOIN tblMenuItems
+ ON tblOrderItems.MenuId = tblMenuItems.MenuId
+ WHERE tblOrders.OrderId <= 2;
```

The results of this cosmetic formatting appear in Figure 9-8.

In Access, you can get a similar effect using the following SQL Statement that employs the Access Format function (see Figure 9-9 for the result):

```
SQLStatement:
+ SELECT Format(OrderTime, 'mm/dd/yy')
+ AS OrderDate, Quantity,
+ Format(Price, 'Currency') AS ItemPrice,
```

(continued)

(continued)

```
+ Format(Price*Quantity, 'Currency')
+ AS ExtendedPrice
+ FROM (tblOrders INNER JOIN tblOrderItems
+ ON tblOrders.OrderId = tblOrderItems.OrderId)
+ INNER JOIN tblMenuItems
+ ON tblOrderItems.MenuId = tblMenuItems.MenuId
+ WHERE tblOrders.OrderId <= 2;
```

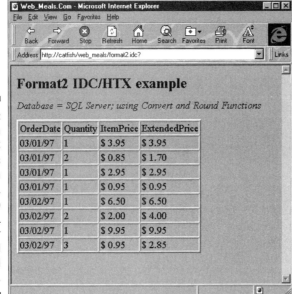

Figure 9-8:
This version
of the IDC
query looks
much
better,
thanks to
the SQL
Server
Convert and
Round
functions.

Filling lists

You can use the results of an IDC query to fill an HTML SELECT control. Doing so makes your HTML forms user-friendly yet up-to-date because the list of values gets created on the fly.

To fill an HTML SELECT control with data from a table, you need to create an IDC file that specifies the query to fill the control and an HTX file that merges that data with a SELECT control. The hard part is creating the HTX file. Here's what the portion of the HTX file that creates the SELECT control should look like:

```
control_label <SELECT NAME="control_name" SIZE=1>
<%BeginDetail%>
<OPTION><%field_name%>
<%EndDetail%>
</SELECT><P>
```

For example, say that you want to improve the AddCustomer.HTML form used earlier in the chapter to add new customers. The tblCustomers table includes a field, FavoriteCategory, that the AddCustomer.HTML form fails to collect. Furthermore, you'd like to limit the user to selecting a category only from the list of categories stored in the tblCategories table.

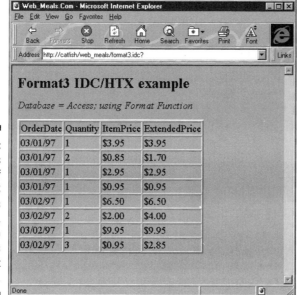

Figure 9-9: This Access version of the IDC query looks good, thanks to the Access Format function.

The NewCustomer.IDC and NewCustomer.HTX files create a dynamic customer form that derives its list of categories from the tblCategories tables. Following is the NewCustomer.IDC file:

```
Datasource: WebMealsSQL
Template: NewCustomer.htx
SQLStatement: SELECT Category
+ FROM tblCategories
+ WHERE Category <> 'Beverage'
+ ORDER BY Category;
Username: webuser
Password:
```

And here's the NewCustomer.HTX file:

```
<HTML>
<HEAD>
<TITLE>Web_Meals.Com New Customer Form</TITLE>
</HEAD>
<BODY background = gray.jpg>
<IMG SRC="web_meals.gif" ALT="web_meals.com logo"
          ALIGN=left>
<FONT COLOR="0000FF">
<BR><BR><H2>Become a Web_Meals.Com Customer!</H2>
<H6><I>This form created by the NewCustomer IDC/HTX files</
          I></H6>
</FONT><BR CLEAR=ALL>
<FORM METHOD="GET" ACTION="AddCustomer.IDC">
First Name <INPUT TYPE="Text" NAME="FirstName" SIZE=25>
Last Name <INPUT TYPE="Text" NAME="LastName" SIZE=25><P>
Address <INPUT TYPE="Text" NAME="Address" SIZE=40><P>
City <INPUT TYPE="Text" NAME="City" SIZE=25>
State <INPUT TYPE="Text" NAME="State" SIZE=4>
Zip Code <INPUT TYPE="Text" NAME="ZipCode" SIZE=15><P>
Phone Num <INPUT TYPE="Text" NAME="Phone" SIZE=25><P>
Select your favorite food category <SELECT
NAME="FavoriteCategory" SIZE=1>
<%BeginDetail%>
<OPTION><%Category%>
<%EndDetail%>
</SELECT><P>
<INPUT TYPE="Submit" VALUE="OK—Sign Me Up!">
<INPUT TYPE="Reset" VALUE="Clear Form">
<P><A HREF=default.html>On second thought,
I don't want to become a customer</A>
</FORM>
</BODY>
</HTML>
```

Notice how the SELECT control is built on the fly with the following HTML
tags mixed in with the special IDC tags:

```
Select your favorite food category <SELECT
NAME="FavoriteCategory" SIZE=1>
<%BeginDetail%>
<OPTION><%Category%>
<%EndDetail%>
</SELECT><P>
```

The browser, however, sees the preceding code only after the IDC merges the HTX file with the results of the IDC query, which produces the following HTML:

```
Select your favorite food category <SELECT
NAME="FavoriteCategory" SIZE=1>
<OPTION>American
<OPTION>Indian
<OPTION>Italian
<OPTION>Polish
<OPTION>Russian
<OPTION>Thai
</SELECT><P>
```

The resulting form appears in Figure 9-10.

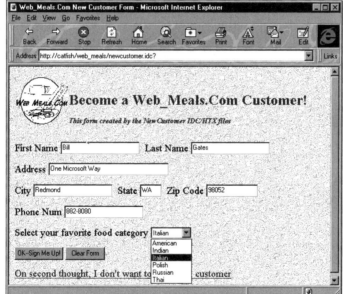

Figure 9-10: I created the Favorite Category Select control on the fly by using an IDC query.

Displaying parameter values

You can display the value of a parameter that was passed to an IDC page from the page linked to the IDC page.

To insert the value of a parameter into an HTX file, use the following syntax:

```
<%idc.parameter_name%>
```

For example, a better version of the confirming page (shown earlier in this chapter in Figure 9-3) may include some of the information the user entered into the form, as shown in Figure 9-11.

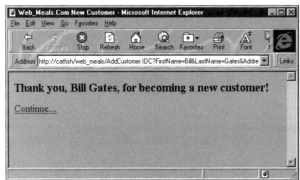

Figure 9-11:
A
personalized
confirmation
message,
thanks to
the use of
parameters.

Following is the HTX file I used to pull off this personalization wonder:

```
<HTML>
<HEAD>
<TITLE>Web_Meals.Com New Customer</TITLE>
</HEAD>
<BODY>
<H3>Thank you, <%idc.firstname%> <%idc.lastname%>,
for becoming a new customer!</H3>
<P><A HREF=default.html>Continue...</A>
</BODY>
</HTML>
```

How IDC Stacks Up against the Alternatives

You may ask how the IDC stacks up against the alternatives. Good question! The IDC is a fast and efficient way to link your databases to your Web server. In Table 9-2, I compare the IDC with alternative technologies.

Table 9-2	How IDC Stacks Up against the Competition	
Alternative	*Advantages Over IDC*	*Disadvantages When Compared with IDC*
Static HTML	Works with any Web server; simple to implement	Only as current as the time you generated the page
CGI Application	Works with more Web servers	Slower than IDC
Active Server Pages	More powerful and flexible than IDC; provides more advanced formatting and processing of data	More difficult to create ASP pages

Ultimately, it's up to you to decide whether to use one technology versus another, but don't make up your mind too soon. The next three parts of this book present several compelling reasons to consider the last alternative from Table 9-2, Active Server Pages. See Chapter 19 for more on alternative technologies.

Part V
The Future Is Here:
Active Server Pages

The 5th Wave — By Rich Tennant

"IT'S ANOTHER DEEP-SPACE PROBE FROM EARTH, SEEKING CONTACT FROM EXTRATERRESTRIALS. I WISH THEY'D JUST INCLUDE AN E-MAIL ADDRESS."

In this part . . .

The most exciting format that the Access Publish to the
Web Wizard supports has to be Active Server Pages
(ASP). You can use this newest Microsoft technology
along with the Access Publish to the Web Wizard to create
Web pages linked to your Access tables, queries, and
forms.

Chapter 10 shows you how to use the wizard to generate
dynamic datasheets from your Access tables and queries.
Chapter 11 shows you how to generate ASP Web pages
that you and others can use to update data in your
Access databases from the comfort of your Web browser.

Chapter 10

Creating Hyperactive Datasheets

• •

• •

*A*ctive Server Pages (ASP) represent Microsoft's newest technology for creating dynamic Web pages. In fact, Active Server Pages are part of the Active Platform — the Microsoft initiative for the next generation of distributed computing.

In this chapter, you explore using the Access Publish to the Web Wizard to create dynamic ASP Web pages that link to your Access databases. I also cover using the Access Publish to the Web Wizard to publish table and query datasheets to the ASP format. Chapter 11 looks at the publishing of forms to the ASP format.

What Can You Publish to the ASP Format?

You can publish a variety of database objects to the ASP format using the Access Publish to the Web Wizard. A summary of the list of objects appears in Table 10-1.

Table 10-1 Access Objects You Can Publish to the ASP Format

Access Object	Publishable?	Comments
Table	Yes	
Query	Yes	Select and Totals queries only. Supports the use of parameters.
Form	Yes	The wizard creates a facsimile of the form.
Report	No	
Macro	No	
Module	No	

The Access Publish to the Web Wizard supports the publishing of tables and queries, including parameter queries, to the ASP format, just as with the IDC format. In addition, you can use the Access Publish to the Web Wizard to publish Access forms that you can use to view and update records.

What's Required to Publish to the ASP Format?

You don't need anything special to publish to the ASP format. However, to use the ASP pages, a Microsoft Web server (Internet Information Server 3.0 or later, Peer Web Services 3.0 or later, or Personal Web Server 1.0 or later), with Active Server Pages installed, must host your pages. Chapter 2 offers more details on obtaining and configuring Microsoft Web servers.

After you install one of the Microsoft Web servers, you must decide where the Web pages will reside on your server. Unlike pure HTML files, ASP pages must reside in a Web directory to which you've assigned both Read and Script rights (Read and Execute rights for pre-Version 4.0 Microsoft Web servers). Chapter 2 also has more information on how to create Web directories.

For the examples in this chapter, I created a virtual Web directory (following the steps from Chapter 2) and used the following name:

```
\inetpub\wwwroot\web_meals
```

and the following alias name:

```
/web_meals
```

All the examples I use in this chapter come from the Meals.MDB database on the CD-ROM, which you can find at the back of this book.

Make sure that you assign both Read and Script access rights (or Read and Execute rights for earlier versions of Microsoft Web servers) to your Web directory using the Internet Service Manager program.

Publishing a Table or Query to ASP

Publishing a table or query to the ASP format is similar to publishing a table or query to the IDC format. (See Chapter 8 for the complete steps.) Because only a few steps differ, I merely highlight the key differences in this section.

✔ To publish ASP pages, select Dynamic ASP (Microsoft Active Server Pages) on page 4 of the Access Publish to the Web Wizard (see Figure 10-1).

✔ When you select the ASP format and click Next, you encounter an extra wizard page (just as when you choose to publish to the IDC format). On this page, which appears in Figure 10-2, you need to answer several additional questions. I describe the questions in Table 10-2.

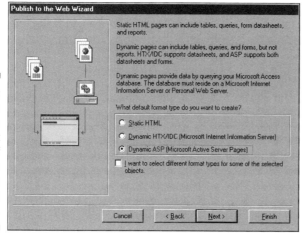

Figure 10-1: You can choose the ASP format on page 4 of the Access Publish to the Web Wizard.

Figure 10-2:
Time to
specify a
data source
and several
other
options.

Table 10-2	ASP Data Source Questions	
Question	**Description**	**Required?**
Data Source Name	Name of the ODBC system data source.	Yes
User Name	Optional user name to use to log into the database.	No
Password	Optional password to use to log into the database.	No
Server URL	URL address where the pages will be located on the Web server.	No
Session Timeout	The number of minutes an inactive session can be left open before the Web server times it out. (The default value is 20 minutes if left blank.)	No

✔ The only required item is the first one, Data Source Name. Here, you need to type in the name of the ODBC system data source on the server that links the page back to the Access database. Don't worry if you haven't yet created the data source — you don't need to create it until you want to use the published Web pages.

✔ Enter values into the User Name and Password items only if your database uses Access security. If not, you can leave these items blank. If the database does require a logon, however, you need to indicate here the user name and password that you want the ASP page to use to log into the database.

✔ You don't need to enter anything into the Server URL text box. You only need to enter the URL if you're publishing a form with an embedded subform (see Chapter 11). Otherwise, leave this blank.

✔ The Server Timeout is also optional and is better left blank unless you have some need to control how quickly the server times out a user session.

✔ The rest of the wizard pages are the same as for the other output formats.

The Wizard Output

The result of using the Publish to the Web Wizard to publish an Access table or query is a single file with the .ASP extension and a root name consisting of the name of the published object plus "_1". That is, *object_name*_1.asp. (If you choose to publish multiple objects, you end up, of course, with multiple ASP files.) For example, if you publish a query with the name qryCustomerAndCategory, the wizard produces the following file:

```
qryCustomerAndCategory_1.asp
```

This ASP file consists of a mixture of server-side VBScript and HTML. When the server executes the ASP file, the ASP engine grabs the data from the data source and creates an HTML file, which it passes back to the Web browser on the client machine.

Post-Wizard Housekeeping

Before you can use your ASP files, you must perform three additional steps. (These steps are very similar to what you need to do when publishing to the IDC format.)

1. **Copy the ASP files to the server.**

   Copy the ASP files from the wizard output folder to a folder on your Web server. Do the same for any .GIF or .JPG files that the template references, if any, that you used. Check out the earlier section in this chapter called "What's Required to Publish to the ASP Format?" for more details on setting up this folder.

2. **Copy or move the Access database to the server.**

   You don't actually have to locate the database on the server, but for the sake of efficiency, it's a good idea to place the Access database on the Web server machine.

3. **Create an ODBC System data source to link the ASP page to the database.**

Create the system data source on the Web server machine. Use the ODBC Data Source Administrator program to set up a system data source that points to the Access 97 database you copied in Step 2. See Chapter 8 for more details on how to set up a data source.

Using the ASP Page

To view the wizard-generated ASP Web page, you need to link to it with your browser. The exact URL you link to, however, varies depending on whether the Web server is on an intranet or the Internet.

On an intranet server

If your Web server is accessible across an intranet, then you link to the ASP page using the following syntax:

```
http://server_name/virtual_directory/page.asp
```

where `server_name` is the machine name of the Web server, `virtual_directory` is the Web folder that hosts the Web page, and `page.asp` is the name of the ASP page that the Access wizard generates. For example, if your server name is `catfish` and the published ASP file is `qryCustomerAndCategory_1.asp` and located in the virtual Web folder, you enter the following URL:

```
http://catfish/Web_Meals/qryCustomerAndCategory_1.asp
```

On an Internet server

If you connect to the Web server across the Internet, then you link to the ASP page using the following syntax:

```
http://www.site_name/server_folder/page.asp
```

where `site_name` is the domain name of the Web server, `server_folder` is the Web folder that hosts the Web page, and `page.asp` is the name of the ASP page that the Access wizard generates. For example, if your site name is web_meals.com and the published ASP file is qryCustomerAndCategory_1.asp and is located in the root folder of the Web server, you enter the following URL:

```
http://www.web_meals.com/qryCustomerAndCategory_1.asp
```

What you get

When you link to the wizard-generated ASP page, the ASP query executes entirely on the server, and the ASP engine creates an HTML page on the fly and returns to your Web browser. Because the Web browser never sees anything but standard HTML, you can use any Web browser — not just a Microsoft browser — as shown in Figure 10-3.

Figure 10-3: The results of the ASP query shown in Netscape Navigator.

Publishing Parameter Queries to ASP

Publishing a parameter query to the ASP format is much like publishing a parameter query to the IDC format. You need to take several key steps prior to invoking the Publish to the Web Wizard.

Preparing the query

As detailed in Chapter 8, you must follow these three steps when constructing your parameter query:

1. **Create a regular select query.**

2. **Enter each parameter into the query grid surrounded by brackets.**

3. **Declare each parameter and its data type by choosing Query⇨Parameters.**

For more information on preparing parameter queries for publishing, see Chapter 8.

Publishing the query

When you publish a parameter query using the Access Publish to the Web Wizard, the wizard prompts you for each parameter as it generates the pages. You don't need to actually enter anything into these prompts — just click OK. What you enter (or fail to enter) doesn't effect the actual publishing of the query.

The resulting files

When you publish a parameter query to the ASP format, you end up with two files:

- The ASP file
- An HTML page that collects the parameters and submits them to the ASP file

For example, when I publish the `qryParamCity` query from Meals.mdb, I end up with these two files:

- qryParamCity_1.asp
- qryParamCity_1.html

Linking to the parameter query page

After you copy the files to the server and set up the data source, you're ready to link to the ASP parameter query page. However, you need to link to the HTML file, not the ASP file. For example, when I link to the qryParamCity_1.html file, I get a parameter prompt page like that shown in Figure 10-4. And when I enter Seattle into the prompt, the ASP query returns a page like that shown in Figure 10-5.

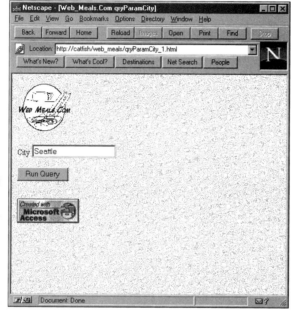

Figure 10-4:
The HTML
page
collects the
value
for the
parameter.

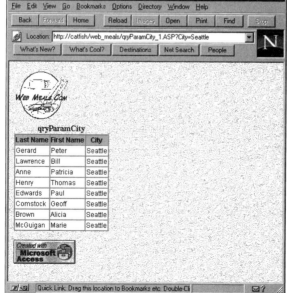

Figure 10-5:
The ASP
parameter
query
returns
these
records.

Is That All There Is to Publishing to the ASP Format?

If you wonder if that's all there is to publishing Access objects to the ASP format using the Access Publish to the Web Wizard, the answer is no. This chapter covers only the publishing of tables and queries. In Chapter 11, you look at how to use the wizard to publish Access forms that you can then use to view and update data in your Access databases.

Chapter 11
Publishing Radioactive Forms

- -

In This Chapter

▶ Publishing Access forms to the Access wizard

▶ Linking to the published forms

▶ Publishing forms with embedded subforms

▶ Understanding which parts of the form are actually published

- -

*T*he real advantage to using the Access Publish to the Web Wizard to publish to the Active Server Pages (ASP) format is apparent when you publish forms. When you publish a form using the ASP format, the wizard generates an ASP page that looks and acts like an Access form. You can use the ASP page to view and update records in the Access database.

This chapter explores the publishing of Access forms to the ASP format and takes a look at the pluses and minuses of the Access-generated ASP pages.

Publishing an Access Form

Publishing an Access form to the ASP format is very similar to publishing a table or query to the ASP format, which I cover in Chapter 10.

Before you start publishing your Access forms to the ASP format, you need to have a few things in place:

✔ You must be using a Microsoft Web server with Active Server Pages installed.

✔ You must have a Web directory setup to hold your ASP files. Assign both Read and Script access rights (or Read and Execute rights for earlier versions of Microsoft Web servers) to this Web directory by using the Internet Service Manager program.

Chapter 2 has more details on obtaining and configuring Microsoft Web servers and creating Web directories. I also discuss configuring your Web server for Active Server Pages in Chapter 10.

Following is a brief look at how to publish a form:

1. **Open an Access database, start the Access Publish to the Web Wizard, and click Next until you reach the fourth wizard page.**

2. **Select the form or forms you want to publish on the second wizard page.**

3. **Select the Dynamic ASP (Microsoft Active Server Pages) publishing option on the fourth wizard page, as shown in Figure 11-1, and click Next.**

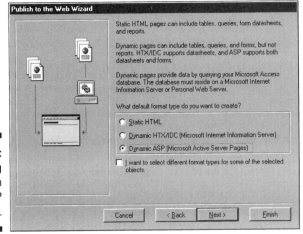

Figure 11-1:
Choosing
to publish
to the ASP
format.

4. **On the fifth page, type the data source name and other optional fields.**

If the form you're publishing contains a subform, tab to the Server URL text box. Type the URL address of the virtual Web directory where the ASP files will be hosted. This address points to the virtual Web directory where you store the files, not the actual files (see Figure 11-2).

For example, if your Web server is accessible across an intranet, then type an address using the following syntax:

```
http://server_name/virtual_directory/
```

If you connect to the Web server across the Internet, then enter an address using the following syntax:

```
http://www.site_name/virtual_directory/
```

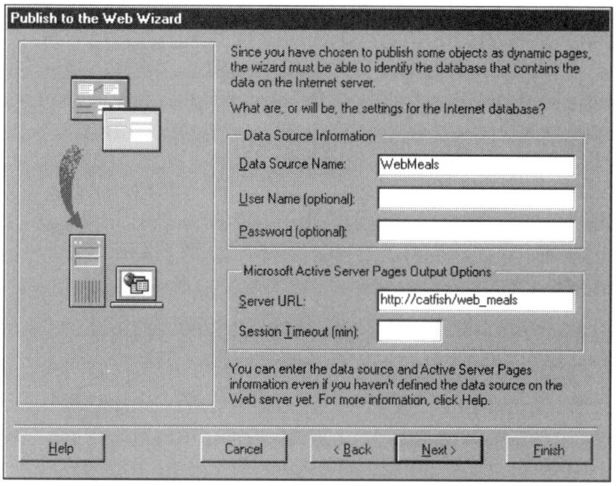

Figure 11-2:
If you're
publishing
a form
with an
embedded
subform,
you need to
type an
address
into the
Server URL
text box.

If the form doesn't contain a subform, you can leave the Server URL text box blank (see Figure 11-3). Entering an address doesn't do any harm, but getting an address wrong is easy. You may as well leave the text box blank. In addition, if you decide later to move the files to a different Web directory, the form won't work if you've entered a server URL here.

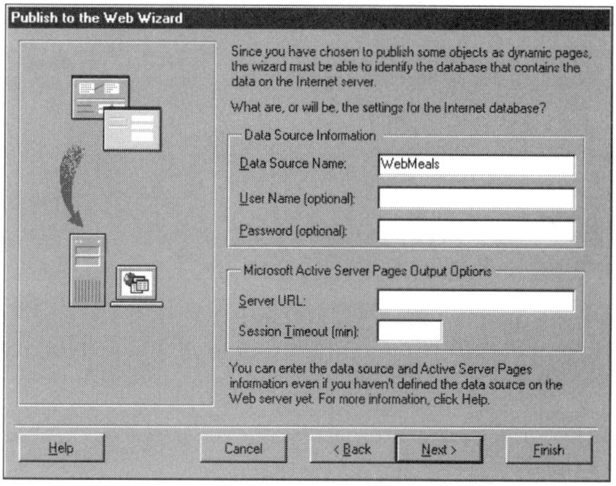

Figure 11-3:
If you aren't
publishing
a form
containing
a subform,
then leave
the Server
URL text
box blank.

5. Click Finish to generate the pages and quit the wizard.

Enter whatever you want on the remaining wizard pages before clicking Finish.

The Published ASP Files

When you use the Publish to the Web Wizard to publish an Access form, you end up with at least two files — perhaps three, if you publish a form with an embedded subform. The files generated by the wizard are

- ✔ **form_1.asp:** This is the main ASP file, the one you link to. The file grabs the data displayed on the form and inserts an HTML Layout control into the Web page.

- ✔ **form_1alx.asp:** This ASP file creates the form displayed by the HTML Layout control.

- ✔ **subform.asp:** This file is created by the wizard only if the published Access form contains a subform. If so, then this file is responsible for grabbing the data for the subform and displaying it in the HTML Layout control.

For example, if you publish a form (with no subform) named frmMenuItems, the wizard generates the following files:

```
frmMenuItems_1.asp
frmMenuItems_1alx.asp
```

If you publish a form named frmOrders that contains an embedded subform named frmOrderItemsSub, you get the following files:

```
frmOrders_1.asp
frmOrders_1alx.asp
frmOrderItemsSub.asp
```

Post-Wizard Housekeeping

Before you can use your ASP files, you must perform three additional steps. These steps are identical to what you need to do when publishing a table or query to the ASP format:

1. **Copy the ASP files to the server.**

2. **Copy or move the Access database to the server.**

3. **Create an ODBC System data source to link the ASP page to the database.**

Chapter 10 gives you all the details on these steps.

Previewing the Results

To view the wizard-published forms, you need to link to the main ASP page. But first, there's a catch.

The ASP files that the Access wizard generates differ in one important way from all the other Web pages that the wizard generates: You can view the ASP files only by using Microsoft Internet Explorer (IE) 3.0 or later. You need Internet Explorer because the wizard-generated ASP files send VBScript code that uses the HTML Layout control to the Web client.

The wizard uses the HTML Layout control to allow precise two-dimensional positioning of items on the page. This control runs only in browsers that support ActiveX controls, which, for now at least, means that you can view the wizard-published forms by using only Internet Explorer Version 3.0 or later.

As is the case in Chapter 10, the exact URL you link to varies, depending on if the Web server is on an intranet or the Internet.

If your Web server is accessible across an intranet, then you link to the ASP page using the following syntax:

```
http://server_name/virtual_directory/form_1.asp
```

where `server_name` is the machine name of the Web server, `virtual_directory` is the Web folder that hosts the Web page, and `form_1.asp` is the name of the ASP page generated by the Access wizard.

For example, if your server name is `catfish` and the published ASP file is `frmEmployees_1.asp` and located in the `Web_Meals` directory, you enter the following URL:

```
http://catfish/Web_Meals/frmEmployees_1.asp
```

If you connect to the Web server across the Internet, then you link to the ASP page using the following syntax:

```
http://www.site_name/virtual_directory/form_1.asp
```

where `site_name` is the domain name of the Web server, `virtual_directory` is the virtual Web directory that hosts the Web page, and `form_1.asp` is the name of the ASP page generated by the Access wizard.

For example, if your site name is `web_meals.com`, and the published ASP file is `frmEmployees_1.asp` and located in the root directory of the Web server, you enter the following URL:

```
http://www.web_meals.com/frmEmployees_1.asp
```

When you link to the wizard-generated ASP page using Internet Explorer, the ASP query executes on the server and the ASP engine generates a Web page consisting of a mixture of HTML and VBScript on the fly and returns the page to the browser. Because the Web page contains VBScript and references to the HTML Layout control, you need to use a Microsoft browser, as shown in Figure 11-4.

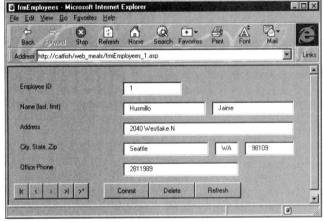

Figure 11-4: The ASP version of the Employees form shown in Internet Explorer 3.02.

If you compare the ASP version of the form with the original Access form (shown in Figure 11-5), you can see that the wizard does an admirable job in converting the Access form into the Web equivalent.

Figure 11-5: The original Access frm Employees form.

If you attempt to view the page in a browser that doesn't support ActiveX controls and VBScript, you get a page that looks similar to the one shown in Figure 11-6.

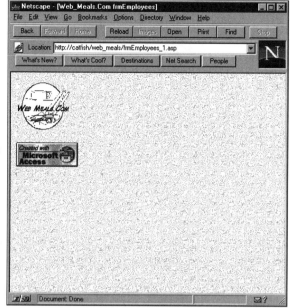

Figure 11-6:
The ASP
page as
seen from
Netscape
Navigator —
not exactly
what you
intended.

Publishing a Form with an Embedded Subform

The trick to successfully publishing a form with a subform is to get the Server URL address on page 5 of the wizard correct. See Figure 11-2 and the discussion in the section "Publishing an Access Form" for more details.

The wizard publishes subforms only in datasheet view and only as read-only HTML tables. To function properly, the published subform must link to the main form using the LinkChildFields and LinkMasterFields properties of the subform control, not custom VBA code. In addition, the wizard doesn't support nested subforms.

For example, the Meals.mdb database contains a form, frmOrders, with an embedded subform (frmOrderItemsSub). The Access version of this form appears in Figure 11-7.

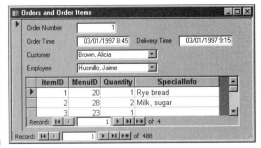

Figure 11-7:
The
frmOrders
Access
form
contains an
embedded
subform.

The Access Publish to the Web Wizard does a good job converting the frmOrders form to an ASP form, as shown in Figure 11-8. As with all published subforms, the subform itself becomes read-only when converted to the ASP format.

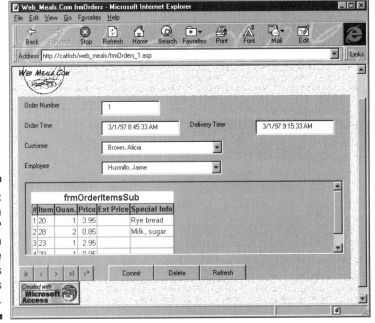

Figure 11-8:
The subform
in the ASP
version
of the
frmOrders
form is
read-only.

Using the Published Forms

The ASP version of your Access form attempts to mimic the look and behavior of the Access form it's based on. However, a few differences crop up in how the ASP version of the form works:

✔ **Navigating around:** Click the navigational buttons at the bottom left of the form to move from one record to another. The buttons behave the same as their Access 97 counterparts. When you navigate to a different record, notice that the entire page is refreshed and repainted. On slower machines, or machines connected to the server over a slow dialup line, the refresh delay is quite noticeable.

✔ **Using combo box and list box controls:** You can use combo controls just as you use them in Access, even when the controls are bound to a lookup table. (See the Customer and Employee fields in Figure 11-8.) Any code linked to events of the controls, however, doesn't work.

Bound list box controls do not behave correctly. When browsing a saved record, the list box doesn't highlight the correct value.

✔ **Updating records:** To update a record, directly edit the values in the controls on the form just as you do in the Access version of the form. Unlike in Access, however, you must also click the Commit button or else you lose your changes. After you commit the changes, the form repositions to the first record in the recordset.

✔ **Deleting records:** Click the Delete button while a record is displayed, and you end up deleting the record from the database after a confirming dialog box appears. After you delete the record, the form repositions to the previous record in the recordset.

✔ **Refreshing records:** If you want the currently displayed record to refresh with any changes made by other users since you began viewing the record, click the Refresh button.

Publishing Better Forms

The code behind the Access Publish to the Web Wizard does some amazing things. A sophisticated algorithm analyzes the Access form and spits out ASP code to simulate the look and feel of the Access form. The wizard hardly does a perfect job, however, and in fact has problems converting certain form elements.

What's published and what's not?

Forms in Access can be quite a bit more complex than tables or queries. As you may guess, the Access Publish to the Web Wizard can't convert everything on a form to a Web page. Table 11-1 summarizes which parts are published and which parts aren't.

**Table 11-1   What Parts of an Access Form Does Access
                    Publish to the Web Wizard Publish?**

Part	Published?	Comments
ActiveX control	Yes	Wizard doesn't support data binding.
Background color of form section	No	
Check box	Yes	
Color and font properties of controls	Yes	
Combo box	Yes	
Command button	Yes	The wizard preserves any hyperlink attached to the command button. (The wizard doesn't publish macros and VBA code attached to the command button.)
Expressions	No	
Format and InputX of form section	No	
Image	No	
Label	Yes	The wizard preserves any hyperlink attached to the label.
Line	No	
List box	Yes	Bound list boxes don't behave properly. (See the earlier section "Using the Published Forms.")
Macros	No	
Option button	Yes	
Option group	Yes	Wizard doesn't publish frame.
Page Break	No	
Picture property of form	No	
Rectangle	No	
Subform	Yes	Only as read-only datasheets.
Tab	No	
Text box	Yes	If the control is bound to a hyperlink field, the hyperlink isn't active.
Toggle button	Yes	

Part	Published?	Comments
Unbound or bound object frame	No	
VBA code	No	

As you can see from Table 11-1, the wizard doesn't publish many parts of a form, including VBA code, macros, images, lines, rectangles, and expressions.

Form-publishing tips

To minimize your headaches when publishing forms, consider the following tips and tricks:

- ✔ **Keep it simple.** The simpler a form is, the better it looks when published.

- ✔ **Make your forms small.** The browser version of the form is usually larger, so the smaller you make your forms, the more likely they will fit within one browser page.

- ✔ **If you have controls too close to the left edge of the form, the wizard may chop off the labels, as shown in Figure 11-9.** Whether or not the wizard wields a hatchet depends on how close your labels are to the left-hand margin, if you're using a template, and the width of the form. If the labels get cut off, open the Access form in design view, move the labels to the right a bit or reduce the width of the form, and republish the form.

- ✔ **By default, the background color of the published form is gray regardless of the color of the original Access form.** If you want to change the background color, open the alx ASP file in Notepad, and search for the first instance of <DIV>. This tag should look something like the following:

```
<DIV ID="frmEmployees_1alx"
STYLE="LAYOUT:FIXED;HEIGHT:222;WIDTH:528;">
```

The <DIV> tag controls the insertion of the HTML Layout control. You can change the color of the HTML Layout control by inserting a BACK-GROUND tag between <DIV> and ID using the standard HTML color values. (For color values, see *HTML For Dummies*, 3rd Edition, by Ed Tittel and Stephen N. James, published by IDG Books Worldwide, Inc.) For example, to change the background color to a yellowish hue, you change the preceding lines of code to:

```
<DIV BACKGROUND="#fce503" ID="frmEmployees_1alx"
STYLE="LAYOUT:FIXED;HEIGHT:222;WIDTH:528;">
```

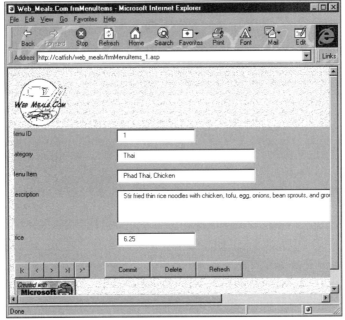

Figure 11-9:
In the published version of the frm-MenuItems form, the wizard cut off the labels on the left side of the form.

✔ **If you move a wizard-generated form to another Web directory and you have hard-coded the Server URL into the ASP files (this is necessary if the form contains an embedded subform), you can do one of two things:**

• Republish the form with the new URL address.

• Search and replace the URL in both the form_1.asp and form_1alx.asp files and replace each `http:` address with the new address.

✔ **If you don't have the HTML Layout control installed on your system and you attempt to view a published Access form, then code attached to the published form attempts to download the control from `www.microsoft.com` and install the control onto your system.** This process may take several minutes, so be patient. The download may fail, however, for a variety of reasons, including:

• Internet Explorer can't download the control because you aren't hooked up to the Internet or you're connected through a firewall. You may be able to circumvent this problem by obtaining a later version of Internet Explorer. IE 3.01 and later versions include the HTML Layout control automatically.

- The security of your Internet Explorer (choose View⇨Options, and click the Security tab) is set to the High setting. Change this value to the Medium setting.

- If you're using IE 3.0, make sure that you select each of the Active Content settings on the Security tab of the Options dialog box.

How Wizard-Generated Pages Stack Up Against the Alternatives

The Access Publish to the Web Wizard makes it easy to publish Access forms to ASP pages that you can use to view and update the records. The pages that the wizard produces, however, have several shortcomings.

✔ You must use a Microsoft Web Server with ASP support installed.

✔ Your Web browser must be Internet Explorer.

✔ You must have the HTML Layout control installed on your machine.

✔ The Web pages are slow and lack any navigational aids beyond the first record, next record, previous record, last record, and new record buttons.

Alternatives to the Access-generated pages are not without shortcomings of their own:

✔ Static HTML doesn't have any of these shortcomings, but you also can't use static HTML to link to or update data stored in a database.

✔ IDC Web pages also must run on a Microsoft Web server, but they are browser-independent. To create the equivalent forms, however, you have to hand-code a lot of IDC and HTX files.

In the next part of this book, you explore another alternative: Microsoft Visual InterDev. You use this powerful tool to produce ASP pages that share many of the strengths of the Access Publish to the Web Wizard-generated pages, while not sharing many of its shortcomings.

Part VI
Coding Active Server Pages

The 5th Wave   By Rich Tennant

"OH, I'LL GET US IN – I USED TO RUN TECH SUPPORT AT AN
INTERNET ACCESS COMPANY."

In this part . . .

The Access Publish to the Web Wizard produces Active Server Pages that only begin to reap the abilities of this nimble dynamic Web page technology. This part shows you how easily you can create ASP pages by hand. In Chapter 12, you explore the anatomy of an Active Server Page and find out how you can use ASP along with the scripting language of your choice to create truly potent pages. Chapter 13 covers the data-access smarts behind ASP: ActiveX Data Objects (ADO). You discover here how to use ADO to retrieve and update records from Access, SQL Server, and other Open Database Connectivity (ODBC) databases.

Chapter 12

Delving into Active Server Pages

· ·

· ·

*T*he ASP specification goes much further than the ASP pages that the Access wizard produces. Using this powerful and flexible server-side scripting technology, you can create interactive data-driven Web applications that do just about anything. In this chapter, you take a look at the code behind ASP Web pages. In the process, you gain a new understanding of the ASP specification and find out how easy it really is to build ASP pages.

What Exactly Is an Active Server Page?

The Active Server Pages specification is a technology built on top of the Microsoft Internet Information Server (IIS) family of Internet servers that provides the framework for producing dynamic Web applications. Unlike the IDC specification that I talk about in Chapters 8 and 9, ASP isn't limited to database connectivity. In addition to its support for database publishing, ASP includes capabilities for providing powerful server-side scripting using a variety of scripting languages, including VBScript and JavaScript. In addition, ASP supports the use of server-side components, and other features that make creating robust client/server Web applications easier.

An Active Server Page is a file with the .ASP extension that consists of regular old HTML along with embedded scripting statements. The ASP Scripting Engine interprets these scripts at the server, processes them, and returns HTML to the Web browser located on the client. Because the browser sees only HTML, ASP pages work with any Web browser (except for the ASP forms produced by the Access Publish to the Web Wizard).

The default scripting language for ASP is VBScript. Access, Visual Basic (VB), and Office developers may be very familiar with VBScript because VBScript is a subset of the Visual Basic for Applications (VBA) language that is behind these products. In addition to VBScript, the ASP Scripting Engine also works with JavaScript and other scripting languages, such as PERL.

Starting Simple

Although you can start exploring ASP by examining the pages produced by the Access Publish to the Web Wizard (see Chapters 10 and 11), these wizard-generated pages are complex and difficult to follow. Understanding how ASP works is easier when you start simple.

In order to be able to run ASP pages, you must be using a Microsoft or compatible server with ASP support. See Chapter 2 for more details.

The following ASP page is about as simple as you can get. (You can find the ASP page on this book's CD-ROM as time1.asp.) The code includes standard HTML, along with embedded ASP scripting code.

```
<HTML>
<HEAD>
<TITLE>Time1.asp Example</TITLE>
</HEAD>
<BODY>
<H2>This page produced on the server at precisely:
<BR> <% = Now() %>
</H2>
</BODY>
</HTML>
```

The ASP script delimiters <% and %> tell the server that the server scripting engine is to interpret the code between these two delimiters prior to sending the page over to the client.

In this example, I use the following VBScript code to insert the current date and time into the HTML on the server. (Now is a built-in VBScript function that returns the current date and time.)

```
<% = Now() %>
```

You use the equal sign within the script delimiters to signify you want to return a value. Because the server's scripting engine interprets this code, the code works with any browser. The browser never sees the script. Instead, the browser sees the following HTML. (The actual HTML varies, depending on when you run the sample.)

```
<HTML>
<HEAD>
<TITLE>Time1.asp Example</TITLE>
</HEAD>
<BODY>
<H2>This page produced on the server at precisely:
<BR> 9/7/97 11:26:15 AM
</H2>
</BODY>
</HTML>
```

The result of this exciting ASP page appears in Internet Explorer 4.0 in Figure 12-1.

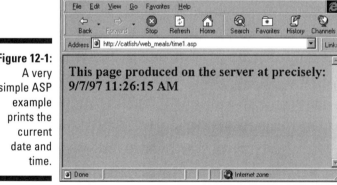

Figure 12-1:
A very simple ASP example prints the current date and time.

Although this first example may seem trivial, try to create the same example using static HTML — you simply can't do it. You could place the current time on a page by using client-side scripting, but then your page works only with certain browsers.

Conditional processing

The default ASP scripting language, VBScript, supports many programming niceties such as conditional processing, looping, string manipulation, arrays, and date and time manipulation. You can do much more than simply print the current date and time.

For example, you may want to print a custom message to your customers based on the time of day by using the VBScript conditional processing statement, If...Then. Time2.asp (also on this book's CD-ROM) represents one example of how you may print such a message:

```
<HTML>
<HEAD>
<TITLE>Time2.asp Example</TITLE>
</HEAD>
<BODY>
<H2>Welcome to Web_Meals.Com</H2>
<HR>
<H2><I><B>
<%If Time() < #12:00:00 PM# Then%>
   Good Morning!
<%ElseIf Time < #6:00:00 PM# Then%>
   Good Afternoon!
<%Else%>
   Good Evening!
<%End If%>
</B></I></H2>
<HR>
</BODY>
</HTML>
```

Time2.asp uses the built-in Time function, which is similar to Now, but returns the current time. Figure 12-2 shows how the preceding code looks if you were to call it up in the morning.

Figure 12-2: I called up this page at 11:27 a.m.; thus, the ASP code behind it displays "Good Morning."

Creating procedures

The server-side VBScript code in time1.asp and time2.asp is interpreted by the ASP scripting engine immediately when the page is processed because I inserted the code into the page as an immediate script. You also can create procedures and call those procedures from an immediate script, as shown in the following example called divide.asp (also on the CD-ROM).

```
<HTML>
<HEAD>
<TITLE>Divide.asp Example</TITLE>
</HEAD>
<BODY>
<H1>
<%
Function Divide(dblNum, dblDenom)
    Divide = dblNum / dblDenom
End Function

Dim dbl1
Dim dbl2

dbl1 = 16
dbl2 = 5
Response.Write dbl1 & " divided by " & dbl2 & _
  " is equal to " & Divide(dbl1, dbl2)
%>
</H1>
</BODY>
</HTML>
```

When divide.asp is processed by the ASP scripting engine, the engine executes the code and sends back the following to the Web browser (shown in Figure 12-3):

```
16 divided by 5 is equal to 3.2
```

In divide.asp, I created a simple function, Divide, which divides two numbers and returns the result of the division. I call this function from an *immediate script.* An immediate script is simply any code outside of a procedure.

All immediate script code is executed by the scripting engine immediately, whereas code contained in procedures is executed only if and when it is called from an immediate script.

You can write HTML to the browser in two ways. The first method is simply to place text or HTML tags outside any ASP script — that is, outside of `<%` and `%>`. Time1.asp and time2.asp use this method. The second technique, as shown in divide.asp, is to use the `Write` method of the `ASP Response` object. This second method is often more convenient in longer procedures.

You can place a script block anywhere on the page. If the script displays text, you should place the script in the part of the page where you want the text to appear. A page can have multiple script blocks. If multiple immediate scripts are on a page, the scripts execute in the order in which you place them on the page.

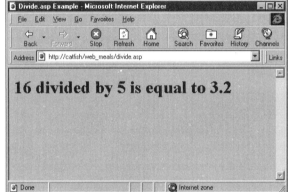

Figure 12-3:
This fascinating ASP page uses a procedure.

Exploring VBScript

VBScript is a lightweight version of the VBA language that Microsoft created with the Web in mind. For readers familiar with VBA, the following is a summary of the major differences between VBA and VBScript:

- ✔ **VBScript is safer than VBA.** Many of the dangerous parts of the language, such as basic file input/output operations, have been removed from VBScript by Microsoft to prevent malicious scripts from wreaking havoc on users' computers.

- ✔ **VBScript has no explicit data types.** You can't define a variable as `String`, `Integer`, `Date`, and so on. You declare all variables in VBScript as the `Variant` data type — the kitchen-sink of data types, which can hold just about anything.

- ✔ **A bunch of other statements and functions have been removed by Microsoft to make VBScript leaner and meaner.** Some missing parts include

    - `Financial` functions

- `File` operations
- User-defined collections
- The `Format` function (fortunately, VBScript replaced most of the functionality of `Format` with several new functions: `FormatCurrency`, `FormatDateTime`, `FormatNumber`, and `FormatPercent`)
- Most error-handling keywords (On Error Resume Next is still available)
- Use of `!` to access members of collections (use `.` instead)

Otherwise, VBScript looks and acts a lot like the VBA language.

If you're familiar with the VBA language in Access, Visual Basic, or Microsoft Office applications, you should have no problem learning ASP's default scripting language, VBScript. (For more on VBScript, pick up a copy of *VBScript For Dummies,* by John Walkenbach, published by IDG Books Worldwide, Inc.)

The following example, color.asp, when executed, displays `Hello There!` with the background color of the page set randomly (see Figure 12-4).

Figure 12-4:
Although you can't see it, the color of the background is currently a steaming hot pink!

```
<HTML>
<%
Function GetRandomColor()
    Dim varColor
    Dim varLen
    Randomize
    varColor= Hex(Rnd()*16777215)
    varLen = Len(varColor)
```

(continued)

(continued)

```
    If varLen < 6 Then varColor = _
    String(6-varLen,"0") & varColor
    GetRandomColor = varColor
End Function
%>
<HEAD>
<TITLE>Color.asp Example</TITLE>
</HEAD>
<BODY BGCOLOR=<% =GetRandomColor() %>>
<HR>
<H1>Hello World!</H1>
<HR>
</BODY>
</HTML>
```

The GetRandomColor function shows off some of the sophisticated capabilities of VBScript; random number generation (notice the Rnd and Randomize keywords); conditional processing (notice the If...Then statement); and string handling (notice the Len and String functions). GetRandomColor returns a random RGB color value. The code sets the background color of the page to the random color value returned by GetRandomColor. Thus, every time the page refreshes, it uses a different background color.

Explicitly declaring your variables in VBScript is always a good idea and helps you avoid making silly typing mistakes.

Although you can use the Option Explicit statement in client-side scripts, the ASP scripting engine doesn't seem to recognize this potentially useful statement for requiring variable declarations.

What About JavaScript?

Because I haven't told it otherwise, the ASP Scripting Engine uses the VBScript interpreter to interpret the sample scripts. When you install ASP, the setup program automatically makes VBScript the default scripting language. You can change the language in a variety of ways.

If you want to change the default scripting language for an ASP page, insert the following statement as the very first line of the file:

```
<%@ LANGUAGE=scripting_language%>
```

One page at a time

To change the default scripting language for a page to JScript (the Microsoft implementation of JavaScript), use the following statement as the first line of the file:

```
<%@ LANGUAGE=JScript%>
```

For example, here's the JavaScript version of the time1.asp page (timej1.asp on the CD-ROM):

```
<%@ LANGUAGE=JScript%>
<HTML>
<HEAD>
<TITLE>TimeJ1.asp Example</TITLE>
</HEAD>
<BODY>
<H2>This page produced on the server (using JavaScript)
at precisely:
<BR>
<% = new Date %>
</H2>
</BODY>
</HTML>
```

The result of running timej1.asp appears in Figure 12-5.

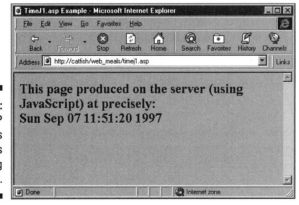

Figure 12-5:
This ASP page uses JScript as its scripting language.

A scripted page

You also can use the <SCRIPT> and </SCRIPT> tags to specify that a section of code on a page should use a scripting language that differs from the default. If you've had experience with client-side scripting, you may notice that this is the same tag you use to indicate a stretch of VBScript or JScript code that should run on the client. To tell ASP to interpret a script on the server, you must include the RUNAT=Server subtag. Using this method allows you to mix and match multiple scripting languages within a single page.

Following is an example of a page that uses the <SCRIPT> and </SCRIPT> tags and a JScript procedure (timej2.asp):

```
<HTML>
<HEAD>
<TITLE>TimeJ2.asp Example</TITLE>
</HEAD>
<SCRIPT LANGUAGE=JScript RUNAT=Server>
function JNow()
{
    var now
    now = new Date()
    Response.Write(now.toString())
}
</SCRIPT>
<BODY>
<H2>This page produced on the server (using JavaScript)
at precisely:
<BR><% = JNow()%>
</H2>
</BODY>
</HTML>
```

Once and for all

If you're a JavaScript programmer at heart, you may want to change the default scripting language to JScript. You can do this for all ASP pages by making a change to the registry.

You need to change the following registry key:

```
HKEY_LOCAL_MACHINE\SYSTEM
\CurrentControlSet
```

```
\Services
  \W3SVC
    \ASP
      \Parameters
```

Change this string key from VBScript to JScript, as shown in Figure 12-6.

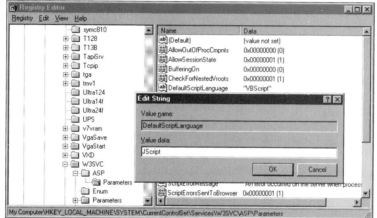

Figure 12-6:
Changing
the default
scripting
language
for Internet
Information
Server.

Changing registry keys can make your system go *boom;* only experienced users should try this. Don't forget that backing up your registry before proceeding is always a good idea.

For more information on programming in JavaScript, see *JavaScript For Dummies,* by Emily A. Vander Veer (IDG Books Worldwide, Inc.).

Is That All There Is?

ASP involves a lot more than this chapter covers. Chapter 13 explores using ASP to get at data and interact with HTML forms. And several chapters in the final part of this book, Part VII, look at more advanced ASP pages you can create using Visual InterDev.

Chapter 13

Activating Your Pages with ADO

● ●

In This Chapter

▶ Understanding ActiveX Data Objects

▶ Creating ADO recordsets

▶ Updating data

▶ Executing stored procedures

● ●

*O*ne of the most compelling reasons for using Active Server Pages is to connect to data. ASP supports data access by using a new Microsoft data-access model called ActiveX Data Objects (ADO). The ADO model enables you to retrieve data using queries, execute action queries and stored procedures, and update records using a data-access model that will make Access and Visual Basic programmers feel right at home.

In this chapter, you discover how to put ASP and ADO together to create powerful and dynamic data-driven Web pages. You also explore how to create ASP pages that interact with HTML forms.

If you're not very comfortable with data-access object models or VBA programming, you may want to pick up a copy of *Access 97 Programming For Windows For Dummies* by Rob Krumm or *Visual Basic 5 For Windows For Dummies* by Wallace Wang (both books are published by IDG Books Worldwide, Inc.).

What's ActiveX Data Objects?

ActiveX Data Objects (ADO) is a lean data-access model (a programmatic language for interacting with databases) that's optimized for access over the Internet and intranets. If you're familiar with other Microsoft data models — that is, if you've used Data Access Objects (DAO) in Access or Remote Data Objects (RDO) in Visual Basic — you'll feel comfortable with ADO. Although you may find many differences between the data access models, you likely will find more similarities than differences.

ODBC, OLE DB, and ADO

ODBC and OLE DB are Windows application programming interfaces (APIs) for accessing data. The older ODBC specification provides data access to primarily relational SQL-based databases, and it does this well. OLE DB, Microsoft's next-generation data-access specification, allows data access to a much broader set of data providers. Those providers include nonrelational database systems, e-mail systems, and CAD/CAM data stores, as well as the classic relational database system.

OLE DB does not replace ODBC. In fact, OLE DB includes a data provider that allows you to use it with ODBC data sources. The important point to realize, however, is that Microsoft plans for OLE DB to go far beyond ODBC in providing universal access to data, no matter how or where it gets stored on the enterprise.

Where does ADO fit into this picture? ADO is a high-level interface to OLE DB. For now, you can conduct business as usual because you can use ADO to access ODBC data sources through OLE DB's ODBC data provider. In the future, however, you will be able to use ADO to access your e-mail system or some other nonrelational data provider.

Microsoft publicly stated that ADO eventually will replace the company's current myriad of data-access models, including DAO and RDO, so keep in mind that ADO is not just for Internet/intranet data access.

The ADO Object Model

The ADO object model, shown in Figure 13-1, is simpler than the DAO and RDO object models.

Figure 13-1: The top-level object in ADO is the Connection object, which contains Command and Recordset objects and the Errors collection.

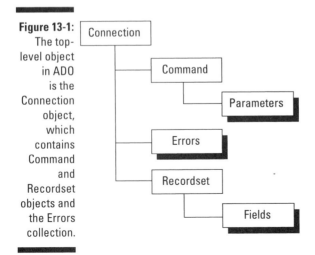

ADO lacks a collection of tables, or any environment, workspace, or engine type object. The major ADO objects and collections are

- ✔ **Connection object:** You use the ADO Connection object to create a connection to a data provider — in the examples in this chapter, this means an ODBC data source. The ADO Connection object is similar to the DAO database object or the RDO rdoConnection object.

- ✔ **Recordset object:** You use the ADO Recordset object to create a set of records from a query. Like the DAO Recordset and the RDO rdoResultset, you can move forward and backward through ADO recordsets. Sometimes, ADO recordsets are called *cursors*.

  ADO always builds recordset cursors on the server.

- ✔ **Command object:** You use the ADO Command object to point to SQL strings, stored procedures, or action queries that you can execute. The Command object is similar to the DAO QueryDef object or the RDO rdoPreparedStatement.

- ✔ **Errors collection:** The ADO Errors collection allows you to loop through the collection of errors that may occur from a failed data-access attempt. Because one data-access statement may produce multiple errors, ADO defines the Errors *collection* rather than a single Error object. The ADO Errors collection is similar to the DAO collection of the same name and the rdoErrors collection.

Accessing Data Using ADO

The following ASP file (emp1.asp) uses ADO to grab a record from the Access 97 WebMeals.mdb database using the WebMeals ODBC system data source. This code uses ADO code to extract a single record from the qryCurrentEmployees query in WebMeals.mdb and display it on the Web page.

Following is the complete emp1.asp page:

```
<HTML>
<HEAD>
<TITLE>Emp1.asp Example</TITLE>
</HEAD>
<BODY>
<H1> Employee #1 </H1>
<%
```

(continued)

(continued)

```
' Declare the variables
Dim rst
Dim varSQL

' Create an empty recordset object
Set rst = Server.CreateObject("ADODB.Recordset")

' Create the SQL statement and stick it in varSQL
varSQL = "SELECT * FROM qryCurrentEmployees " & _
 "WHERE EmployeeID = 1"

' Fill the recordset with records based on the
' SQL statement in varSQL and the WebMeals
' data source
rst.Open varSQL, "WebMeals"

' Display the data
%>

<B>Name:</B> <%= rst("FirstName") %>
   <%= rst("LastName") %>
<BR><B>Address:</B> <%= rst("Address") %>
<BR><B>City/State/Zip:</B> <%= rst("City") %>,
 <%= rst("State") %>
   <%= rst("ZipCode") %>

<%
' Clean up the objects
rst.Close
%>
</BODY>
</HTML>
```

You can see the preceding code in action in Figure 13-2.

If you want to run this example, you need to create a System data source called WebMeals on your Web server machine that points to the WebMeals.mdb database. Take a look at Chapter 8 for more details on creating the WebMeals data source.

Figure 13-2:
This page
uses ADO
code to
extract a
single
record
from the
qryCurrent
Employees
query and
display it on
the Web
page.

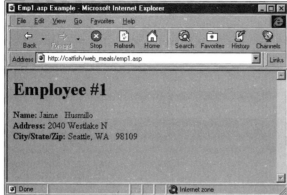

Pure HTML

The emp1.asp file seems to contain a lot of code, but the ASP code is actually quite simple if you break it down into several smaller parts. The first part of the ASP page is just pure HTML:

```
<HTML>
<HEAD>
<TITLE>Emp1.asp Example</TITLE>
</HEAD>
<BODY>
<H1> Employee #1 </H1>
```

Declaring variables

In this stretch of code, I declare two variables. Remember that all variables are variants in VBScript (the default ASP scripting language), so you don't find As Datatype in the VBScript Dim statement.

```
<%
' Declare the variables
Dim rst
Dim varSQL
```

Creating the recordset object

You create the recordset in several steps:

1. **Create an empty** Recordset **object:**

```
Set rst = Server.CreateObject("ADODB.Recordset")
```

If you're used to DAO or RDO in VBA, this way of creating objects may seem strange. VBA allows you to *early bind* your objects — when you write your code, you can set a reference to the object model's type library. (Sometimes, this reference gets created automatically.) You avoid having to use the CreateObject function. Unfortunately, because the VBScript language doesn't support early binding, you must create all objects using the CreateObject function.

You create ASP objects using the Server object, which provides access to methods and properties of the Web server. (For more information on the ASP server object, take a look at Chapter 17.)

2. **Add an** SQL **statement into the** varSQL **variable:**

```
varSQL = "SELECT * FROM qryCurrentEmployees " & _
  "WHERE EmployeeID = 1"
```

For Access data sources, you can reference both tables and queries in your SQL statements.

3. **Use the** Recordset **object's** Open **method to fill it with the records returned by executing the** SQL **statement from** varSQL.

The second argument, in this example "WebMeals", tells ADO the name of the data source to use:

```
rst.Open varSQL, "WebMeals"
%>
```

Displaying the data

To display the data from the record returned by the recordset, you must use a mixture of HTML and VBScript. The HTML provides the labels for the data; the VBScript provides the values from the recordset using the names of the fields from the Access query:

```
<B>Name:</B> <%= rst("FirstName") %>
   <%= rst("LastName") %>
<BR><B>Address:</B> <%= rst("Address") %>
<BR><B>City/State/Zip:</B> <%= rst("City") %>,
 <%= rst("State") %>
   <%= rst("ZipCode") %>
```

You can insert a nonbreaking space into your HTML by using the   sequence of characters.

Clean-up time

The last section of code closes the Recordset object and ends the HTML:

```
<%
rst.Close
%>
</BODY>
</HTML>
```

Now that wasn't so bad, was it?

Flattening the Object Model

In ADO, the object hierarchy has less emphasis. This means that, unlike DAO and RDO, you don't have to work your way down the object hierarchy just to create an object. I took advantage of this fact in emp1.asp by directly creating the rst recordset without first creating a connection.

What's the advantage of this flatter object model? You have fewer lines of code and less use of memory. I save a bit of memory because I avoided creating a Connection object. Memory use is especially critical if hundreds or thousands of clients simultaneously use your Web page.

In many cases, however, you need to explicitly create a Connection object because it's more efficient when you perform multiple recordset or command operations to work with a single connection instead of having to repeatedly close and recreate connections.

Recordset options galore

The Open method of the recordset object allows you to create different kinds of recordsets. The syntax of the Open method follows:

```
recordset.Open Source, ActiveConnection, _
  CursorType, LockType, Options
```

Source

The first argument of the Open method, Source, represents the source of the recordset. In this case, I used an SQL string in emp1.asp, but I also could have used the name of a table or a server-stored procedure.

ActiveConnection

In the second argument, ActiveConnection, you can do one of the following:

- ✔ Use a connection string, which creates a new connection for the sole purpose of creating the recordset.
- ✔ Point to an active Connection object that you previously created.

CursorType

You use the third argument, CursorType (optional), to specify the type of recordset to create. A summary of the possible values of this argument appears in Table 13-1.

Table 13-1	Possible CursorType Values	
Value	*Constant*	*Description*
0	adOpenForwardOnly	Forward-only recordset cursor (the default)
1	adOpenKeyset	Keyset recordset cursor
2	adOpenDynamic	Dynamic recordset cursor
3	adOpenStatic	Static recordset cursor

The default recordset cursor is a forward-only recordset. Unlike DAO recordsets, you can update all ADO recordsets, even the static and forward-only recordsets. The different types of recordsets vary in how your recordset reflects changes made by other users.

Changes to the records made by other users in *static* and *forward-only* recordset are invisible to you. That is, when you create a static or forward-only recordset, you are totally unaware of any changes made by other users. If you don't need to move backward through the recordset, use the forward-only recordset because it consumes less memory and is faster than the static cursor.

Forward-only recordsets don't support methods such as MovePrevious, MoveFirst, or MoveLast. Also, forward-only recordsets don't support the use of the RecordCount property.

The *keyset* recordset is very similar in behavior to the DAO dynaset. The number of records in a keyset recordset never changes. You never find out about additions that other users make, nor do records deleted by other users disappear from your recordset (although the deleted records become inaccessible). However, you do get notification when existing records get updated.

The *dynamic* recordset has no DAO counterpart. This type of recordset is totally dynamic. When you have a dynamic recordset open, you get notices of recordset additions, deletions, and updates. While the dynamic recordset is the most functional, be aware that it's also the most expensive in terms of memory and speed.

The recordset is maintained by the Web server, not the client. When I say that a recordset is notified of updates, I am not referring to the list of records on the Web page that are not connected to the data. The data can change, however, when the user refreshes the Web page or moves to another page that displays records from the recordset.

LockType

The fourth argument, also optional, specifies the type of locking to employ. A summary of the possible lock types appears in Table 13-2.

Table 13-2	Possible LockType Values	
Value	*Constant*	*Description*
1	adLockReadOnly	Read only (the default)
2	adLockPessimistic	Pessimistic locking
3	adLockOptimistic	Optimistic locking
4	adLockBatchOptimistic	Optimistic locking with batch updates

Set LockType to 1 (read only) if you aren't updating records.

Generally, if you're updating records, you should set LockType to 3, *optimistic locking*. All data providers support this type of locking. When you choose optimistic locking, the record is locked by the data provider only while ADO physically updates the record. In contrast, a Locktype of 2 provides *pessimistic locking* (if the data provider supports it). In this type of locking, the record is locked by the data provider while you edit the record. When you use pessimistic locking, you increase you chances of freezing other users out of the locked records, so it's usually best to use optimistic locking. Some data providers, such as SQL Server 6.5, do not offer pessimistic locking.

Setting the LockType argument to 4 tells ADO that you want to employ batch updating. This form of updating allows you to download multiple records, update them locally, and submit them back to the data provider in a single batch. Many data providers do not support batch updating.

Options

You use the optional Options argument to indicate the type of Source argument you are providing to the Open method. You can set Options to any of the options in Table 13-3.

Table 13-3		Possible Options Values
Value	*Constant*	*Description*
1	adCmdText	Command text (SQL statement)
2	adCmdTable	Table, view, or saved select query
4	adCmdStoredProc	Stored procedure or saved action query
8	adCmdUnknown	Unknown (the default)

If you submit an SQL string as the Source argument, then set Options to 1.

If you set the Source argument to the name of a table, select query or view, you need to use a value of 2. Not all data providers allow you to use the adCmdTable option.

If you want to call a stored procedure or saved action query, you need to set Options to 4.

By default, Options is set to a value of 8 (unknown). In this case, ADO attempts to infer the source type from its contents. As you may guess, this option is less efficient and should be avoided.

Constants — what constants?

The constants listed in Tables 13-1, 13-2, and 13-3 are not predefined for you by VBScript as they are when you use ADO from VBA (with a reference to the ADO type library). You can use these constants in two ways in your code:

✔ Define your own constants using the constants from the tables.

✔ Include the adovbs.inc "include" file in your code. (If you use JavaScript, you can include the adojavas.inc include file instead.)

You can find these include files in the Program Files\Common Files\
System\Ado folder on your Web server. (Older versions of the
Microsoft Web servers place these files in the \Inetpub\wwwroot\
ASPSamp\Samples folder.)

To incorporate an include file in your ASP file, use a server-side `include`
statement like the following:

```
<!--#include virtual="/ASPSAMP/SAMPLES/ADOVBS.INC"-->
```

You need to place this preceding statement outside of any script. For
example:

```
<%
Dim con
Dim rst
Dim strSQL
%>
<! #include virtual="/ASPSAMP/SAMPLES/ADOVBS.INC"->
<%
Set con = Server.CreateObject("ADODB.Connection")
' ...
```

If you need only a few constants, however, using the entire advobs.inc
include file is probably overkill and wastes a lot of memory.

Another recordset example

The emp1.asp example displays a single record on the Web page. More
typically, you want to display a group of records on a single page using an
HTML table — as shown in a second example, cust1.asp. This example
draws its records from the SQL Server version of the Meals database.

Following is the complete ASP file:

```
<HTML>
<HEAD>
<TITLE>Cust1.asp Example</TITLE>
</HEAD>
<BODY>
<H1> Our Customers </H1>
<%
' Declare the variables
Dim con
Dim rst
```

(continued)

(continued)

```
Dim strSQL
' Declare the Open method constants
Const adOpenStatic = 3
Const adLockReadOnly = 1
Const adCmdText = 1

' Create a Connection object and point it to
' the WebMealsSQL data source passing it
' a username and password
Set con = Server.CreateObject("ADODB.Connection")
con.Open "WebMealsSQL", "WebUser", ""

' Create the Recordset object and fill it with
' the records from the SQL statement, using the
' already established connection
' Since this page is used to create an HTML table,
' a static, read-only recordset is created
strSQL = "SELECT * FROM tblCustomers " & _
  "ORDER BY LastName, FirstName"
Set rst = Server.CreateObject("ADODB.Recordset")
rst.Open strSQL, con, adOpenStatic, _
  adLockReadOnly, adCmdText
' Only display table if there are records
' in the recordset
If Not rst.EOF Then
    ' Display the header
%>
    <TABLE BORDER>
    <TR>
        <TD><B>Firstname</B></TD>
        <TD><B>Lastname</B></TD>
        <TD><B>City</B></TD>
    </TR>

<%
    ' Loop through the recordset until there
    ' aren't anymore records
    Do While Not rst.EOF
        ' Display the record values
%>
        <TR>
            <TD><%= rst("FirstName") %></TD>
            <TD><%= rst("LastName") %></TD>
            <TD><%= rst("City") %></TD>
        </TR>
<%
```

```
            ' If you forget this next statement,
            ' you'll keep printing the same record
            ' and create a very, very large table!
            rst.MoveNext
      Loop

Else
%>
    <B>No records in recordset!</B>
<%
End If

' Clean up time
rst.Close
con.Close
%>
</TABLE>
<BR><A HREF="adomenu.html">[Return to home page]</A>
</BODY>
</HTML>
```

You can see the result of executing cust.1asp in Figure 13-3 as it appears in Internet Explorer 4.0.

If you want to run this example, you need to create a System data source called WebMealsSQL on your Web server machine that points to the WebMeals SQL Server database. Chapter 9 gives you more details on creating the WebMealsSQL data source.

In the next few sections, I highlight some of the key pieces of code in cust1.asp.

Declaring variables and constants

After the requisite HTML header, the VBScript code in cust1.asp declares its variables and several constants that the Open method uses:

```
<%
Dim con
Dim rst
Dim strSQL
Const adOpenStatic = 3
Const adLockReadOnly = 1
Const adCmdText = 1
```

Using constants in your VBScript code instead of arbitrary numbers is always a good idea. This practice makes your code more readable.

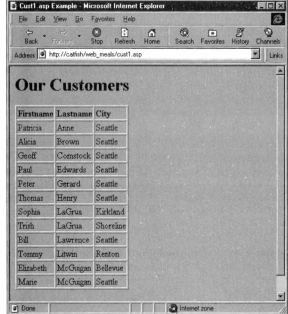

Figure 13-3:
This page
uses ADO
code to fill
an HTML
table with
records
from the
tblCustomers
table.

Opening a connection

The following code from cust1.asp creates a connection object and opens it:

```
Set con = Server.CreateObject("ADODB.Connection")
con.Open "WebMealsSQL", "WebUser", ""
```

Because the WebMealsSQL data source points to an SQL Server database, you must provide username and password arguments. For Access databases, these arguments are optional.

The first argument of the Connection object's Open method, ConnectionString, may refer to either an ODBC data source name (DSN) or a detailed ADO connection string. All the examples in this chapter use the former, but in some cases you may need to provide further information. You need a detailed ADO connection string when you're using a non-ODBC data provider. See the ADO documentation for more information on ADO connection strings.

Creating the recordset

This section of code creates the recordset using an SQL statement and links it up to the existing Connection object:

```
strSQL = "SELECT * FROM tblCustomers " & _
  "ORDER BY LastName, FirstName"
Set rst = Server.CreateObject("ADODB.Recordset")
rst.Open strSQL, con, adOpenStatic, _
  adLockReadOnly, adCmdText
```

What if the recordset doesn't contain any records?

Cust1.asp includes the following If...Then...Else statement to handle the case where the query returns no records:

```
If Not rst.EOF Then
    ' ...create the table ...
Else
%>
    <B>No records in recordset!</B>
<%
End If
```

The preceding code uses the EOF property of the recordset to check if any records are present. If the query returns an empty recordset, ADO sets the EOF property to True, otherwise it sets EOF to False. If the query returns no records, the Web page looks like the one shown in Figure 13-4.

Displaying the table

If the recordset contains at least one record (rst.EOF = True), then the code creates the table header:

```
%>
    <TABLE BORDER>
    <TR>
            <TD><B>Firstname</B></TD>
            <TD><B>Lastname</B></TD>
            <TD><B>City</B></TD>
    </TR>
```

Figure 13-4:
When the
query
returns no
records, the
Web page
reports as
much.

After the code creates the header, it needs to loop through each of the records and plug the `FirstName`, `LastName`, and `City` values into the rows of the HTML table. You do this by using a `Do While` loop and the `MoveNext` method of the recordset:

```
<%
   Do While Not rst.EOF
%>
        <TR>
                <TD><%= rst("FirstName") %></TD>
                <TD><%= rst("LastName") %></TD>
                <TD><%= rst("City") %></TD>
        </TR>
<%
        rst.MoveNext
   Loop
```

Don't forget the `MoveNext` method. (Does this sound like a voice of experience speaking?) If you do, then the `Do While` loop prints the same record in an infinite loop, producing a Web page of infinite length — probably not what you intended.

Updating Data

Using ADO, you can update records, add new records, and delete records. The following sections demonstrate how to accomplish these feats with several examples.

Adding records to a recordset

To add a new record to an ADO recordset, you use the `AddNew` and `Update` methods of a `Recordset` object. First, though, you need to create a `Recordset` object (see the section "Creating the recordset" earlier in this chapter). After you create a non-read-only recordset, you're ready to add a new record. The code to add a record should look something like this:

```
rst.AddNew
    rst("field1") = value1
    rst("field2") = value2
    ' ...
rst.Update
```

Adding a new record is always a three-step process:

1. **Call the `AddNew` method to tell ADO you want to add a new blank record.**

2. **Set the values of one or more fields for the new record.**

3. **Call the `Update` method to save the new record to the database.**

The next example consists of two files: an HTML file that captures a new record using an HTML form (addcust1.html); and an ASP file (addcust1.asp) that adds the new record to the `tblCustomers` table using the `AddNew` and `Update` methods. Following is the addcust1.html file:

```
<HTML>
<HEAD>
<TITLE>Addcust1.html Example</TITLE>
</HEAD>
<BODY>
<H1> Adding A New Customer </H1>

<FORM METHOD="POST" ACTION="Addcust1.ASP">
<TABLE>
```

(continued)

(continued)

```
   <TR><TD>First Name:</TD>
        <TD><INPUT NAME="FirstName" SIZE=20></TD></TR>
   <TR><TD>Last Name:</TD>
        <TD><INPUT NAME="LastName" SIZE=20></TD></TR>
   <TR><TD>Address:</TD>
        <TD><INPUT NAME="Address" SIZE=40></TD></TR>
   <TR><TD>City:</TD>
        <TD><INPUT NAME="City" SIZE=20></TD></TR>
   <TR><TD>State:</TD>
        <TD><INPUT NAME="State" SIZE=6></TD></TR>
   <TR><TD>ZipCode:</TD>
        <TD><INPUT NAME="ZipCode" SIZE=10></TD></TR>
</TABLE>
<BR><INPUT TYPE="SUBMIT" VALUE="Save Record">
<INPUT TYPE="RESET" VALUE="Reset Fields">
<BR><BR><A HREF="adomenu.html">Abandon edits
and return to home page</A>
</FORM>
</BODY>
</HTML>
```

The addcust1.html page is shown in Figure 13-5.

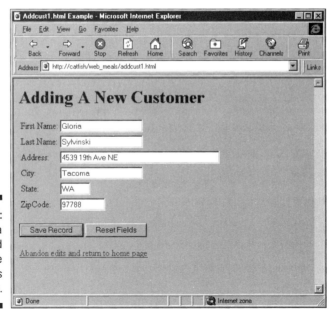

Figure 13-5:
Adding a new record to the tblCustomers table.

And following is the addcust1.asp file to which addcust1.html posts its data to:

```
<HTML>
<HEAD>
<TITLE>Addcust1.asp Example</TITLE>
</HEAD>
<BODY>
<H1> Adding A New Customer </H1>
<%

Dim con
Dim rst
Const adOpenKeyset = 1
Const adLockOptimistic = 3

' Create the objects
Set con = Server.CreateObject("ADODB.Connection")
Set rst = Server.CreateObject("ADODB.Recordset")

' Open the connection to the Meals database
con.Open "WebMealsSQL", "WebUser", ""

' Create a keyset recordset based on the
' tblCustomers table with optimistic locking
rst.Open "SELECT * FROM tblCustomers", con, _
 adOpenKeyset, adLockOptimistic

' Create a new blank record
rst.AddNew

   ' Set the fields to the user-entered values
   ' from the html form used to collect the data
   rst("FirstName")= Request.Form("FirstName")
   rst("LastName")= Request.Form("LastName")
   rst("Address")= Request.Form("Address")
   rst("City")= Request.Form("City")
   rst("State")= Request.Form("State")
   rst("ZipCode")= Request.Form("ZipCode")

' Save the new record to the database
rst.Update

Response.Write "<B>Thank you!</B>"

rst.Close
```

(continued)

(continued)

```
con.Close
%>
<BR><A HREF="adomenu.html">Return to home page</A>
</BODY>
</HTML>
```

Because addcust1.asp needs to update data, I created a keyset recordset with optimistic locking enabled:

```
rst.Open "SELECT * FROM tblCustomers", con, _
  adOpenKeyset, adLockOptimistic
```

Values from the calling HTML form get sucked into the code using the Response object, as in:

```
rst("FirstName")= Request.Form("FirstName")
```

When you successfully submit the new record, the addcust1.asp page looks like the one shown in Figure 13-6.

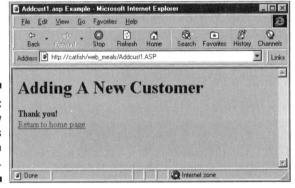

Figure 13-6: A new record has been added.

What about handling errors?

The code in update1.asp assumes that the new record is always successfully added to the tblCustomers table. Unfortunately, the fact that the record was added at this point is not a foregone conclusion. Several things can and will (from time to time) go wrong. For example, the update may fail for the following reasons:

- ✔ You lack the correct permissions to update the records
- ✔ A referential integrity or index error occurs

> ✔ A field that doesn't accept nulls is left blank
>
> ✔ You save a string value to a numeric field
>
> ✔ You attempt to save a value that is too large for a field
>
> ✔ A check constraint (SQL Server) or a validation rule (Access) fails

Always remember the most important rule of computing: If something can go wrong, it will go wrong — especially when you're on vacation!

So what happens if you encounter an error while saving the record? The ASP scripting engine prints an error to the page, as shown in Figure 13-7. The message varies, depending on the type of error. No matter what the error, the result isn't very professional looking.

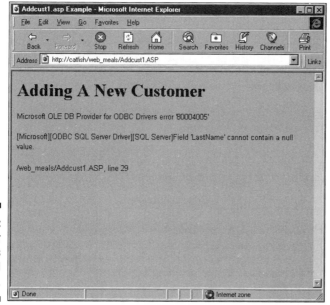

Figure 13-7:
An error message as displayed by default.

VBScript error handling

Unlike its cousin VBA, VBScript has limited custom error-handling capabilities. VBScript doesn't support the use of procedure-level error handlers. The error-handling capabilities of VBScript consist of the ability to turn off the default error handling (which allows you to intercept the errors and handle them yourself) with

```
On Error Resume Next
```

and the ability to turn default error handling back on with

```
On Error GoTo 0
```

In addition, when you turn off the default error handling, you can use the VBScript `Err` object to get information about the error. For example, you can check if an error has occurred with an `If...Then` statement like the following:

```
If Err.Number <> 0 Then
   ' You know an error has occurred.
End If
```

Whenever you check its value, `Err.Number` equals

- ✔ 0 if no error has occurred, or
- ✔ a long integer containing the error number of the error that has occurred

You also have access to the error message that VBScript would have displayed had it reported the message itself. You find this message stored in the `Description` property of the `Err` object. You can display the message with the following code:

```
Response.Write Err.Description
```

You must test the value of `Err.Number` immediately after any statement that may trigger an error because `Err.Number` resets after each statement and thus contains only information regarding the most recent error (or lack of one).

The ADO errors collection

In addition to the VBScript `Err` object, the ADO `Connection` object has an `Errors` collection that may contain multiple entries regarding the last ADO error. The `Errors` collection's `Count` property tells you how many errors, if any, are in the collection. Thus, with code like this, you can display all the errors that may have occurred from an ADO operation. (In the following example, `con` points to an active ADO `Connection` object.)

```
varErrorCount = con.Errors.Count
If varErrorCount > 0 Then
   For varI = 0 To varErrorCount - 1
         Response.Write "<BR><I>" & _
         con.Errors(varI).Description & "</I>"
   Next
End If
```

Which one should I use?

Why use the ADO Errors collection when you can use the simpler VBScript Err object? A particular ADO operation sometimes may generate a series of errors. In these cases, the ADO Errors collection provides additional information on the problem. In most cases, however, the VBScript Err object and the ADO Errors collection return the same information, so you're often fine if you use the simpler Err object.

No matter which form of error reporting you decide to use, you must use the VBScript On Error Resume Next statement to tell VBScript you want to intercept the errors that VBScript normally handles.

An error-handling example

If you decide to implement custom error handling in your ASP pages, be prepared for a bunch of extra code. Because VBScript lacks any way to define a procedure-level error handler, you need to check for the occurrence of an error after every VBScript statement — or at least after every VBScript statement that you think may cause an error.

One way to lessen the error-handling load is to create a function to take care of some of the tedium of handling errors. I created such a function in a modification to the addcust1.asp file named addcust2.asp. The complete code for addcust2.asp is on the CD-ROM at the back of this book. Here, I highlight just the key parts of the ASP page.

The HandleErrors function follows:

```
Function HandleErrors(varNum, varDesc)
   On Error Resume Next
   If varNum <> 0 Then
         Response.Write "<BR><B>The following " & _
          "error occurred:</B><BR>"
         Response.Write varDesc
         HandleErrors = 1
   Else
         HandleErrors = 0
   End If
End Function
```

The main code from addcust2.asp calls HandleErrors immediately after every statement that may cause an error. For example, the code calls HandleErrors after the Update method:

```
rst.Update
varErrors = varErrors + _
  HandleErrors(Err.Number, Err.Description)
```

The main code passes `HandleErrors` the error number and the description. I define a variable, *varErrors*, to keep track of the number of errors that occur. This approach works because `HandleErrors` returns a 0 if no error occurs or a 1 if an error occurs. At the end of the main code, I then know whether the record addition succeeded and I can display the status of the record addition to the user:

```
Response.Write "<BR><BR>"
If varErrors = 0 Then
    Response.Write "<B>Record added!</B>"
Else
    Response.Write "<B>Record could not be " & _
        "added because of errors!</B>"
End If
```

The same error that occurs in Figure 13-7 appears in Figure 13-8 using a custom error-handling routine.

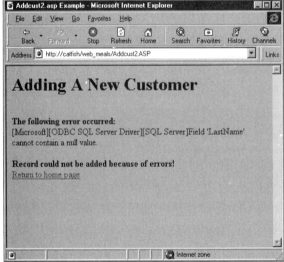

Figure 13-8:
This error message is more professional looking and makes it clearer that the record didn't get added.

Going to the trouble of handling errors has two advantages:

- ✔ You can display better, more user-friendly information to the user.
- ✔ You can react to the error and branch in your code appropriately.

You don't have to display the VBScript or ADO error message to the user. You can always check to see which error has occurred (using `Err.Number`) and then display more user-friendly versions of some of the most common errors.

Updating a record in a recordset

Unlike DAO and RDO, there is no `Edit` method of a recordset in ADO to indicate when you want to begin editing a record. The code to edit a record in ADO should look something like the following:

```
rst("field1") = value1
rst("field2") = value2
' ...
rst.Update
```

Editing a record is a three-step process:

1. **Move to the record you want to edit.**

2. **Set the values of one or more fields for the record.**

3. **Call the Update method to save the changes to the database.**

In fact, even Step 3 is optional. If you forget to use the Update method to save your changes and move to another record, ADO automatically saves your edits for you. Wow!

How, then, do you abandon your edits? Fortunately, ADO recordsets have a method, `CancelUpdate`, which you can use to throw away your edits. Using the `CancelUpdate` method couldn't be easier:

```
rst.CancelUpdate
```

The CD-ROM at the back of this book includes an example that you can use to update records in the tblCustomer table of the SQL Server Meals database. This example uses three files:

- ✔ **Update.asp:** This page displays a list of customers and lets you click on a customer to edit the associated record.

- ✔ **UpdRec.asp:** This page displays the current data from the customer record using an HTML form and includes buttons to edit or delete the record.

- ✔ **UpdAct.asp:** This page either saves the changes or deletes the record.

In this section, I discuss the updating portion of the example files. Later in this chapter, I discuss the delete functionality of the example files.

Update.asp

Much of the code in Update.asp is identical to the code from cust1.asp discussed in the "Another recordset example" section earlier in the chapter, so I don't show the complete page here. (You can also find it on this book's CD-ROM.) You can use the following section of code to display the values in a standard HTML table:

```
<%
    ' Loop through the recordset
    Do While Not rst.EOF
        ' Display the record values
%>
        <TR>
            <!-Create a hyperlink in the left column
            that passes the CustomerId to the
            UpdRec.asp page                           ->
            <TD><A HREF="UpdRec.asp?CustomerId=
            <%= rst("CustomerId") %>">
            <%= rst("Name") %></A></TD>
            <TD><%= rst("City") %></TD>
            <TD><%= rst("State") %></TD>
        </TR>
<%
        ' Move to the next record
        rst.MoveNext
    Loop
```

The preceding example uses the `<A>` tag to create a hyperlink that displays the customer's name from the `Name` field. The URL for this hyperlink is constructed from the UpdRec.asp page and a query string consisting of `"CustomerId="` and the value of the `CustomerId` for that record.

This `<A>` tag sends HTML to the browser that looks like the following (for the record with a `CustomerId` = 7):

```
<A HREF="UpdRec.asp?CustomerId=7">Alicia Brown</A>
```

Take a look at Figure 13-9 to see how update.asp appears in Netscape Navigator.

UpdRec.asp

The code behind UpdRec.asp is responsible for displaying the values from the requested record, as well as two submit buttons that determine the action to take on the record.

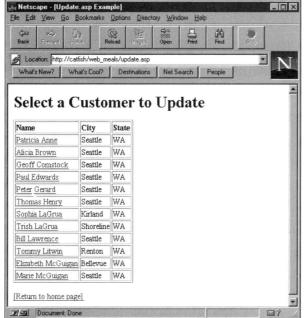

Figure 13-9:
The
Update.asp
page lets
you select
any
customer
for
updating.

Following is the complete UpdRec.asp file:

```
<HTML>
<HEAD>
<TITLE>UpdRec.asp Example</TITLE>
</HEAD>
<BODY>
<H1> Customer Record Update Page </H1>
<%
' Declare the variables
Dim con
Dim rst
Dim strSQL
' Declare the Open method constants
Const adOpenStatic = 3
Const adLockReadOnly = 1
Const adCmdText = 1

' Create a Connection object and point it to
' the WebMealsSQL data source
Set con = Server.CreateObject("ADODB.Connection")
con.Open "WebMealsSQL", "WebUser", ""
```

(continued)

(continued)

```
' Create a recordset with one record in it
' based on the CustomerId passed to this page
' from the update.asp page
strSQL = "SELECT * FROM tblCustomers " & _
 "WHERE CustomerId =" & Request("CustomerId")
Set rst = Server.CreateObject("ADODB.Recordset")
rst.Open strSQL, con, adOpenStatic, _
 adLockReadOnly, adCmdText

' Only display form if there is a matching
' record
If Not rst.EOF Then
%>
   <FORM METHOD="POST" ACTION="UpdAct.ASP">
   <INPUT Type="HIDDEN" NAME="CustomerId"
   Value="<% = rst("CustomerId") %>">
   <TABLE>

   <TR><TD>CustomerId:</TD><TD>
   <B><I><% = rst("CustomerId") %></I></B>
   </TD></TR>

   <TR><TD>First Name:</TD><TD>
   <INPUT NAME="FirstName"
   Size=20 Value="<% = rst("FirstName") %>">
   </TD></TR>

   <TR><TD>Last Name:</TD><TD>
   <INPUT NAME="LastName"
   Size =20 Value="<% = rst("LastName") %>">
   </TD></TR>

   <TR><TD>Address:</TD><TD>
   <INPUT NAME="Address"
   Size=40 Value="<% = rst("Address") %>">
   </TD></TR>

   <TR><TD>City:</TD><TD>
   <INPUT NAME="City"
   Size =20 Value="<% = rst("City") %>">
   </TD></TR>

   <TR><TD>State:</TD><TD>
   <INPUT NAME="State"
```

```
      Size =6 Value="<% = rst("State") %>">
      </TD></TR>

      <TR><TD>ZipCode:</TD><TD>
      <INPUT NAME="ZipCode"
      Size =10 Value="<% = rst("ZipCode") %>">
      </TD></TR>
      </TABLE>
      <BR><INPUT TYPE="SUBMIT" Name="Submit"
      VALUE="Save Changes">
      <INPUT TYPE="SUBMIT" Name="Submit"
      VALUE="Delete Record">
      </FORM>

<%
Else
%>
      <B>No record was found matching
      this CustomerId!</B>
<%
End If

' Clean up time
rst.Close
con.Close
%>

<A HREF="update.asp">[Abandon edits and select
 another customer]</A>
  
<A HREF="adomenu.html">[Return to home page]</A>
</BODY>
</HTML>
```

The UpdRec.asp page creates a recordset based on the CustomerId value passed to the page by the Update.asp page (see Figure 13-10). The SQL for the recordset follows:

```
strSQL = "SELECT * FROM tblCustomers " & _
  "WHERE CustomerId =" & Request("CustomerId")
```

The following statement sets up the form to post the data to the UpdAct.asp page when the user clicks the Submit button:

```
<FORM METHOD="POST" ACTION="UpdAct.ASP">
```

The form displays the `CustomerId` value as regular HTML text rather than as a form field to prevent the user from changing the value. I also include, however, a hidden control on the form that contains the `CustomerId` value so that the value can be passed along to the UpdAct.asp page:

```
<INPUT Type="HIDDEN" NAME="CustomerId"
Value="<% = rst("CustomerId") %>">
```

A good way to pass along information between pages is to store it in hidden controls.

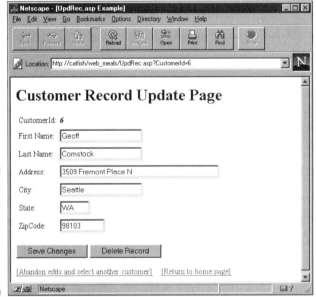

Figure 13-10:
You can edit a customer record using the UpdRec.asp page.

The UpdRec.asp page contains two Submit buttons. Because I include `Name` subtags for both Submit buttons and give them the same name — in this example, `Submit` (but there's nothing special about this name) — UpdRec.usp posts the name and value pair to UpdAct.asp. This technique allows the code in UpdAct.asp to tell which button the user clicks. This trick doesn't work unless you include the `Name` subtag in the `Submit` button tags.

UpdAct.asp

The UpdAct.asp page completes the update operation by opening a recordset based on the edited record from UpdRec.asp and saving the updated values back to the record. Much of this code is similar to the two other pages (Update.asp and UpdRec.asp), so in this section I highlight only key portions of the code. (The complete page is on the CD-ROM.)

In this portion of code from UpdAct.asp, the LockType argument of the rst.Open method is set to adLockOptimistic to allow for editing:

```
rst.Open strSQL, con, adOpenStatic, _
  adLockOptimistic, adCmdText
```

The following If...Then...Else statement determines which of the Submit buttons on UpdRec.asp the user clicked:

```
If Request("Submit")= "Save Changes" Then
```

The updated values carry over from UpdRec.asp, and the Update method saves the changes to the database in this stretch of code:

```
rst("LastName") = Request("LastName")
rst("FirstName") = Request("FirstName")
rst("Address") = Request("Address")
rst("City") = Request("City")
rst("State") = Request("State")
rst("ZipCode") = Request("ZipCode")
rst.Update
```

The UpdAct.asp page is shown in Figure 13-11.

Figure 13-11: A successfully updated customer record.

Deleting a record from a recordset

Deleting a record in ADO is pretty simple. You use the Delete method of the Recordset object to delete the current record. The code looks like the following:

```
rst.Delete
```

Deleting a record is a two-step process:

1. **Move to the record you want to delete.**

2. **Call the** `Delete` **method to delete the record from the database.**

   Following is the code from UpdAct.asp that deletes the record:

```
If Request("Submit")= "Save Changes" Then
    '...
Else
    ' Delete record
    rst.Delete
    '...
End If
```

You can't get much simpler than that! Figure 13-12 shows the resulting page.

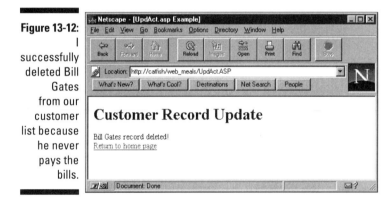

Figure 13-12:
I successfully deleted Bill Gates from our customer list because he never pays the bills.

Executing Queries and Stored Procedures

The ADO `Command` object makes it easy for you to execute Access action queries or server-stored procedures. You can use the `Command` object in one of two ways:

- ✔ With stored procedures that don't return records or Access action queries
- ✔ With stored procedures that return records

To execute a `Command` object on a stored procedure that doesn't return records or an Access action query (which never returns records), you use the following syntax:

```
cmd.Execute RecordsAffected, Parameters, Options
```

When you need to create a recordset for a stored procedure, you use this syntax instead:

```
Set rst = cmd.Execute(RecordsAffected, Parameters, Options)
```

If you pass a variable to the Execute method's RecordsAffected argument, the Execute method returns the number of records affected by the action query or stored procedure. Using RecordsAffected is a good way to determine if the action query or stored procedure succeeded.

You can use the Parameters argument to pass an array of parameters to the Execute method. In most cases, setting the parameter values prior to using the Execute method is better, however, because when you use the argument, you must construct the array of parameters.

You can use the Options argument to tell the Execute method the type of command you are executing. The possible values are the same as for the Recordset object's Open method, which I list in Table 13-3. You can also use the CommandType property of the Command object to set this value prior to using the Execute method.

All the Execute arguments are optional.

A stored procedure example

The UpdAct.asp file (from earlier in the chapter) creates a recordset to delete a record. In most cases, using an action query or stored procedure to perform this sort of activity is much more efficient than using a recordset. In this section, I demonstrate how to delete a record using a stored procedure. The stored procedure example on the CD-ROM uses two files:

- ✔ **updatesp.asp:** This page displays a list of customers and lets you click on a customer to edit the associated record.
- ✔ **sp.asp:** This page executes a stored procedure using a Command object.

Because the updatesp.asp file is almost identical to the update.asp file discussed in a previous section of this chapter, I don't present it here (but you can find the file on the CD-ROM). The only real difference in the file is that it calls sp.asp instead of updrec.asp with the following code:

```
<TD><A HREF="Sp.asp?CustomerId=<%= rst("CustomerId") %>">
   <%= rst("Name") %></A></TD>
```

The code in the sp.asp file deletes the requested record by calling the procDeleteCustomer stored procedure in the SQL Server version of the Meals database. This stored procedure accepts a single parameter, the CustomerId of the record to delete.

Following is the complete sp.asp file:

```
<HTML>
<HEAD>
<TITLE>Sp.asp Example</TITLE>
</HEAD>
<BODY>
<H2> Customer Record Delete </H2>
<H3> (Using a SQL Server Stored Procedure) </H3>
<%
Dim con
Dim varRecords
Const adCmdStoredProc = 4
Const adInteger = 3

' Create a Connection object and point it to
' the WebMealsSQL data source
Set con = Server.CreateObject("ADODB.Connection")
con.Open "WebMealsSQL", "WebUser", ""

' Create a Command object and link it to the
' Connection object already established
Set cmd = Server.CreateObject("ADODB.Command")
Set cmd.ActiveConnection = con

' Point the Command object to the stored
' procedure and pass the single parameter
cmd.CommandText = "procDeleteCustomer"
cmd.CommandType = adCmdStoredProc
cmd.Parameters(1) = Request("CustomerId")

' Execute the stored procedure
cmd.Execute varRecords

' If varRecords is 0 then the stored
' procedure was not executed successfully.
If varRecords >= 1 Then
   Response.Write "Record deleted!"
Else
   Response.Write "Record delete failed!"
End If

' Clean up time
con.Close
```

```
%>
<BR><A HREF="adomenu.html">Return to home page</A>
</BODY>
</HTML>
```

You create the `Command` object with this code from sp.asp:

```
Set cmd = Server.CreateObject("ADODB.Command")
```

After you create the `Command` object, you need to link it to a previously created `Connection` object with code like the following:

```
Set cmd.ActiveConnection = con
```

The next two statements identify the stored procedure:

```
cmd.CommandText = "procDeleteCustomer"
cmd.CommandType = adCmdStoredProc
```

If the stored procedure has any parameters, you can set the values of the stored procedures using the `Command` object's `Parameters` collection. Although the `Parameters` collection begins numbering with 0, SQL Server reserves the first parameter, parameter 0, for the return value of the stored procedure, even if you haven't explicitly defined a return value. Thus, the first input parameter is parameter 1. Following is the code in sp.asp used to pass the `CustomerId` (from the updatesp.asp page) to the stored procedure:

```
cmd.Parameters(1) = Request("CustomerId")
```

This next statement executes the stored procedure, sticking the number of records affected by the stored procedure into the `varRecords` variable:

```
cmd.Execute varRecords
```

To determine whether the stored procedure worked, all you need to do is check the value of `varRecords` like this:

```
If varRecords >= 1 Then
   Response.Write "Record deleted!"
Else
   Response.Write "Record delete failed!"
End If
```

An action query example

Executing an Access action query in ADO is very similar to executing a stored procedure. In fact, the code is virtually identical. The updateaq.asp and aquery.asp files on the CD-ROM demonstrate how to execute an Access delete query using an ADO Command object.

The only significant difference in executing an Access action query is in how the parameters are numbered. Because Access action queries lack any return value, the first input parameter in Access queries is parameter 0, not parameter 1 as with SQL Server stored procedures.

Following is the code from aquery.asp that executes an Access delete query named qryDeleteCustomer. The query contains a single parameter:

```
Set con = Server.CreateObject("ADODB.Connection")
con.Open "WebMeals"

Set cmd = Server.CreateObject("ADODB.Command")
Set cmd.ActiveConnection = con
cmd.CommandText = "qryDeleteCustomer"
cmd.CommandType = adCmdStoredProc
cmd.Parameters(0) = Request("CustomerId")

cmd.Execute varRecords
```

That was easy.

Part VII
A Virtual Web Publishing Studio: Visual InterDev

In this part . . .

*V*isual InterDev is an exciting new Microsoft product for developing dynamic, data-driven Web sites. Using this virtual Web publishing studio, you can create Web pages that practically jump off your users' screens. Think of Chapter 14 as your orientation guide to Visual InterDev. Here you find out how to use Visual InterDev to create a new Web project and Web pages and edit existing pages using the editor of your choice. In Chapter 15, you take a hard look at the Visual InterDev Data Form Wizard. This wizard produces full-featured data forms for browsing and updating data stored in Access, SQL Server, and other Open Database Connectivity (ODBC) data sources.

In Chapter 16, you dig in a little deeper, exploring the Data Range, Data Command, and Include designer controls that come with Visual InterDev. This chapter shows you how to use these controls along with the SQL Query Designer to create custom Web pages linked to your databases. Chapter 17 introduces a powerful Visual InterDev and ASP feature: Active Server Objects. This chapter shows you how to take advantage of Active Server Objects to persist information across the pages of your Web application, retrieve data from prior Web pages, work with *cookies,* and extend your ASP pages using ActiveX Automation servers.

Chapter 14

Are You Ready for Visual InterDev?

In This Chapter

▶ Understanding the Visual InterDev architecture

▶ Getting around the Visual InterDev IDE

▶ Creating a project

▶ Editing pages

▶ Previewing pages

*V*isual InterDev is a next-generation Web development tool from Microsoft that makes easy work out of creating and managing dynamic intranet and Internet Web applications. The Visual InterDev environment is especially adept at helping you create database-driven Web sites, particularly those using Active Server Pages.

Visual InterDev may at first appear to be complex and difficult to master. Appearances, however, can be deceiving. You can use this chapter to make the transition to this powerful Web development tool as smooth and effortless as possible. In this chapter, you get to know the Visual InterDev integrated development environment and discover that this seemingly complex product is actually quite easy to learn and use.

Why Visual InterDev?

All this talk of "advanced development environment" and "database-driven this or that" may beg the question "Why Visual InterDev?" You can certainly choose from other options, including Microsoft FrontPage and a host of Web development tools from other companies. (See Chapter 18 for a list of alternatives.)

Visual InterDev has several advantages over the alternative Web development solutions. Visual InterDev:

✔ Offers a database-centric development environment; most development tools lack strong database tools

✔ Is closely integrated with Active Server Pages and Internet Information Server

✔ Offers two Web page editors: the FrontPage WYSIWYG (what-you-see-is-what-you-get) visual editor, and the color-coded Visual InterDev Source Editor; Visual InterDev lets you hook in other page editors, too

✔ Supports both design-time and run-time ActiveX controls

✔ Can craft both server-side and client-side scripting using JavaScript or VBScript

✔ Integrates with source code control tools to provide a multideveloper development

✔ Includes powerful database and query design tools

✔ Has site-management features

✔ Includes several multimedia content authoring tools, including Microsoft Image Composer and Microsoft Music Producer, as well as the Microsoft Media Manager tool for managing this content

✔ Lets you preview Web sites using any Web browser

Why not just use the Access and SQL Server wizards to generate your Web pages? These products lack the Web management and editing tools of Visual InterDev. You may find it handy to use these products *and* Visual InterDev together. Create your pages using the Access and SQL Server wizards and use Visual InterDev to tie it all together into one cohesive Web site. On the other hand, you can do it all in Visual InterDev, too. After you get comfortable with Visual InterDev, you may find that Visual InterDev and its wizards and other database tools produce friendlier and more powerful database-driven Web pages than the Access and SQL Server wizards. The choice is yours.

The Visual InterDev Way

Visual InterDev uses an architecture and terminology that may confuse you at first — I certainly got confused! The next few sections describe some of the key parts to the Visual InterDev architecture.

Webs

All the files that make up a Web application stored on a Web server are called a *Web*. These files become the Web site that you see when you link to the Web site's URL address.

Projects

When you create a Web (or edit an existing Web) in Visual InterDev, the development tool creates a *project file* on your client workstation (the machine you're running Visual InterDev from). The project file points to the Web directory on the Web server that holds the Web. Visual InterDev uses this project file — which has a file extension of .dsp (for developer studio project) — to store information about the Web.

Visual InterDev is project-oriented rather than file-oriented. In Visual InterDev, you must always work within a project. You can't edit an individual HTML or ASP file, for example, without creating the file within a project or adding it to an existing project.

The Web and the local project file together make up a *Web project*. A Web project, however, is not the only kind of project you can create with Visual InterDev. You also can create a *Database project,* which you can use to directly interact with an ODBC database such as Access, SQL Server, or Oracle.

Workspaces

A workspace in Visual InterDev is a container for one or more projects. The workspace file has a file extension of .dsw (for developer studio workspace). You can group multiple projects together into a single workspace. Grouping projects allows you to view more than one project at a time in the Visual InterDev editor.

If you use other tools from the Microsoft Visual Studio suite, such as Visual J++ or Visual C++, you can create a single workspace that combines projects from Visual InterDev and these other tools.

A Product with More Than One View

Visual InterDev is part of the Microsoft Visual Studio suite, and as a member in good standing, it uses the *Developer Studio* integrated development environment (IDE). Two other Visual Studio members, Visual J++ and Visual C++, share the Developer Studio IDE. (Visual Basic and Visual FoxPro use their own IDEs.)

The Developer Studio IDE consists of a series of windows. A typical Visual InterDev editing session appears in Figure 14-1. The *Project Workspace window* appears on the left side of the screen; one or more *document windows* appear on the right side of the screen.

Project Workspace window   Infoviewer Topic window   Document windows

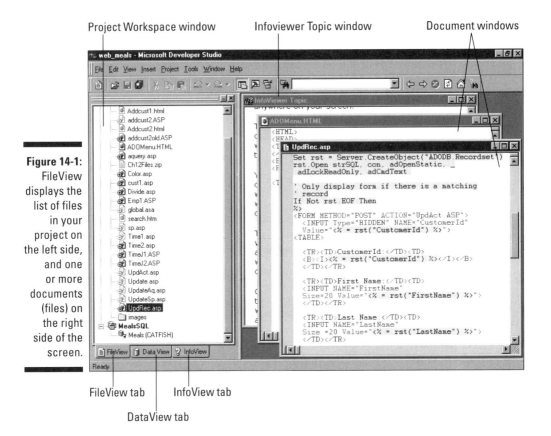

Figure 14-1:
FileView
displays the
list of files
in your
project on
the left side,
and one
or more
documents
(files) on
the right
side of the
screen.

FileView tab   InfoView tab

DataView tab

Initially, the Project Workspace window contains only one tab, the InfoView tab. As you create projects, additional tabs appear. Click one of the tabs to switch to that view. Following is a brief description of each view:

- **FileView:** This is the main view that lists the projects of the current workspace (see Figure 14-1).

- **DataView:** Here you can view the objects of any databases you added to the workspace as either database projects or data connections. When you change to this view, you're using the Microsoft Visual Database Tools that ship with Visual InterDev and Visual Studio (see Figure 14-2).

- **InfoView:** Use this view to browse through and search the excellent online documentation system (see Figure 14-3). I describe this view in this chapter.

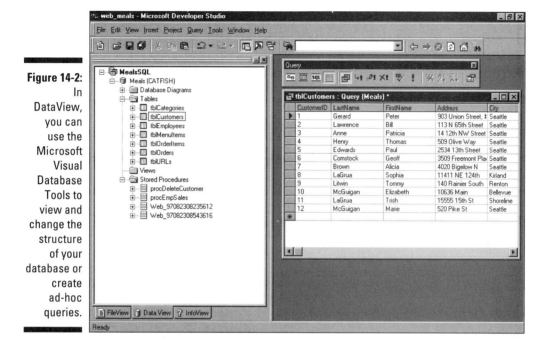

Figure 14-2:
In DataView, you can use the Microsoft Visual Database Tools to view and change the structure of your database or create ad-hoc queries.

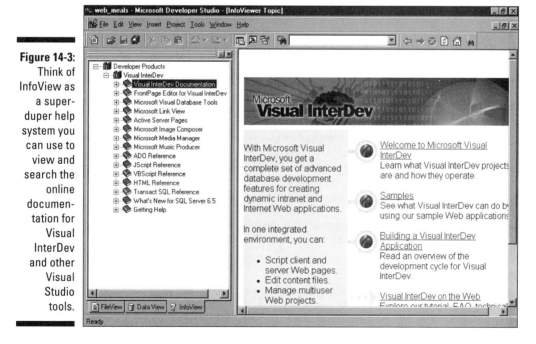

Figure 14-3:
Think of InfoView as a super-duper help system you can use to view and search the online documentation for Visual InterDev and other Visual Studio tools.

The Wonderful World of InfoView

Getting to know any product, especially one as complex as Visual InterDev, can be a chore. However, thanks to InfoView, Developer Studio's fantastic help system, the chore is a bit easier to accomplish.

When you switch to InfoView, click the Developer Products entry on the left side of the screen, and you see a list of entries on myriad InfoView topics, including Visual InterDev, the FrontPage Editor, the Visual Database Tools, Active Server Pages, ADO, VBScript, HTML, and other related topics (see Figure 14-3).

Drilling down to a page

In InfoView, Visual InterDev displays a list of topics in the Project Workspace window. A book icon to the left of each entry indicates topics, which don't have associated text. You must drill down the list of topics (by single-clicking the plus sign or double clicking the book icon or the topic title) until you get to a page icon. When a page icon appears, double-click either the page icon or the page title to view the page in the InfoViewer Topic window on the right side of the screen.

For example, in Figure 14-4, I expanded the list of topics to display the list of pages on the topic OverView: Text Editor and double-clicked the About Syntax Coloring page. You can see the About Syntax Coloring page in the InfoViewer Topic window on the right side of the screen.

Searching the InfoView system

You can search for information on a topic in the vast InfoView help system by choosing Help⇨Search. When you choose that command, a tabbed dialog box appears, offering you the choice of performing a search on either a list of predetermined keywords (select the Index tab) or a free-form search of the contents (select the Query tab).

InfoView puts a powerful help system at your finger tips. Take the time to explore this help system — it will be well worth the effort.

Creating a Web Project

Creating content for your Web site is the reason you bought Visual InterDev. Before you can create or edit the files associated with a Web site, however, you must first create a Web project. The following steps show you how to create a new Web project:

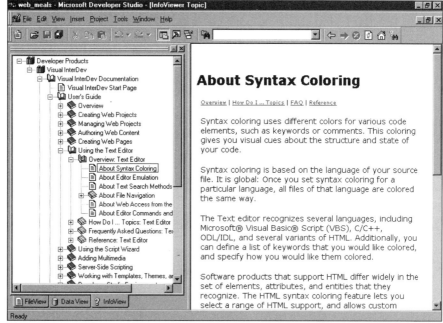

Figure 14-4:
Drilling
down to the
About
Syntax
Coloring
page of the
InfoView
help
system.

1. **Choose File⇨New to display the New dialog box.**

   Click the Projects tab and select Web Project Wizard in the list of project types (see Figure 14-5).

2. **Type the name of the project into the Project name text box and select a location for the project file.**

3. **Choose whether you want to create a new workspace or create the project in an existing workspace.**

   Typically, you want to choose to create a new workspace with the same name as the project. You can, however, opt to create the project in an existing workspace, if you like.

   Visual InterDev creates the Web Project file (*project*.dsp) in the location you specify in the Location text box of the New dialog box. Visual InterDev also stores local working copies of your Web site here, although the original files remain on your Web server.

4. **Click OK to start the Web Project Wizard.**

5. **On Page 1 of the two-page Web Project Wizard, type either the name of the Web server machine if the server is on a local area network or the URL of the server if you're using a remote server (see Figure 14-6).**

Figure 14-5:
The Visual
InterDev
New dialog
box.

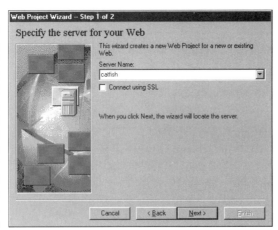

Figure 14-6:
In Step 1 of
the Web
Project
Wizard, you
must
specify the
name of the
Web server
that will
host the
Web site.

6. Select the SSL check box if you want to communicate with the Web server using the secure sockets layer.

SSL is a security encryption protocol for communicating over the Internet. Choosing the SSL option is probably wise if you're connecting to a Web server over the public — and thus insecure — Internet.

7. Click Next to connect to the Web server.

Establishing the connection may take several minutes — even longer if the Web site contains many existing pages or the server is located at a remote site.

After Visual InterDev successfully connects to the Web server, it displays Page 2 of the wizard.

Before you can create a Visual InterDev Web on a Web server, you need to set it up properly. The server must

- Run Internet Information Server 3.0 or a compatible server with ASP and ADO installed (see Chapter 2)

- Have the FrontPage server extensions installed (this comes with Visual InterDev but must be installed separately)

- Be using ODBC 3.0 or later (this should be installed automatically when you install ASP support)

8. Select whether you want to create a new Web or connect to an existing one; then type the name of the Web site you want to create (see Figure 14-7).

- Select Create a new Web if you want to create a new Web site or if you want to manage an existing Web site with Visual InterDev.

- Select Connect to an existing Web only when you want to point to an existing Visual InterDev Web created in another project.

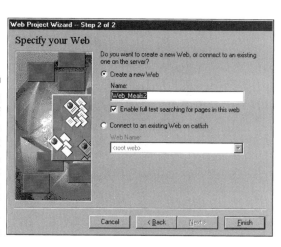

Figure 14-7: In Step 2 of the Web Project Wizard, you must specify the name of the Web.

9. **If you want Visual InterDev to create a full-text-searching facility for your Web site, check the Enable full text searching for pages in this web check box.**

When you select this option, Visual InterDev creates a search page (search.htm) that lets users search for pages on your Web site using a free-form text search. The easiest way to determine whether you want this page as part of your Web site is to select the option and see what it looks like — if you don't like it, you can always delete search.htm later.

10. **Click Finish when you're ready for the wizard to create your Web.**

After the Web Project Wizard finishes creating your Web project, the wizard displays your project in the IDE.

When the Web Project Wizard creates a new Web, it creates the necessary Web directory on the Web server and even sets the appropriate permissions for the Web directory.

You also can use the Projects tab of the New dialog box to run other project wizards, some — like the Departmental Site Wizard — which create entire Web site applications (see Figure 14-5). Table 14-1 summarizes the project wizards.

Table 14-1	Visual InterDev Project Wizards
Project Wizard	*Description*
Database Project	Creates a database project that you can use to manage any ODBC data source
Departmental Site Wizard	Creates an entire Web site for a company department or division
New Database Wizard	Creates a new SQL Server database
Sample Application Wizard	Installs one of the Visual InterDev sample applications and creates a Web to host the sample application
Web Project Wizard	Creates a new blank Web project

Creating Pages

Web sites consist of multiple files or pages. Visual InterDev supports several different types of files. You create these files by choosing File➪New and selecting the type of file from the Files tab of the New dialog box (see Figure 14-8). Table 14-2 lists a summary of the files you can create using the New dialog box.

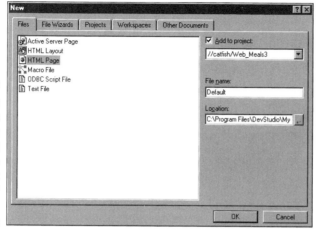

Figure 14-8:
Using the
New dialog
box, you
can create
different
types of
files.

Table 14-2	Visual InterDev Files	
File Type	*Default Extension*	*Description*
HTML Page	HTM	The standard HTML page that we all know and love
Active Server Page	ASP	A server-side scripting page (Chapter 12 has more detail on this type of file.)
HTML Layout	ALX	The specifications for an HTML Layout ActiveX control that allows you to visually place controls on a page with precise 2-D positioning. This requires your users to use Internet Explorer.
Text File	TXT	A plain-old text file
ODBC Script File	SQL	A text file containing SQL statements
Macro File	DSM	A macro file used to automate the Developer Studio IDE

The next few sections explore creating several of the more common of these files.

Creating a new HTML page

To create a new HTML page, follow these steps:

1. Choose File⇨New.

The New dialog box appears (refer to Figure 14-8).

2. **Choose HTML Page from the New dialog box.**

3. **Type a name for the new page in the File name text box (see Figure 14-8) and click OK.**

   Visual InterDev automatically fills in the Location and Add to project drop-down list.

Editing your page

Visual InterDev inserts the new page into your project and displays it in a document window on the right side of the screen (see Figure 14-9). The new HTML page includes a header telling you where it came from with the HTML comment `<!- Insert HTML here ->` highlighted for you.

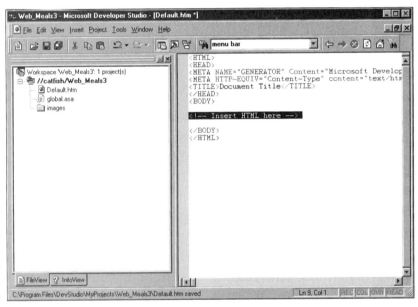

Figure 14-9: A freshly created HTML page, complete with a header that tells you Developer Studio created the page.

After you insert a new HTML page into your Visual InterDev project, the only thing left to do is to create the actual HTML. At this point, you can create the content for the page using the color-coded Visual InterDev Source Editor or the special Visual InterDev edition of the popular FrontPage Editor — it's your choice. In fact, Visual InterDev even lets you use other third-party editors with its files.

✔ **Visual InterDev Source Editor:** To edit an HTML file using the default editor, double-click the filename in the Project Workspace window. (The default editor is the editor that launches when you double-click a file.) When Visual InterDev is initially installed, the default editor is set to be the Visual InterDev Source Editor.

✔ **FrontPage Editor:** To edit an HTML file using the FrontPage Editor, right-click the file and select Open With from the pop-up menu. The Open With dialog box appears. Select the FrontPage Editor and click Open (see Figure 14-10).

Figure 14-10:
Use the
Open With
dialog box
to edit files
with your
favorite
editor.

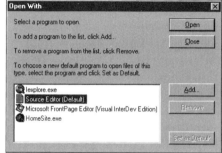

✔ **Third-party editor:** To edit an HTML file using a third-party editor, right-click the file and select Open With from the pop-up menu. The Open With dialog box appears. Click Add and select the third-party editor you'd like to use.

You can also set any editor to be the default editor in the Open With dialog box by selecting the editor's name in the list box and clicking the Set as Default button.

If you make changes to the page using the Source Editor, be sure you choose File⇨Save (or click the big disk icon on the toolbar) to save changes before opening the file with a different editor. Otherwise, you may lose your changes.

Choosing the right editor

The Visual InterDev Source Editor is a lean and mean color-coded HTML and scripting code editor. It doesn't try to hide HTML or scripting code from you. The Visual InterDev Source Editor is a nice editor to use if you're comfortable with HTML. The Source Editor designates different parts of a file using various (but customizable colors). This differentiation makes it easy, for example, to tell the difference between an HTML tag (by default colored purple on white) and server-side scripting (by default colored black on yellow). Figure 14-11 displays a sample page in the Source Editor.

The Visual InterDev Source Editor doesn't have many of the niceties for automating the creation of HTML tables and forms that are standard features of FrontPage and other *visual* Web editors. The FrontPage Editor is a user-friendly WYSIWYG (what-you-see-is-what-you-get) editor. With the FrontPage Editor, for example, you can create an HTML table with a few clicks of the mouse, as shown in Figure 14-12.

Figure 14-11:
The Visual
InterDev
Source
Editor color
codes your
Web pages.

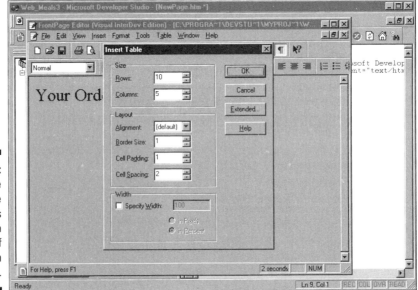

Figure 14-12:
The
FrontPage
Editor takes
the tedium
out of
creating an
HTML table.

TIP

To change the colors used by the Visual InterDev Source Editor, choose
Tools➪Options and click the Format tab of the Options dialog box (see
Figure 14-13).

Figure 14-13:
You can use
the Format
tab of
Options
dialog box
to alter
various
editor
settings.

When you edit existing files using the FrontPage Editor, it tends to reformat your code according to its own wacky rules. FrontPage Editor also inserts its header into your code without asking if it's okay. Upon occasion, these unwanted edits have been known to make ASP code not work. Thus, you may want to avoid using the FrontPage Editor to edit a page that contains scripting code.

Creating a new ASP page

To create a new ASP file, follow these steps:

1. **Choose File⇨New.**

   The New dialog box appears.

2. **Choose Active Server Page from the New dialog box.**

3. **Type a name for the new page in the File name text box and click OK.**

   Visual InterDev automatically fills in the Location and Add to project drop-down list.

These steps are almost the identical sequence for creating an HTML page.

Importing existing files

To import an existing HTML, ASP, or other file into a project, follow these steps:

1. **Right-click the name of your project in the Project Workspace window.**

2. **From the pop-up menu, choose Add Files.**

   The Insert Files into Project dialog box, shown in Figure 14-14, appears.

3. Select the files you want to import and click OK to import the files.

You can use the standard multiple-selection shortcuts to select multiple files (Ctrl+click or Shift+click).

Visual InterDev copies the selected files to your Web server as well as your local Web project working directory.

Previewing Your Pages

You won't get very far creating Web pages without previewing your creations every so often (unless you like lots of surprises). Visual InterDev makes the previewing process easy.

Using the built-in InfoViewer browser

To preview a page using the built-in InfoViewer browser (the default Visual InterDev browser), follow these steps:

1. Right-click the file in the Project Workspace window.

2. From the pop-up menu, choose Preview in Browser.

After a brief delay, the selected page appears in the InfoViewer browser (see Figure 14-15). You don't have to worry about getting the hyperlink correct. Visual InterDev automatically loads the server version of the file using the HTTP protocol.

Visual InterDev always previews the server version of a file.

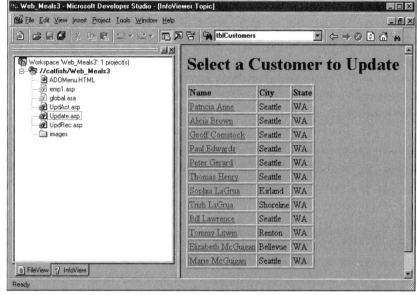

Figure 14-15:
Previewing
a page
using the
built-in
InfoViewer
Web
browser.

The InfoViewer Web browser is an ActiveX control that contains the Microsoft Internet Explorer Version 3.01 Web browser. Thus, the display of any page should look the same as in the standalone version of IE 3.01.

You can change formatting settings of the InfoViewer browser using the InfoViewer tab of the Options dialog box.

Using another browser

To preview a page using another browser installed on your computer, do the following steps:

1. **Right-click the file in the Project Workspace window.**

2. **From the pop-up menu, select Browse With.**

   The Browse With dialog box, shown in Figure 14-16, appears.

3. **Select your favorite browser; click Open.**

   After a brief delay, the selected Web browser launches and the file appears in the browser. Again, Visual InterDev is smart enough to load the server version of the file using the HTTP protocol.

Figure 14-16:
Use this
dialog to
browse a
page using
any Web
browser
installed on
your
system.

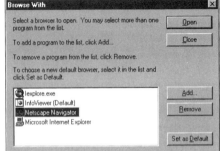

> If you like, you can make any browser the default browser by selecting the
> Web browser program in the Browse With dialog box and clicking the Set as
> Default button.

Working with Working Copies

When you create a Visual InterDev Web project, Visual InterDev creates a
working directory for the project and stores the project file in the *working
directory.* When you open a Web file in the Developer Studio IDE, Visual
InterDev makes a *working copy* of the file on the server and stores this
working copy on your local computer in the project's working directory. In
addition, if you create subfolders (or subdirectories) for your Web site,
Visual InterDev duplicates the folder structure on your local machine.

For the most part, you don't ever have to worry about the details because
Visual InterDev takes care of automatically synchronizing the server and
local working copies of files. For example, when you open a Web file in
Visual InterDev, a working copy of the file is retrieved from the server if a
copy isn't already located in your working directory. And when you save
changes to Web files in Visual InterDev, the program saves changes to both
the working copy and the server copy of the file. Isn't that special?

The Project Workspace window visually indicates which Web files in your
project currently have local working copies. A file that is undimmed indicates that you have downloaded a local working copy of the file. If a file is
dimmed, however, this indicates that no working copy of the file is currently
stored on your computer.

Sometimes you may need to override the automatic synchronization of
changes. To do so, select the file in the Project Workspace window and right-
click your mouse (see Figure 14-17). On the pop-up menu, select one of the
choices summarized in Table 14-3.

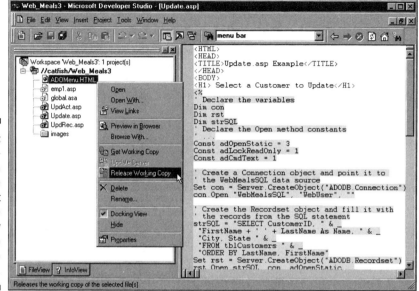

Figure 14-17:
Right-clicking a file in the Project Workspace window brings up this pop-up menu.

Table 14-3	Working Copy Menu Commands	
Command	***Description***	***Use When . . .***
Get Working Copy	Retrieves a local working copy of the selected file from the server. If a local working copy already exists on your workstation, the local working copy is overwritten with the server copy after a confirming dialog box.	You want to retrieve a local working copy file without editing it. Or when you want to discard your local unsaved changes and refresh your local working copy with the server version of the file.
Update Server	Updates the server with the current local working copy version of the file. Only enabled when you have turned off automatic server updates.	When you have turned off automatic updating and want to save local changes to the server.
Release Working Copy	Deletes the local working copy of a file. If you have unsaved changes, a dialog box will ask you first whether you want to save them before the file is deleted.	When you no longer need a working copy of a file.

The Update Server menu command is normally unavailable because Visual InterDev, by default, saves all edits to both the local working copy and the server copy of files. In some cases, however, you may want to turn off the automatic synchronization process. You can do so by choosing Tools➪ Options and unchecking the Update server when files are saved check box on the Web Projects tab of the Options dialog box.

You may want to turn off automatic updating when you are working with a remote server or making changes that you don't want rolled out immediately.

Chapter 15

Discovering the Data Form Wizard

. . . .

In This Chapter

▶ Running the Visual InterDev Data Form Wizard

▶ Using the forms produced by the Data Form Wizard

▶ Creating lookup fields

▶ Creating fields that display images

▶ Creating hyperlink fields

. . . .

*O*ne of the more difficult tasks in creating a database-enabled Web site is creating a user-friendly *data form* for viewing and updating database records. Although the Access 97 Publish to the Web Wizard generates a suitable data form, the Access data form has several shortcomings. The principal drawback is the Access data form's dependency on the HTML Layout Control, and thus on Internet Explorer. Fortunately, Visual InterDev includes the Data Form Wizard, which produces an attractive data form with excellent functionality and browser independence.

This chapter takes a look at the Visual InterDev Data Form Wizard in detail. You explore running the Data Form Wizard, using the ASP pages that the wizard produces, and taking advantage of several of the wizard's advanced features.

The Visual InterDev Data Form Wizard

The Data Form Wizard creates a series of ASP pages that users can use to browse and update data in an ODBC data source using a form-like interface. The ASP pages that the Data Form Wizard produces serve the same purpose as the ASP pages produced by publishing an Access form using the Access Publish to the Web Wizard. The data form produced by the Data Form Wizard, however, has several advantages over its Access-produced counterpart:

✔ Works with most Web browsers.

✔ Is faster than the Access-published form because it doesn't depend on the HTML Layout control.

✔ Has more features than the Access-published form. For example, the data form produced by the Data Form Wizard supports both form and list views, as well as filtering. The form also supports the display of images and hyperlinks.

Figure 15-1 displays an example of the sort of form you can produce using the Visual InterDev Data Form Wizard.

Running the Wizard

The Data Form Wizard is a file wizard that constructs the ASP files and adds them to the current project.

Follow these steps to create a data form using the Data Form Wizard:

1. **Choose File⇨New and click the File Wizards tab of the New dialog box.**

2. **Select Data Form Wizard from the list of file wizards, as shown in Figure 15-2.**

   Type a name for the file in the File name text box. (This name actually forms the prefix for the three ASP files the wizard produces.)

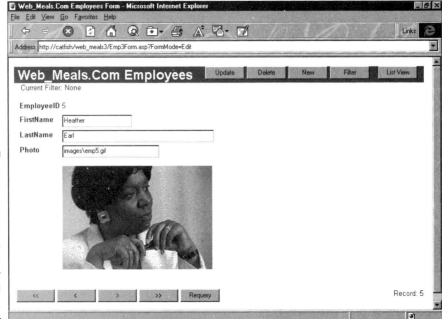

Figure 15-1:
The Data Form Wizard generated this attractive and fully functional form.

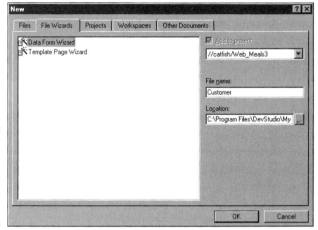

Figure 15-2:
Launching
the Data
Form
Wizard.

3. Click OK to launch the wizard.

4. On step 1 of the wizard, create or select an existing data connection (see Figure 15-3).

You use a *data connection* to connect your project to an ODBC data source.

If your project has an existing data connection, you may reuse it by selecting the data connection from the drop-down list.

If your project doesn't have any existing data connections or you want to create a data connection to a different data source, click New to create a data connection. (See Chapter 16 for more details on creating a data connection.)

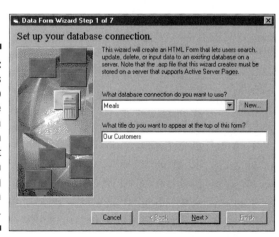

Figure 15-3:
Use this
page to
create
a data
connection
or select
from an
existing
data
connection.

5. **In the lower text box of the step 1 page, type a title for the data form; click Next to proceed to the second page.**

6. **On step 2, choose the type of record source for your form and click Next.**

   You can select from four different types of record sources, as shown in Figure 15-4.

   • Table

   • Stored Procedure

   • View

   • SQL Statement

   The next page of the wizard (step 3) varies, depending on your choice of record source type from the last step.

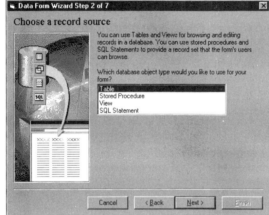

Figure 15-4:
Selecting the type of record source for the data form.

7. **Select a data source and click Next.**

   • If you select *Table* or *View* in step 2, you get to choose the table or view and the fields from the table or view you want to include on the form (see Figure 15-5).

   • If you select *Stored Procedure* in step 2, you choose the name of the stored procedure here. If the stored procedure has any parameters, the wizard lists them in a datasheet on the page.

   How you type the value of a parameter isn't entirely clear because you can't actually type the value directly into the datasheet and the instructions don't give you any hints. Try this undocumented method: Double-click the parameter to pop up a little dialog box, which you can use to type in a value (see Figure 15-6).

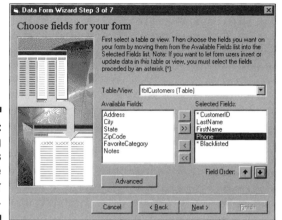

Figure 15-5:
Selecting
fields
from the
customer
table.

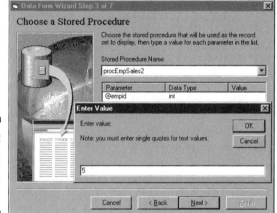

Figure 15-6:
Entering
a stored
procedure
parameter.

If the parameter is a text value, make sure that you surround the parameter with single quotation marks as follows:

```
'Jersey City'
```

- If you select *SQL Statement* in step 2, you need to type the SQL statement in step 3, as shown in Figure 15-7.

8. On step 4 of the wizard, specify edit options for the form (see Figure 15-8).

The first question you answer is "Would you like users to be able to edit information in your form?" If you want the form to be read-only, then select the No option button. Otherwise, select the Yes option button.

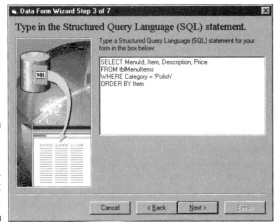

Figure 15-7:
Entering
an SQL
statement
in step 3.

If you select the Yes option button, you answer several additional questions that determine whether users can modify existing records, insert new records, and delete records. You also must decide whether users receive a *feedback page* after each update. Offering such a page generally is a good idea. (For more information on feedback, see the section "Updating records," later in this chapter.)

Your answer to the last question on the page determines whether the form includes a Filter button that lets users filter the records in the form using a Query by Form-type feature. This feature is especially useful if you expect the query supplying records for the form to return a large number of records.

On the fifth step of the wizard, you select various viewing options for the form (see Figure 15-9).

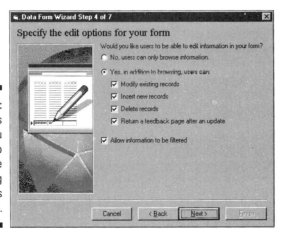

Figure 15-8:
On this
page, you
get to
fine-tune
the editing
capabilities
of the form.

9. Select the desired options and click Next.

The form that the wizard produces supports two basic views: *Form View* and *List View*. In Form View, the page displays one record at a time for browsing and editing. In List View, the page displays a read-only list of records. By default, both views are enabled, but you can choose to disable one of them. (You can't disable both — a data form without anything to do isn't that useful.)

If you choose to enable List View, you also decide whether List View hot-links to Form View. This feature is handy if you decide to enable both views. Users can use List View to quickly browse through the records, selecting a particular record and clicking on a hot-linked record number to pull that record up in Form View.

Another choice that is applicable only if you enable list view concerns the *paging* of records. If you select this option, then List View presents only a selectable subset of records — by default 10 — along with paging controls to allow users to navigate to another subset of records. If you opt against paging, all the records appear on a single list-view page.

Regardless of which views you select, you also must decide whether the data form includes a status line. This data form uses the status line to display information on the currently applied filter.

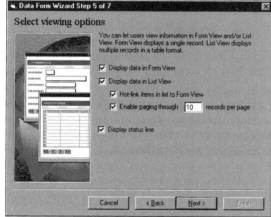

Figure 15-9: Selecting various viewing options on step 5 of the wizard.

10. On the sixth step of the wizard, select the theme for the page (see Figure 15-10) and click Next.

The theme describes the look and feel of the data form. Visual InterDev ships with five themes:

- Bluemood
- Bluerose
- Grid

- Redside

- Raygun

You can create your own themes or install additional themes from Microsoft and third parties. Notice the Fresh theme in the list of themes in Figure 15-10 — I downloaded this theme from the Visual InterDev Web site. (A good place to look for additional themes is the Visual InterDev Web site at `www.microsoft.com\vinterdev\`.)

When you click the name of a theme, the wizard displays a facsimile of the theme to give you an idea of how the form looks using that theme.

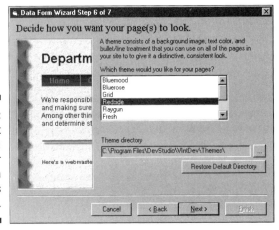

Figure 15-10: You must select a theme for the data form on this wizard step.

11. **Step 7 is a true no-brainer; click Finish to complete the wizard and have it generate your data form (see Figure 15-11).**

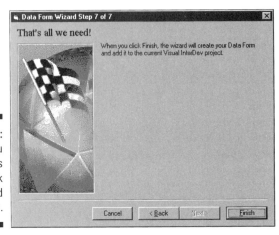

Figure 15-11: When you get to this step, click Finish and you're done.

Using the Data Form

The Data Form Wizard produces the following ASP files (where *name* is the file name you type into the New dialog box):

- ✔ *name*Form.asp: This file creates the Form View data form, but only if you enable Form View.

- ✔ *name*List.asp: This file creates the List View data form, but only if you enable List View.

- ✔ *name*Action.asp: This file filters, updates, inserts, and deletes records in Form View. The file also generates the optional feedback page after updates. The file always gets created, even when you don't enable Form View.

The HTML form code that produces the data form gets generated on the fly by server-side ASP code at *run time*. This means that the Data Form Wizard doesn't generate any HTML form code at design time that you can edit to move around the position of items.

Form View

The Visual InterDev Data Form Wizard produces an attractive and functional data form, as shown in Figure 15-12.

In the header of the form is the form title, a status line containing information about any filters applied to the form, and the editing buttons (Update, Delete, New, and Filter). Some elements may not appear — for example, the status line — if you choose not to include them.

The detail area of the form contains standard HTML form controls for each included field. If a field is of the Bit (SQL Server) or Yes/No (Access) data type (for example, the Delivered and Canceled fields in Figure 15-12), the wizard is smart enough to create radio button controls for the field.

The footer area of the form contains navigational buttons you can use to move from one record to another or requery the form's recordset.

Updating records

Updating a record is as simple as directly modifying the fields on the form and clicking the Update button to save your changes.

If you opted for the feedback option when you ran the wizard, the browser displays a feedback page that lists the newly updated values. The feedback page looks something like the one shown in Figure 15-13.

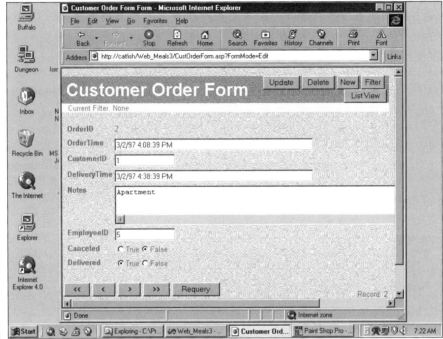

Figure 15-12: This data form for taking orders uses the bluemood theme.

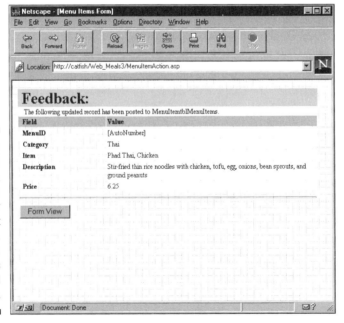

Figure 15-13: An optional feedback page displays for certain edit operations. This data form uses the Grid theme.

Inserting records

If you click the New button, a blank record in which you can type a new record appears. Click the Insert button to save your new record or click Cancel to abandon the new record.

When you click the Insert button, the browser displays a feedback page confirming your action (if you have enabled the feedback option).

Deleting records

When you click the Delete button, the record that is currently on display gets deleted. The browser displays a feedback page confirming the record deletion (if you enabled the feedback option).

When you click the Delete button, the record is deleted immediately without any confirming dialog.

Filtering records

When you click the Filter button, the filter form appears (see Figure 15-14). Type any values you want to use to filter the recordset and click the Apply button to apply the filter and display the filtered recordset in Form View. Click the Cancel button to return to Form View without applying the filter.

Figure 15-14:
This filter, when applied, limits the displayed records to Italian menu items greater than $6.

The status line on the data form reveals when a filter is in effect, as shown in Figure 15-15.

List View

List View displays a read-only list of records, as shown in Figure 15-16. Recall from Step 5 of the wizard (refer to Figure 15-9), that you can enable paging of records. The data form in Figure 15-16 shows the result of enabling paging with a page size set to 15 records.

This data form, shown in Figure 15-16, hot-links to Form View. If you click a record's record number — the number appearing in the # column — that record displays in Form View.

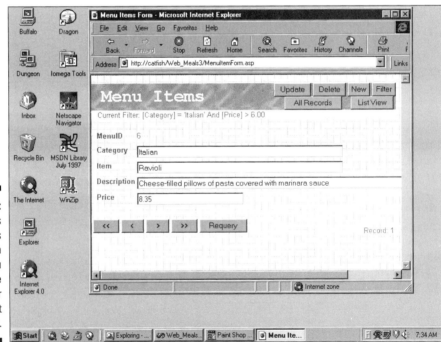

Figure 15-15:
The status line of this data form informs you of the criteria for the current filter.

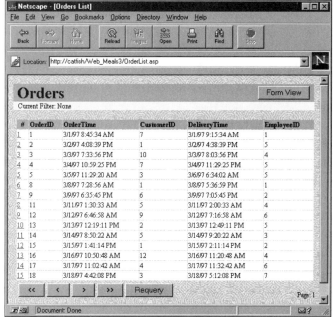

Figure 15-16:
The Orders
data form in
List View
with a page
size of 15.

Advanced Wizard Features

The Visual InterDev Data Form Wizard offers several advanced features.
Perhaps you want to spice up your forms with custom labels and cool
lookup fields. Or maybe you want to add an image or a URL field. This
section covers these bases.

Custom labels

If you click the Advanced button on step 3 of the Data Form Wizard (see
Figure 15-5), you get whisked off to the Advanced page. On the advanced
page, you can change the label of any or all of the fields you select. To create
a custom label for a field, follow these steps:

1. **Click the field in the list box.**

2. **Type the new label in the Alternative Field Label text box (see
   Figure 15-17).**

3. **Click OK to return to the main step 3 wizard page from the
   advanced page.**

You're done. Customizing is that simple.

Figure 15-17:
The
Advanced
Options
page of the
Data Form
Wizard lets
you create
custom
labels and
lookup
fields.

Lookup fields

You also can create lookup fields on the Advanced Options page of the Data Form Wizard. Follow these steps to create a lookup field:

1. **Click the field in the list box.**

2. **Select the name of the table that you want to serve as the source for the lookup list, using the Look-up Table combo box.**

3. **Select the name of the field from the look-up table that links to the lookup field using the Corresponding key ID field combo box.**

   The lookup field and the linked field must share the same data type.

4. **Select the name of the field from the look-up table that you wish to display in the lookup list using the Display this field combo box.**

   For example, in Figure 15-17, I created a lookup field for the CustomerID field. Figure 15-18 shows what this lookup field looks like on a data form.

5. **Click OK to return to the *main* step 3 wizard page from the advanced page.**

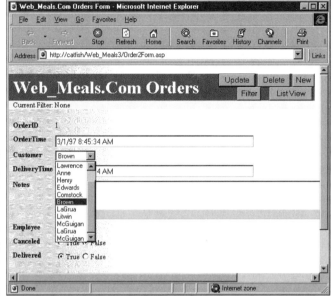

Figure 15-18:
You can use
a lookup
field to make
it easier
to select
lookup
values.

Image and URL fields

The Data Form Wizard gives special treatment to fields with the following prefixes:

- **img:** If you have a field with this prefix and if the values in this field point to GIF or JPG image files, then the wizard displays the images on the form using the <IMG> HTML tag.

- **url:** If you have a field with this prefix, then the wizard creates a hyperlink for this field using the <A> HTML tag.

For example, the img_Photo field in Figure 15-19 contains the names of files that point to GIF images.

The data form shown in Figure 15-19 also includes a field named url_EmailAddress, so the Data Form Wizard makes that field a hyperlink. If you click the word Go (to the right of the e-mail address), your default e-mail program launches, with the displayed address in the TO: address field.

Figure 15-19:
This data
form
contains an
image and
an url field.

Chapter 16

Designing with Designer Controls

● ●

In This Chapter

▶ Understanding designer controls

▶ Taking advantage of designer controls in your applications

▶ Creating data connections

▶ Creating tables of data using the Data Range controls

▶ Creating a parameterized delete query using the Data Command control

▶ Using the SQL Query Designer

● ●

*A*lthough you can build Active Server Web pages by hand — coding them from scratch — you can avoid some of that hand coding, thanks to the tools built into Visual InterDev. Mind you, you can't completely avoid the coding, but by using these tools, you can minimize the time you spend writing scripts and instead spend that time designing better Web applications.

This chapter takes a look at several Visual InterDev designer controls you can use to create better ASP pages. In addition, this chapter explores the use of the SQL Query Designer.

What's a Designer Control?

A *designer control* (also known as a design-time control) is an ActiveX control that writes server-side script, client-side script, or HTML for you at design time. For example, you may use the Data Command control to write the server-side ASP script to update all area codes for Redmond, Washington, from 206 to 425.

Designer controls do nothing more than write code at design time. Designer controls are not the code itself, nor does the client ever see them.

Why use designer controls?

You certainly don't have to use designer controls. They can, however, alleviate some of the drudgery of writing ASP code.

For example, one file on the book CD, cust1.asp (from Chapter 13), takes 77 lines of ASP and HTML code to create an HTML table listing the dozen or so customer records. You can create the same ASP page using the Data Range Header and Data Range Footer controls and only a few lines of custom code.

How do designer controls differ from wizards?

You can use both Visual InterDev designer controls and Visual InterDev wizards to develop Web applications. However, the two differ in several aspects:

✔ Like the wizards, the designer controls write application code, but unlike the code that wizards generate, the designer controls generate only a portion of a Web page, not a whole page — or, in the case of the Data Form Wizard, several pages.

✔ You don't have to know anything about active server pages or VBScript code to use wizards such as the Data Form Wizard. In contrast, the user of a designer control must understand active server pages in order to use the controls.

✔ Although the designer controls do less for you, they also give you finer control because you can drop them into a Web page wherever you like. In contrast, wizards such as the Data Form Wizard generate complete pages that are more difficult — if not impossible — to modify and add to.

Deciding which one to use isn't necessarily an either/or decision. In many applications, you may want to take advantage of both wizards *and* designer controls.

Using the Data Range Controls

The Data Range controls write ASP code that grabs a range of records from a data source and returns the records to you in a format that's easy to display on a Web page. You can use these controls to return a single record or a group of records in a form, a table, or a list format. In addition, like the Data Form Wizard (discussed in Chapter 15), the Data Range controls support record paging.

Visual InterDev has two Data Range controls:

✔ **Data Range Header control.** Writes the server script code that creates an ADO recordset and starts a loop to move through all the records in the recordset. (See Chapter 13 for a discussion of ADO.)

✔ **Data Range Footer control.** Writes the server script code that ends the loop that the Data Range Header control started and displays the optional paging controls.

In most applications, you use the Data Range controls together. However, nothing precludes you from using the Data Range Header control but writing the code that the Data Range Footer code produces, for example, by hand.

Creating the data connection

Before you can use the Data Range controls (or the Data Command control), you must first create a *data connection.*

To create a data connection, follow these steps:

1. **Right-click the project file name in the Project Workspace window.**

2. **From the pop-up menu, choose Add Data Connection.**

   The Select Data Source dialog box, shown in Figure 16-1, appears.

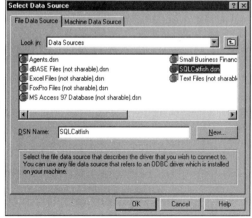

Figure 16-1: Selecting the data source for a data connection.

3. Select a data source.

Select the name of an existing file data source or machine data source or click the New button to create a new data source.

In most cases, you're better off creating or using an existing file data source rather than a machine data source. You can use a machine data source only on a single machine. When you use a file data source, Visual InterDev creates what's called a *DSN-less connection*. In other words, your code works at both design-time and run-time without having to create any additional data sources. The code works even if the server that hosts your Web site is different from the one you use when designing your application.

4. Click OK to create the data connection.

If the data connection points to a server database, a login dialog box appears.

5. Type a user name and password, if prompted, and click OK.

If the data source points to a password-protected database, you get a prompt for a user name and password. Enter values and click OK. (These values are for design-time access to the database; you get the opportunity to enter different run-time values in the next step.)

Visual InterDev displays the Data Connection Properties window, shown in Figure 16-2.

Figure 16-2:
The
Properties
window for
the Meals
data
connection.

Data Connection Properties

General | Run-Time

Data Connection
Name: Meals
Connection String: DRIVER=SQL Server;SERVER=catfish;UID=sa;

Connection Builder...

Connection Timeout: 15
Command Timeout: 30

Type: SQLSRV32.DLL
User: dbo
Login: sa

6. Click the Run-Time tab and enter a default run-time user name and password.

Click the Run-Time tab of the Data Connection Properties window to adjust the default user name and password that will be used at run time when users connect to your Web site using a Web browser.

7. Close the Data Connection Properties window.

Click the x icon in the upper-right corner of the window to close the window.

A data connection is the Visual InterDev equivalent of an ADO `Connection` object, which I cover in detail in Chapter 13. When you create a data connection, Visual InterDev adds code to the project's global.asa file to create and maintain the connection for the duration of the user connection to your Web site. For example, if you use the same data connection on six different ASP pages and a user visits all six pages, the data connection gets created only once — when the user first connects to your Web site. The application reuses the data connection, which reduces the load on your Web server and greatly improves performance. Chapter 17 offers more detail on the global.asa file.

If you ever need to adjust the properties for a data connection, right-click the data connection in the Project Workspace window. (You may have to first click the plus sign to the left of the global.asa file to unhide the data connection.) Next, choose Properties from the pop-up menu (see Figure 16-3).

Figure 16-3:
Displaying
the
Properties
window for
the Meals
data
connection.

Creating an HTML table with the Data Range controls

Once you establish a data connection (see the section "Creating the data connection," earlier in this chapter), follow these steps to create an HTML table of records by using the Data Range controls:

1. **Create a new ASP page or open an existing ASP page in a document window.**

   Take a look at Chapter 14 to get the full scoop on how to create or open the page.

2. **Create the skeleton for an HTML table with a border, two rows, and one column for each field that you want to display.**

   In the first row of the table, enter the text for the table header. (You will use the second row in a later step to display the record values.) When you finish, the skeleton looks something like the following:

   ```
   <TABLE BORDER>
     <TR>
     <!-Table header goes here->
     </TR>
     <!-Data Range Header control goes here->
     <TR>
     <!-Table detail goes here->
     </TR>
     <!-Data Range Footer control goes here->
   </TABLE>
   ```

   You may want to use the FrontPage editor to create the table.

3. **Insert the first ActiveX control.**

   Position the cursor right after the header record: between the first `</TR>` tag and the second `<TR>` tag. (I mark this location in the above HTML code with the `<!-Data Range Header control goes here->` comment.) Right-click and choose Insert ActiveX Control from the pop-up menu, shown in Figure 16-4. The Insert ActiveX Control dialog box, shown in Figure 16-5, appears.

4. **Click the Design-time tab, select the Data Range Header control, and then click OK.**

   The Properties window for the control appears (see Figure 16-6).

5. **Click the Advanced tab and change the cursor type, if appropriate.**

   At this point, you need to decide if you want the page to use the record paging controls or if you want all the records to appear on a single Web page.

   If you have more than a few dozen rows, using record paging is a good idea. But if you decide to use record paging, you need to change the type of cursor (recordset) that the Data Range Header control uses from a forward-only cursor to either a keyset or static cursor. (See Chapter 13 for a look at the different types of cursors.) You need to change the type of cursor because you can't move backwards using a forward-only cursor. (That should be obvious, by the name, shouldn't it?) Anyway, to change the cursor, in the Advanced tab of the Properties window, select Keyset or Dynamic from the Cursor Type drop-down list.

If you decide against using paging, skip ahead to the next step.

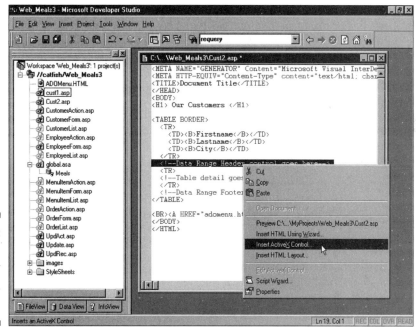

Figure 16-4:
Inserting an ActiveX control into your ASP code.

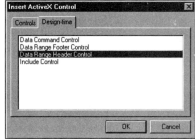

Figure 16-5:
The Insert ActiveX Control dialog box displays a list of ActiveX designer controls.

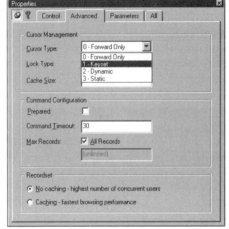

Figure 16-6:
To use record paging, you must use a keyset or static cursor.

6. Click the Control tab and type a descriptive name for the control.

In the Control tab (see Figure 16-7), you can set several additional options, including the ID (name) of the control. You can keep the default name (DataRangeHdr1) or change it to something more descriptive, as I do in Figure 16-7.

Figure 16-7:
Setting various control options for the Data Range Header control.

7. Select a data connection from the Data Connection drop-down list.

If you haven't yet created any data connections, none will appear in the list and you won't be able to go any further. If this happens to you, close the Properties and Data Range control windows (see Steps 13 and

14 for details) and choose Edit⇨Undo to undo the ASP code created by
the bad data connection. Now go create the data connection (see the
earlier section "Creating the data connection") and start over at Step 1.

8. Select a Command Type.

In the Command Type combo box, you must select the type of
command that you will use to create the recordset. Command Type
can be

- 0 - SQL
- 1 - Stored procedure
- 2 - Table
- 3 - View

If you don't want to base the recordset on an existing stored procedure,
table, or view, select SQL to create a new ad-hoc query.

9. Select the Command Text.

If you select a command type of stored procedure, table, or view,
choose the name of the object from the Command Text drop-down list.
If you select SQL, you need to click the SQL Builder button to create the
query. (See "Using the SQL Query Designer," later in this chapter, for
more details.)

10. Select record paging, if appropriate.

If you want to use record paging, click the Record Paging check box and
enter the number of records to display on each page in the Page Size
text box. In addition, you can adjust the location of the paging controls
(left justified, right justified, or centered) using the Bar Alignment
combo box.

If you're not using paging, skip ahead to the next step. (For more
details on record paging, see Step 5.)

11. Select the Range Type.

Under Range Type, select one of the following choices from the drop-
down list to match the type of data range you want to produce:

- 0 - Text
- 1 - Form
- 2 - Table

The goal of this section is to produce a table. In theory, this setting
affects how the Copy Fields button works. In practice, however, Visual
InterDev gets things only half right because, for tables, you have to
modify the pasted field code, which I explain in a bit.

12. Copy the field references and then click OK.

Click the Copy Fields button to reveal the Copy Fields dialog box, shown in Figure 16-8. Select the fields that you want to display in the table. When you click OK, you return to the Properties window.

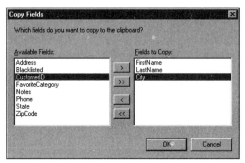

Figure 16-8: Selecting the fields to copy to the detail section of the table.

13. Close the Properties window.

Click the x icon in the upper-right corner of the window to close the window.

Visual InterDev displays a cute little Data Range Header control. Figure 16-9 shows what the control looks like, but it doesn't do much good to look at it. The control is kind of like a door — all the work is done when you close it!

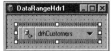

Figure 16-9: Doesn't the control look cute?

14. Close the Data Range Header control window to generate the data range header code.

Click the x icon in the upper-right corner of the window to close the window.

When you close the Data Range Header control, the control rewards you by generating a whole mess of ASP code (see Figure 16-10).

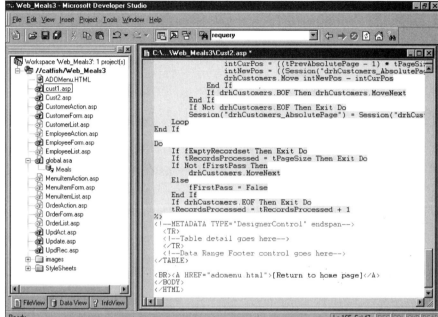

Figure 16-10:
And this is
only part of
the ASP
code written
by the cute
little Data
Range
Header
control.

15. Paste the field references into the table.

Place the cursor in the table detail area, *between* the first $\langle/\text{TR}\rangle$ tag
and the second $\langle\text{TR}\rangle$ tag. (In Figure 16-10, I mark this location with the
$\langle!-\text{Table detail goes here}-\rangle$ comment.) Right-click and choose
Paste from the pop-up menu.

Visual InterDev pastes references to the fields you selected in Step 12 to
your table.

16. Fix up the field references.

The pasted field references from the last step aren't in the right format
for a table. The references will look something like the following after
you copy them to your code:

```
<TR>
<%= drhCustomers("FirstName") %><br>
<%= drhCustomers("LastName") %><br>
<%= drhCustomers("City") %><br>
</TR>
```

Indent each row, insert a `<TD>` tag at the beginning of each row, and replace the `<br>` tag at the end of each row with a `</TD>` tag. The code should now look similar to the following:

```
<TR>
   <TD><%= drhCustomers("FirstName") %></TD>
   <TD><%= drhCustomers("LastName") %></TD>
   <TD><%= drhCustomers("City") %></TD>
</TR>
```

Now you're ready to insert the Data Range Footer control.

17. Insert the second ActiveX control.

Place the cursor in the table detail area, between the second `</TR>` tag and the `</TABLE>` tag. (In Figure 16-10, I mark this location with the `<!-Data Range Footer control goes here->` comment.) Right-click and choose Insert ActiveX Control from the pop-up menu.

18. Select the Data Range Footer control.

Click the Design-time tab in the Insert ActiveX Control dialog box, choose Data Range Footer Control, and then click OK.

19. Adjust the control's properties, if needed, and close the Properties window.

This time, a simpler and less friendly Properties window displays (I guess Microsoft was running short on time) for the Data Range Footer control (see Figure 16-11). Adjust any properties you want (none *require* adjustment) and close the window using the close icon in the upper-right corner of the window.

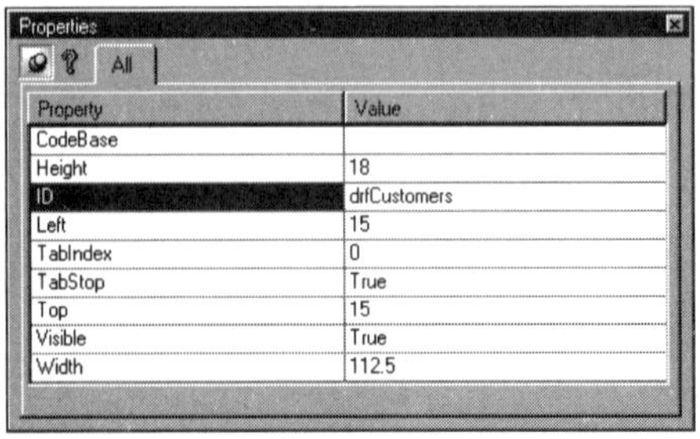

Figure 16-11:
The Data Range Footer control has a plainer-looking Properties window.

20. Close the Data Range Footer control window to generate the data range footer code.

That's it. You're finished. Go ahead and preview your page in the browser of your choice. The table will look something like the example shown in Figure 16-12. Your mileage will vary with your own data and settings. For example, if you choose not to employ the paging controls, you see all the records on a single page with no paging controls.

Figure 16-12: The little Data Range Header and Footer control elves wrote the ASP code behind this table.

After you generate an ASP script using a designer control, you can adjust the properties for the control by right-clicking anywhere in the script and choosing Edit Design-time Control from the pop-up menu. After you finish adjusting the properties, close the control window, and the control regenerates the script using your updated property settings.

Creating an HTML form with the Data Range controls

You also can use the Data Range controls to create a data form with or without paging controls. You may want to use the Data Range controls rather than the Data Form Wizard to produce a form for several reasons, including:

✔ You want more control over the positioning of items on the form

✔ You want a simple read-only form

✔ The data form is only one element of a larger Web page

In each of the preceding cases, the pages produced by the Data Form Wizard don't suffice. You could always grow your own form, writing the ASP code yourself to read the records from the database, but why not use the Data Range controls to write the ASP code for you?

Creating a form using the Data Range controls is similar to creating a table using the Data Range controls.

Follow these steps to create a data form using the Data Range controls:

1. **Create a data connection.**

   See the steps in this chapter's section called "Creating the data connection" for more details.

2. **Create a new ASP page or open an existing ASP page in a document window.**

   See Chapter 14 for details on how to create an ASP page.

3. **Insert a Data Range Header control and change its cursor type to** `keyset` **using the Advanced tab.**

   See this chapter's section called "Creating an HTML table with the Data Range controls" for more details.

4. **Set the Command Type and Command Text to your liking.**

   Once again, see the steps under "Creating an HTML table with the Data Range controls" for more details.

5. **Set the Range Type to** 1 - Form.

6. **Select record paging with a page size of 1.**

   Check the Record Paging check box and enter a Page Size of 1 (see Figure 16-13). You may want to adjust the location of the paging controls using the Bar Alignment combo box, too. A Bar Alignment of left justified usually works best.

7. **Copy the field references.**

   For details, take a look at this chapter's section called "Creating an HTML table with the Data Range controls."

8. **Close the Properties window.**

9. **Close the Data Range Header control window to generate the header code.**

10. **Paste the field references into the code.**

    Place the cursor immediately *after* the code inserted by the Data Range Header control. The following comment, which appears in the code, indicates the end of the control:

```
<!—METADATA TYPE="DesignerControl" endspan—>
```

Right-click and choose Paste from the pop-up menu.

Visual InterDev pastes references to the fields you selected in Step 7 in the correct format for an HTML form (see Figure 16-14).

Figure 16-13:
Data Range
Header
control
settings for
a data form.

Figure 16-14:
The pasted
field
references
for a form
are wide but
functional.

11. **Enter labels for the fields and adjust any subtags to your liking.**

    Insert a label for each field at the beginning of the line to the left of the `<INPUT>` tag.

    At this time, you may also want to adjust some settings for each field. For example, you may want to adjust the `SIZE` subtags for the fields to more appropriate sizes.

12. **Insert a Data Range Footer control into the code right after the field references.**

    See the steps in this chapter's section called "Creating an HTML table with the Data Range controls" for more details.

13. **Close the control's Properties window.**

14. **Close the Data Range Footer control window to generate the footer code.**

Save your page. If you preview this Web page with the browser of your choice, you will see a data form that bears some resemblance to the one shown in Figure 16-15. With a little extra formatting, this form may actually look halfway decent.

The Data Range controls produce a read-only form. However, with a little work, you can adapt it for updating data, too. See Chapter 13 for ideas on how you can accomplish this.

Figure 16-15: This ASP code behind this form was also written by the Data Range controls.

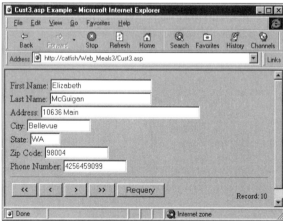

Using the SQL Query Designer

At times, you may want to create a recordset based on an ad-hoc query rather than an existing table, view, or stored procedure. For example, you may want to apply some special criteria to the recordset or sort it differently than the data that's stored in the table.

One way to create an ad-hoc query is to directly enter the SQL statement into the `Command Text` property of the Data Range (or Data Command) control. If you're comfortable with SQL and don't mind entering a potentially lengthy statement into a tiny little text box, this option is for you. On the other hand, you may prefer to create the query using the SQL Query Designer that's part of Visual InterDev and Visual Studio.

Starting the SQL Query Designer

You can use the SQL Query Designer with both the Data Range Header and Data Command controls. To start the SQL Query Designer, open the control's Properties window, set Command Type to `0 - SQL`, and click the SQL Builder button (see Figure 16-16).

Figure 16-16: When you click the SQL Builder button, Visual InterDev launches the SQL Query Designer.

Exploring the SQL Query Designer

When you first start the SQL Query Designer, the screen is quite busy. Before you proceed, you may find it less busy if you close the Data Connection Properties window and maximize the Query Builder document window.

The user interface of the SQL Query Designer should look familiar to those of you who've created queries in Microsoft Access or Microsoft Query. (The latter is part of Microsoft Excel.) Figure 16-17 shows a typical Query Designer session.

Grid pane

Query designer toolbar   Diagram pane

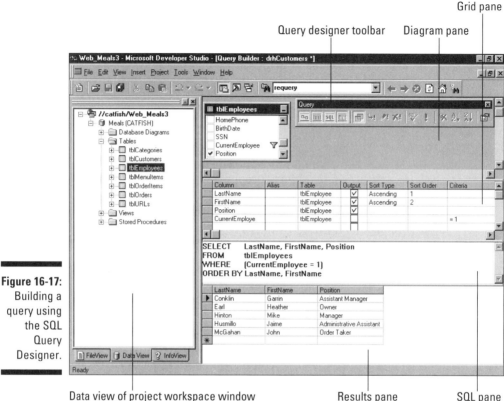

Data view of project workspace window   Results pane   SQL pane

Creating an ad-hoc query

To create a query in the SQL Query Designer, follow these steps:

1. **Add the desired tables to the diagram pane.**

    Drag the tables you want to include in the query from the Project Workspace window to the diagram pane of the Query Builder document window.

    If you include multiple tables for which you've previously established relationships, the Query Designer automatically joins the tables together. If you want to join together two tables without an existing relationship, drag the linking field from one of the tables to the other to create the temporary join.

    To remove a table from the diagram pane, right-click the window's title bar and choose Remove from the pop-up menu.

2. **Select the fields to include in the query.**

    Select the fields you want included in the recordset by clicking the check boxes to the left of the field names in the diagram pane.

3. Set any criteria or sorting of the fields in the grid pane.

If you're used to the Access query grid, this pane may give you pains! The basic difference between the two query grid panes is that the fields go down the screen in Access, while in Visual InterDev the fields go across the screen. Otherwise, the two panes are nearly identical. Well, almost, anyway.

4. Execute the query.

Execute the query by choosing Tools⇨Run. Alternately, click the Run (the exclamation point icon) toolbar button.

The query results appear in the results pane.

If you prefer your SQL straight up, choose View⇨Show Panes to close the diagram and grid panes — or click the Show Diagram Pane (first from the left) and Show Grid Pane (second from the left) toolbar icons until the icons appear raised — and enter your SQL directly into the SQL pane.

Returning to the Properties window

When you perfect your query, place the cursor in the Query Builder document window, and close the query document window by either choosing File⇨Close or clicking the document window's close icon.

When you close the query document window, Visual InterDev displays a confirmation dialog box like the one shown in Figure 16-18. Click Yes to update the designer control's Command Text and return to the designer control.

Figure 16-18:
Closing the
SQL Query
Designer
produces
this dialog
box.

At this point, the designer control window may be hidden by other windows. You may need to select the designer control window by using the list of open windows on the Window menu.

Back in the Properties window for the designer control, Visual InterDev has updated the Command Text to the SQL produced by the SQL Query Designer, as shown in Figure 16-19.

Figure 16-19:
When you close the SQL Query Builder, it updates the control's Command Text.

What else can you do?

You can do lots more with the SQL Query Designer, including:

- Creating Group By queries that aggregate or summarize data
- Creating parameter queries (see the following section)
- Creating action queries that update, insert, or delete records (also discussed in the following section)
- Creating Union queries
- Executing SQL Server stored procedures

Using the Data Command Control

You use the Data Command control to execute a SQL command, which may or may not return a recordset. The Data Command control may be useful in two situations:

- You want to create a recordset, but your needs don't require the kind of loop through a recordset that the Data Range controls produce.
- You want to execute a stored procedure or action query that doesn't return a recordset.

For example, you may use the Data Command control to create the ASP code to delete a record from a table. (This ASP code doesn't require a recordset.)

Creating a delete query with a parameter

To use the Data Command control to execute a delete action query with a parameter, follow these steps:

1. **Create a data connection.**

   See the steps in the section "Creating the data connection" for more details.

2. **Create a new ASP page or open an existing ASP page in a document window.**

3. **Insert a Data Command control into your ASP page.**

   See the steps in this chapter's section called "Creating an HTML table with the Data Range controls" for more details on how to insert a designer control on a page.

4. **Set the Command Type.**

   Select SQL from the Command Type drop-down list (see Figure 16-20).

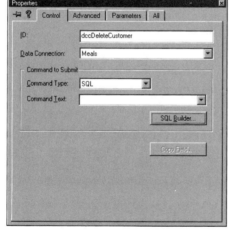

Figure 16-20:
The
Properties
window for
a Data
Command
control.

5. **Click the SQL Builder button to open the SQL Query Builder.**

6. **Create the Delete query.**

   To change the query from the default type (Select) to Delete, choose Query➪Change Type➪Delete or click the Create Delete Query toolbar button (the eighth button from the left).

7. Create the parameter.

To create a parameter, enter the parameter in the criteria for a field surrounded by brackets. For example, to enter a parameter for the CustomerId field with the name CustID, you enter the following into the Criteria column of the CustomerId field:

```
[CustID]
```

8. Close the query document window to update the Command Text for the Data Command control.

You can close the query document window by either choosing File⇨Close or clicking the document window's close icon.

9. Close the Data Command control's Properties window.

10. Close the Data Command control window to generate the ASP code.

For example, I used the Data Command control to generate the following ASP code to delete a record from the tblCustomer table:

```
<%
Set Meals = Server.CreateObject("ADODB.Connection")
Meals.ConnectionTimeout = _
  Session("Meals_ConnectionTimeout")
Meals.CommandTimeout = Session("Meals_CommandTimeout")
Meals.Open Session("Meals_ConnectionString"), _
  Session("Meals_RuntimeUserName"), _
  Session("Meals_RuntimePassword")
Set cmdTemp = Server.CreateObject("ADODB.Command")
Set dccDeleteCustomer = _
  Server.CreateObject("ADODB.Recordset")
cmdTemp.CommandText = "DELETE FROM tblCustomers " & _
  WHERE (CustomerID = " & CustID & ")"
cmdTemp.CommandType = 1
Set cmdTemp.ActiveConnection = Meals
dccDeleteCustomer.Open cmdTemp, , 0, 1
%>
```

Passing the parameter to the script

The Data Command control generates code that references the parameters you created using the SQL Query Designer. Before you can use the page with the parameters, however, you need to add code that supplies the parameters to the ASP code.

For example, in order to supply the parameter for the script from the last section, you must add the following code at the beginning of the script:

```
CustID = Request.Form("CustomerID")
```

This preceding line of code sets the `CustID` variable to the `CustomerID` value posted to this ASP form from the previous Web page. All you need to do now is to create an HTML or ASP page containing an HTML form that collects the `CustomerID` value and posts it to the page containing the Data Command control. (See Chapter 13 for examples on how to do this.)

Using the Include Control

The Include control is a very simple designer control that you can use to copy code from *include files* to your ASP page. Why would you want to do this? Say that you use the same server-side script or chunk of HTML on several forms. Using the Include control, you only have to write the code once, save it to a file, and then *include* that file on as many pages as you like.

To use the include control, follow these steps:

1. **Create a new ASP page or open an existing ASP page in a document window.**

2. **Insert an Include control into your ASP page wherever you'd like to include the Include File.**

   See the steps under "Creating an HTML table with the Data Range controls" for more details on how to insert a designer control on a page.

   Visual InterDev displays the Properties window for the Include control (see Figure 16-21).

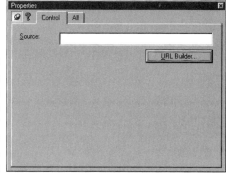

Figure 16-21:
The Properties window for an Include control.

3. Click the URL Builder button to build the include path.

When you click URL Builder, Visual InterDev displays the Edit URL dialog box (see Figure 16-22).

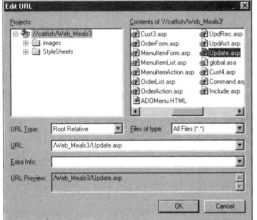

Figure 16-22: You use this busy dialog box to create the path to an include file.

4. Select the type of URL to include.

The Include control can create two different types of URL addresses to point to the Include file. You can select a URL Type of:

- **Doc Relative:** This creates an Include File directive; use this type of URL to include a path relative to the document containing the `Include` control.

- **Root Relative:** This creates an Include Virtual directive; use this type of URL to include a path relative to the virtual Web site root.

5. Select the Include file and click OK to close the Edit URL dialog box.

Navigate to the Include file using the Projects and Contents of controls of the Edit URL dialog box.

6. Close the Include control's Properties window.

7. Close the Include control window to generate the Include directive.

For example, I generated the following Include directive by using a Doc Relative URL:

```
<!--#INCLUDE FILE="Update.asp"-->
```

You may nest `Include` references. That is, an Include file may include other Include files.

Include files merge into the ASP file before any server script processes. Therefore, you can't conditionally include an include file. In addition, any scripts you include must be whole scripts containing both starting and ending script delimiters; you can't include part of a script.

Editing the Scripts Produced by Designer Controls

You have two ways to edit the scripts produced by the designer controls:

- ✔ Right-click anywhere in the ASP script, choose Edit Design-time Control from the pop-up menu, and modify the properties using the control's Properties window. After you edit the properties and close the control window, the control (using the updated settings) regenerates the script.
- ✔ Directly edit the code in the ASP file.

 If you use the Properties window to update a script, you lose any changes you made directly to the script.

If you made extensive edits to the ASP code in a script produced by one of the designer controls, you can prevent yourself from inadvertently wiping out your edits by deleting the METADATA comments from the ASP file. When you do this, you break the link between the designer control and the ASP script and thereafter can no longer edit the script using the control.

Chapter 17

Scripting Active Server Objects

· ·

In This Chapter

▶ Understanding Active Server objects

▶ Using the Session object to manage the state of a user session

▶ Retrieving user values with the Request object

▶ Displaying information using the Response object

▶ Reading and writing cookies

▶ Extending the Active Server with the Server object

· ·

*T*he real power behind Active Server Pages comes to the forefront when you start using the Web server's Active Server objects. Using the Active Server objects, you can manage the state of a user session, grab form data, and perform other more advanced capabilities such as running an external server application.

Chapter 17 shows you how you can maintain information across the pages of your Web application using the Session object. You also explore using the Application object to create a session-hit counter; and, using the Request and Response objects, to read and write cookies. Finally, this chapter shows you how you can use the Server object to manipulate external components.

What's an Active Server Object?

The Active Server Pages engine (the ASP engine built into Microsoft and compatible Web servers) exposes five built-in objects that you can manipulate in your server-side scripts. For example, you can use the Request object to retrieve values posted to an ASP page, the Response object to send text to the browser, or the Server object to *instantiate* (execute a copy of) ADO objects. Table 17-1 summarizes the five objects.

Table 17-1	The ASP Objects
Object	**Description**
Application	Shares information among all users of an application. An ASP application consists of all the .ASP files in a virtual directory and its subdirectories.
Request	Retrieves values from the client browser. Contains five collections (ClientCertificate, Cookies, Form, QueryString, and ServerVariables).
Response	Sends output to the client browser. Contains one collection, Cookies. You can use the Response object's Write method to write text to the browser.
Server	Provides access to several methods and properties of the server, including utility functions such as HTMLEncode. Using the Server object's CreateObject method, you can create objects on the server, including the ADODB object for performing data access and the MS.TextStream object for reading and writing information to files.
Session	Stores information about a user session that persists between pages. The Session object has several properties and methods, including the SessionID property.

You're not limited to using the five built-in ASP objects, however. By making use of the Server object's CreateObject method, you can instantiate other objects from your ASP applications. (This is discussed later in this chapter in the section "Extending ASP with the Server Object.")

Managing State with the Session Object

Traditional client/server programmers take for granted the fact that a user session *persists* from one screen to another of an application, maintaining the *state* of the user session. Not so in Web applications! Unlike persistent LAN connections, HTTP transactions between a Web server and a Web client are independent of one another. That independence makes it difficult to track a single-user session — or maintain a user's state — from one page of your application to another.

Web application programmers often spend an inordinate amount of time and energy managing state by keeping information in hidden form variables on Web pages. Although still a reasonable solution to the problem, this approach requires a lot of work. Fortunately, the Active Server Session object makes state management a nonissue.

A Session object allows you to maintain state information across all the pages of your Web application for a single user session. Table 17-2 summarizes the Session object's properties and methods.

Table 17-2		Session Object Properties and Methods
Type	*Name*	*Description*
Property	SessionID	Returns a Long Integer that is used to uniquely identify the session.
Property	Timeout	Specifies the number of minutes that a session can remain idle before the server terminates it. Defaults to 20 minutes.
Method	Abandon	Destroys the current Session object after all script commands on the current page are processed by the server. Subsequent pages get a new Session object.

In addition to the built-in properties and methods of the session, you can store and retrieve information to custom session properties.

The Abandon method is useful during development when you want to start a new session. You may find it useful to create a page containing the following script:

```
<%Session.Abandon%>
```

Pull up this page (containing the preceding script) in your browser any time you want to begin a new session.

What defines a session?

The Active Server (the ASP engine) automatically starts a session when a new user links to a page in your application. A session continues to exist as long as the same user jumps from page to page. A session terminates, by default, if the user hasn't made any HTTP requests in the past 20 minutes. You can use the Timeout property to adjust the timeout interval of a session. For example, the following sets the timeout interval to 10 minutes:

```
<%Session.Timeout = 10%>
```

How and when does the Session object work?

How does this magic work? In a word: cookies. A *cookie* is a mechanism that allows a Web server to store information on the client machine that the server can later read back. Web sites commonly use cookies to retain information about users between visits. The Active Server uses a cookie to store a session identifier on user machines.

Here's how the Session object works: When a user requests a page of your application, the Active Server checks the HTTP header for a SessionID cookie. If the Active Server doesn't find a cookie, the Active Server engine generates a unique SessionID and saves it to the client's machine as a temporary cookie. If the SessionID cookie is found, however, the Active Server looks for any active sessions with a matching SessionID, and if found, associates that page with the active session.

The SessionID cookie is temporary. That is, the browser deletes the cookie from the user's machine when the browser closes down.

You also can use your own cookies in your applications. See "Writing Values with the Response Object" and "Reading Values with the Request Object," later in this chapter, for more details.

What happens when the browser doesn't support cookies?

The Active Server session-management capabilities don't work if the Web browser doesn't support cookies or if the user opts to inactivate or reject cookies. In an intranet scenario, this dependency on cookies may not be so much of an issue if you can dictate browser standards. On an Internet Web server or an intranet where you don't have control over browser selection, however, you have to deal with the possibility that Active Server Session objects don't work.

If you can't guarantee that cookies are always enabled by users, you probably want to check to see whether cookies are enabled early in your application and either tell users that they can't use your application unless they use a browser that supports cookies or have an alternate set of pages for cookieless browsers.

Head over to this chapter's section called "Writing Values with the Response Object" for an example that demonstrates how to check if cookies are enabled. If you determine that cookies aren't enabled, you can then branch to a set of pages that pass information around using hidden form fields or some other *hack* for manually managing state.

The online Visual InterDev 1.0 documentation incorrectly states that the `Session` object works even when cookies are turned off. Not true. It's possible, however, that a future version of Visual InterDev or ASP will support the `Session` object for cookieless browsers. One can hope, at least!

Saving session data

In addition to its built-in properties and methods, the `Session` object lets you create user-defined properties of the session object. Think of these user-defined properties as session-level variables to which you can read and write values.

For example, you may want to save to a session variable the fact that a user prefers text pages using code like this:

```
<%
Session("PagePref") = "text"
%>
```

Alternately, you can use the following style syntax instead:

```
<%
Session.PagePref = "text"
%>
```

On subsequent pages, you can display a text or graphical version of a page based on the value of the `PagePref` session property. Following is an example of what one of those pages may look like:

```
<HTML>
<HEAD>
<TITLE>SessionVar2.asp Example</TITLE>
</HEAD>
<BODY>

<%
If Session("PagePref")="graphics" Then
%>
    <body background="images\gray.jpg">
    <img src="images\web_meals.gif"
    alt="web_meals.com logo"> <br>
    <H1>Graphics Version of Page</H1>
```

(continued)

(continued)

```
<%
Else
%>
    <H1>Text Version of Page</H1>

<%
End If
%>
```

Figure 17-1 shows the graphical version of this sample page. Figure 17-2 shows the text version of the same page.

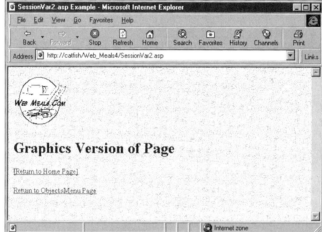

Figure 17-1:
The graphical version of a simple page.

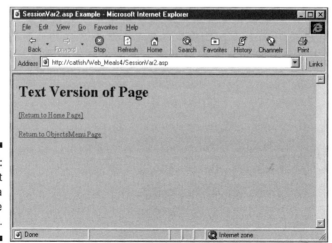

Figure 17-2:
The text version of a simple page.

What about Global.asa?

When you use Visual InterDev to create a new Web project, Visual InterDev creates an ASP page named global.asa. This special ASP page lets you define variables and objects that have session scope. In addition, you can include special event procedures in global.asa that execute whenever a session starts or ends.

Global.asa also lets you define variables, objects, and event procedures at the application level. To get the full scoop on this use of global.asa, take a look at the section "Sharing across Sessions with the Application Object," later in this chapter.

Session events

You can place ASP code into two global.asa session event procedures:

- ✔ `Session_OnStart`. This event fires at the start of a session but before any requested application pages are sent to the user by the server.

- ✔ `Session_OnEnd`. This event fires at the end of a session right after the server abandons or times the session out.

A session event procedure example

The following global.asa file places several `Session` property assignments inside of the `Session_OnStart` event procedure. This approach is a good way to initialize default values for session properties:

```
<SCRIPT LANGUAGE="VBScript" RUNAT="Server">
Sub Session_OnStart
    Session("PagePref") ="graphics"
    Session("BackColor") = "gray"
    Session("HitHomePage") = "False"
    Session.TimeOut = 30
End Sub
</SCRIPT>
```

All code contained in the global.asa file must be part of a session event procedure, an application event procedure, or an object declaration.

Global.asa and data connections

When you create a data connection, Visual InterDev places the data connection properties in global.asa. For example, Visual InterDev created the following code when I added the Meals data connection to a Web project:

```
<SCRIPT LANGUAGE=VBScript RUNAT=Server>
Sub Session_OnStart
    '==Visual InterDev Generated - DataConnection startspan==
    '-Project Data Connection
    Session("Meals_ConnectionString") = _
      "DRIVER=SQL Server;SERVER=catfish;UID=sa;" & _
      "APP=Microsoft (R) Developer Studio;" & _
      "WSID=BUFFALO;DATABASE=Meals"
    Session("Meals_ConnectionTimeout") = 15
    Session("Meals_CommandTimeout") = 30
    Session("Meals_RuntimeUserName") = "WebUser"
    Session("Meals_RuntimePassword") = ""
    '==Visual InterDev Generated - DataConnection endspan==
End Sub
</SCRIPT>
```

Notice that Visual InterDev doesn't store the ADO Connection object itself in global.asa; it merely sets several properties of the connection here. Although you can create the Connection object in the Session_OnStart event procedure, I don't recommend doing so because you immediately tie up a data connection for the entire duration of the session (by default, for 20 minutes). This session is created and maintained for the full 20 minutes even if the user links to your page and then immediately links to a URL outside of your application without ever hitting any page that needed data.

A better way to handle Connection objects that you use on multiple pages is to declare them the first time you use them as session scope properties and thereafter reuse the session properties. The Visual InterDev Data Form Wizard and Data Range Header control do exactly this.

For example, following is an excerpt from the code produced by the Data Form Wizard in the CustomerForm.asp example from Chapter 15:

```
If IsEmpty(Session("rsCustomertblCustomers_Recordset")) _
  Then
    fNeedRecordset = True
Else
    If Session("rsCustomertblCustomers_Recordset") _
    Is Nothing Then
        fNeedRecordset = True
    Else
```

```
              Set rsCustomertblCustomers = _
              Session("rsCustomertblCustomers_Recordset")
      End If
   End If

   If fNeedRecordset Then
      Set Meals = Server.CreateObject("ADODB.Connection")
      Meals.ConnectionTimeout = _
        Session("Meals_ConnectionTimeout")
      Meals.CommandTimeout =
        Session("Meals_CommandTimeout")
      Meals.Open Session("Meals_ConnectionString"),_
        Session("Meals_RuntimeUserName"), _
        Session("Meals_RuntimePassword")
      Set cmdTemp = Server.CreateObject("ADODB.Command")
      Set rsCustomertblCustomers = _
        Server.CreateObject("ADODB.Recordset")
      cmdTemp.CommandText = "SELECT ""CustomerID"", _
        ""LastName"", ""FirstName"", ""Phone"", _
        ""Blacklisted"" FROM dbo.""tblCustomers"""
      cmdTemp.CommandType = 1
      Set cmdTemp.ActiveConnection = Meals
      rsCustomertblCustomers.Open cmdTemp, , 1, 3
   End If
   On Error Resume Next
   If rsCustomertblCustomers.BOF And _
    rsCustomertblCustomers.EOF Then _
      fEmptyRecordset = True
   On Error Goto 0
   If Err Then fEmptyRecordset = True
   If fNeedRecordset Then
      Set Session("rsCustomertblCustomers_Recordset") _
        = rsCustomertblCustomers
   End If
```

Notice that the first few lines of code check to see whether the
rsCustomertblCustomers_Recordset object already exists:

```
If IsEmpty(Session("rsCustomertblCustomers_Recordset")) _
Then
   fNeedRecordset = True
```

The Connection and Recordset objects are then created only when they
don't already exist. In this way, you delay creating a Connection object until
you need to, but never have to create the same Connection object (and
Recordset object in this example) twice. The Access Publish to the Web
Wizard generates ASP pages that contain similar code.

Sharing across Sessions with the Application Object

The Application object enables you to set properties that are available to all users of an application. The object has no built-in properties, but does have two methods, which I summarize in Table 17-3.

An application begins when the Active server starts or restarts. As the Web server comes up, the server begins each of its applications. An application consists of all of the pages in a virtual Web directory and includes all of its subdirectories. An application ends when the Web server stops.

Table 17-3		Application Object Methods
Type	*Name*	*Description*
Method	Lock	Prevents other sessions from modifying any Application properties or objects.
Method	Unlock	Releases the lock of properties and objects applied by the Lock method.

Because the Application object is accessible from any session, you should always use the Lock and Unlock methods to bracket all Application property and object assignments.

You may use the Application object to store static data that rarely changes. For example, you can read static lookup tables into an array maintained at the Application level. Then, these lookup values are available to all application users without your having to recreate the array for each session.

Application events

You can place ASP code into two global.asa application event procedures:

- ✔ Application_OnStart: This event fires at the start of an application, right before the first Session_OnStart procedure occurs for an application.
- ✔ Application_OnEnd: This event fires as the application quits, right before the Web server shuts down.

Creating a hit counter

One use for the `Application` object is in creating an application session-hit counter. Because the `Application_OnStart` event procedure gets called only when the application begins, this event procedure makes a convenient place to initialize a hit counter.

Following is a global.asa file that I used to create a session (or user) hit counter:

```
<SCRIPT LANGUAGE="VBScript" RUNAT="Server">
Sub Session_OnStart
    Application.Lock
            Application("HitCounter") = _
            Application("HitCounter") + 1
    Application.UnLock
End Sub

Sub Application_OnStart
    Application.Lock
            Application("HitCounter") = 0
            Application("StartDate") = Date()
    Application.UnLock
End Sub
</SCRIPT>
```

The following excerpt from an ASP page (HitCounter1.asp) displays the session-hit counter:

```
<H2> You are the #
<% = Application("HitCounter")%>
user to visit this application since
<% = Application("StartDate")%>.
</H2>
```

Figure 17-3 shows what a session-hit counter page may look like.

Figure 17-3:
The
Application
and
Session
objects help
create a
simple
session-hit
counter.

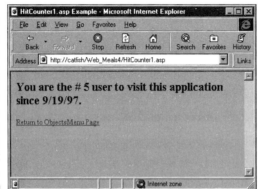

Writing Values with the Response Object

The Response object lets you manipulate the Web page sent back to the user. You can also use the Response object to manipulate the HTTP header information that the server sends along with a Web page to the user. The Response object is a busy little beaver of an object having numerous properties, methods, and collections. Table 17-4 summarizes these properties, methods, and collections.

Table 17-4		Properties, Methods, and Collections of the Response Object
Type	**Name**	**Description**
Collection	Cookies	Writes to the collection of cookie values.
Property	Buffer	Determines whether HTML is sent to the client as the script gets processed (False is the default), or whether the page gets buffered and sent to the client only after the entire script processes (True).
Property	ContentType	Tells the browser how it should treat the page. The default is text/HTML. If you want to send a page to the client without any processing of tags, you can set ContentType to text/plain.
Property	Expires	Sets the number of minutes until the page expires. If the user returns to the page prior to expiration, the cached version of the page displays.
Property	ExpiresAbsolute	Sets the date and time that the page should expire.

Type	Name	Description
Property	Status	Sets the status line of the HTTP header sent to the client. For advanced use only.
Method	AddHeader	Adds a new header to the HTTP response. For advanced use only.
Method	AppendToLog	Appends a string to the server log file.
Method	BinaryWrite	Writes characters to the HTTP header without the normal character conversion. For advanced use only.
Method	Clear	Erases any buffered HTML response output. Only available when Buffer is set to True.
Method	End	Stops the processing of the script and sends any buffered output to the client.
Method	Flush	Sends buffered output immediately to the client. Only available when Buffer is set to True.
Method	Redirect	Immediately causes the browser to connect to another URL without processing the current page. Redirect causes an error if used after content has been sent to the browser.
Method	Write	Writes text to the client.

Wow, that's a lot of properties, methods, and collections. Many of them are for pretty advanced use, however. You may never use anything but the Response object's Write method. Other popular items include the Redirect method and the Cookies collection.

Writing text

You use the Write method of the Response object to write text to the client from within a script. This approach is often more convenient than terminating the script to display a few lines of text. For example:

```
<%
If Session("PagePref")="graphics" Then
   Response.Write "<BODY background=""gray.jpg"">"
   Response.Write "<H1>Graphical Version</H1>"
Else
   Response.Write "<H1>Text Version</H1>"
End If
%>
```

If you need to include embedded quotes within the `Write` string, just double each embedded quote, as shown in this example.

Saving cookies

The `Response` object's `Cookies` collection makes it easy for you to save information to cookies on the client machine. (Reading the values back requires you to use the `Request` object, which I cover in the section "Reading Values with the Request Object," later in this chapter.)

For example, the following code (from trysomecookies.asp) writes a cookie named `FavoriteTVShow` to the client machine:

```
<%
' this is a temporary cookie
Response.Cookies("FavoriteTVShow") = "Mad About You"
%>
```

Because I didn't specify an `Expires` property, `FavoriteTVShow` is a temporary cookie that gets deleted when the Web browser quits. To make a permanent cookie, you use code like the following instead:

```
<%
' this cookie is good until 12/31/1998
Response.Cookies("FavoriteMovie").Expires = _
  "December 31, 1998"
Response.Cookies("FavoriteMovie") = "Il Postino"
%>
```

You also can create arrays of cookies to place together similar information. For example, in this code from Cookie2.asp, three form variables (posted from cookie1.asp) get saved together under the WebMeals key:

```
<%
Dim varFirstName
Dim varLastName
Dim varColor

varFirstName = Request.Form("FirstName")
varLastName = Request.Form("LastName")
varColor = Request.Form("Color")

Response.Cookies("WebMeals").Expires = _
```

```
"December 31, 1997"
Response.Cookies("WebMeals")("FirstName") = _
 varFirstName
Response.Cookies("WebMeals")("LastName") = _
 varLastName
Response.Cookies("WebMeals")("Color") = _
 varColor
%>
```

Redirecting Johnny through the front door

You can use the `Response` object's `Redirect` method to immediately switch to another URL. This method is useful, for example, in making sure that users always enter your application through a *front-door* page.

To set up a front-door routine, you need to follow these steps:

1. **Create a session property that you can use to track if someone enters through the front door (your home page).**

   For example, add code like the following to your global.asa file:

   ```
   Sub Session_OnStart
       Session("HitHomePage") = "False"
   End Sub
   ```

2. **Add code to the top of each nonhome page to check to see whether the user has gone through the front door; if not, redirect the user through the front door.**

   For example, add code like the following (from nonhomepage.asp on the CD-ROM) to the top of the file:

   ```
   <%
   If Session("HitHomePage") = "False" Then
       Response.Redirect "homepage.asp"
   End If
   %>
   ```

   The preceding code must appear at the very top of the page, before any content is sent back to the client by the server. If the code appears after any content, an error occurs.

3. **When a user goes through the front door (your home page), set the session property used to track if someone enters through the front door to `True`.**

Once a user has entered your home page once, you set the session property used to track whether they've been to the home page to True to ensure that you don't redirect the user to the home page again, which can be quite annoying.

For example, add code like the following (from homepage.asp) to the top of the home page file:

```
<% Session("HitHomePage") = "True"%>
```

When you implement a front-door routine, and users attempt to link to any page other than the front door page without first going through the front door, they never see the page. Instead, the front-door page comes up in the user's browser.

Reading Values with the Request Object

The Request object represents the flip side of the Response object. You use the Response object to send information to the client; you use the Request object to retrieve information from the client.

The Request object contains five collections, which I summarize in Table 17-5. Request doesn't have any properties or methods.

Table 17-5		Collections of the Request Object
Type	*Name*	*Description*
Collection	ClientCertificate	Retrieves values from the client certificate that the client sends to the server as part of the HTTP header.
Collection	Cookies	Retrieves values from the Cookies collection.
Collection	Form	Retrieves form field values posted from the previous page.
Collection	QueryString	Retrieves values from the HTTP query string (the part of the URL that follows the ?).
Collection	ServerVariables	Retrieves other predefined HTTP header variables. For example, REMOTE_ADDR returns the IP address of the client.

The most commonly used Request collection is the Form collection. You see countless examples in this book that use this collection to retrieve values posted from an HTML form.

Retrieving form fields

Retrieving the value of a form field is a piece of cake (that's right, I said cake, not cookie!). In prior chapters (as well as this chapter), I use various examples that look like this:

```
<% = Request.Form("FormField")%>
```

A good use for the `Request` object in database Web applications is for passing username and password values to a database connection. For example, you can use this code (from custpw.asp) to collect a username and password from the Web user:

```
<body>
<form method="POST" Action="Cust.asp">
    <p>Username: <input type="text"
    size="20" name="UserName"></p>
    <p>Password: <input type="password"
    size="20" name="Password"></p>
    <p><input type="submit" name="Submit"
    value="Login">
    <input type="reset" name="Reset"
    value="Reset"></p>
</form>
</body>
```

The preceding form appears in action in Figure 17-4.

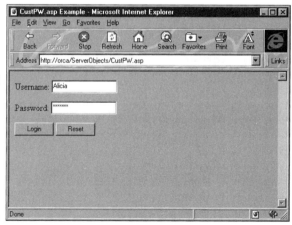

Figure 17-4:
The password field on this login form is a password type input field.

After the user is prompted for the username and password on your login page, you use ASP code like the following (from cust.asp on the CD-ROM) to establish the connection, using the Request object's Form collection:

```
Set Meals = Server.CreateObject("ADODB.Connection")
    Meals.Open Session("Meals_ConnectionString"), _
      Request.Form("UserName"), Request.Form("Password")
```

Reading cookies

Writing cookies isn't very useful if you can't read those values back at a later time. Using the Request object's Cookies collection, you can read cookie values off the client's machine.

For example, the following code (taken from cookie3.asp) displays the values of the three WebMeals cookies written by my earlier cookie2.asp example. (See this chapter's section called "Writing Values with the Response Object.")

```
<H1>Cookie Values</H1>
<%
Dim varFirstName
Dim varLastName
Dim varColor

varFirstName = Request.Cookies("WebMeals")("FirstName")
varLastName = Request.Cookies("WebMeals")("LastName")
varColor = Request.Cookies("WebMeals")("Color")

Response.Write "FirstName = " & varFirstName & "<BR>"
Response.Write "LastName = "& varLastName & "<BR>"
Response.Write "FavoriteColor = "& varColor & "<BR>"
%>
```

Checking whether cookies are enabled

Because the Session object depends on cookies being enabled on the client machine, you may want to check to see if cookies are enabled early in your application. If cookies aren't enabled, branch to a noncookie version of your application or, at the very least, let the user know that the application functionality may be affected.

Checking to see whether cookies are enabled is a matter of performing the following two steps:

1. **Attempt to write a cookie to the user's machine.**

   You can write the cookie with code similar to the following (from cookiecheck1.asp on the CD-ROM):

   ```
   <%
   Response.Cookies("Test").Expires = Date() + 1
   Response.Cookies("Test") = "this is a test"
   Response.Redirect "CookieCheck2.asp"
   %>
   ```

2. **Attempt to read back the cookies.**

   If the read fails, the client isn't accepting cookies.

   You need to read the cookies on a subsequent page because if you attempt to read a cookie from the same page in which you wrote the value of that cookie, ASP helps you by providing that cookie from memory.

   Following is an example of code you may use to read back the cookie (from cookiecheck2.asp):

   ```
   <H1>Test to See if Cookies Are Working</H1>
   <H3>
   <%
   If Request.Cookies("Test") = "this is a test" Then
     Response.Write "You have cookies enabled."
   Else
     Response.Write "You are either using a browser "
     Response.Write "that doesn't support cookies "
     Response.Write "or cookies are disabled."
   End If
   %>
   </H3>
   ```

Grabbing data from the Query string

Sometimes passing information from one page to another without using forms is more convenient. For example, you may want to pass a parameter from one page to another using syntax like the following:

```
Response.Redirect "MenuItem.asp?FormMode=Edit"
```

On the next page, you may retrieve and display the `querystring` information using code like the following:

```
Form Mode: <% = Request.QueryString("FormMode") %>
```

Server variable anyone?

You can retrieve various parts of the HTTP header using the `ServerVariables` collection of the `Request` object.

For example, the following code (from servervars.asp) retrieves the IP address of the Web client and the name and version number of the IIS software running on the Web server from the HTTP header:

```
<%
Response.Write "Server Variable REMOTE_ADDR: " & _
  Request.ServerVariables("REMOTE_ADDR") & "<BR>"
Response.Write "Server Variable SERVER_SOFTWARE: " & _
  Request.ServerVariables("SERVER_SOFTWARE") & "<BR>"
%>
```

Figure 17-5 shows what this page may look like when hosted on a Web server running Peer Web Services 3.0.

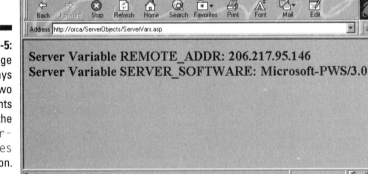

Figure 17-5: This page displays two elements of the `Server-Variables` collection.

The `ServerVariables` collection has many other elements. For a complete listing, see the Visual InterDev online documentation.

Extending ASP with the Server Object

The `Server` object provides access to additional properties and methods of the Active Server itself. Table 17-6 summarizes these properties and methods.

Table 17-6   Properties and Methods of the Server Object

Type	Name	Description
Property	ScriptTimeout	The number of seconds a script may run before being terminated by the server. Does not include time spent while a server component (for example, ADO) processes.
Method	CreateObject	Instantiates (creates a running copy of) non-built-in components such as ADO and other ActiveX components.
Method	HTMLEncode	Encodes a string so that any HTML delimiters or tags get treated as plain text.
Method	MapPath	Returns the fully qualified physical path of a server file. The existence of the file is not checked. If the string that you pass to MapPath starts with a backward or forward slash, then MapPath returns the path relative to wwwroot; otherwise MapPath returns a path relative to the directory where the current asp file is executing.
Method	URLEncode	Encodes a string so that it can be used as part of a URL.

A MapPathing example

Here's some code from (mappath.asp) that demonstrates the use of the MapPath method of the Server object:

```
<H1>MapPath Example</H1>
<%
Const conFile = "images\gray.jpg"

Response.Write "This script is executing from " & _
 "this virtual directory: '"
Response.Write _
 Request.ServerVariables("SCRIPT_NAME") & _
 "'<BR><BR>"

Response.Write "MapPath of '" & conFile & "': "
Response.Write _
 Server.MapPath(conFile) &  _
 "<BR>"
```

(continued)

(continued)

```
Response.Write "MapPath of '\" & conFile & "': "
Response.Write _
  Server.MapPath("\" & conFile) &  _
  "<BR>"
%>
```

The preceding page appears in Figure 17-6.

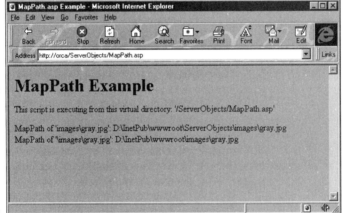

Figure 17-6:
This page
demonstrates
how to
use the
MapPath
method.

Encoding we will go

The `Server.HTMLEncode` method is useful for sending strings back to the client that you don't want the browser's HTML engine to interpret.

For example, the following ASP code (from encode.asp on the CD-ROM)

```
<%
Const conString = "<strong>This is exciting.</strong>"
Response.Write "The HTMLEncoded string: " & _
  Server.HTMLEncode(conString) & "<BR>"
%>
```

returns to the browser:

```
<strong>This is exciting.</strong>
```

You can use a similar method anytime a user passes a URL to you that you want to use. Using the method ensures that any special characters get converted into legal URL characters.

For example, this ASP code (also from encode.asp)

```
<%
Response.Write "The URLEncoded string: " & _
  Server.URLEncode(conString) & "<BR>"
%>
```

returns to the browser:

```
%3Cstrong%3EThis+is+exciting%2E%3C%2Fstrong%3E
```

Doesn't that string look fun? Encode.asp appears in Figure 17-7.

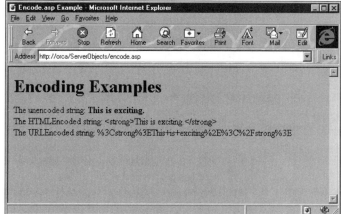

Using components

The Server's `CreateObject` method lets you extend the Active Server by moving beyond the built-in objects to use functionality supplied by other components. Wow!

Any objects you instantiate using the `Server.CreateObject` method get created on the Web server and are thus never seen by the client.

In Chapter 13 (and later chapters of this book), you explore using the ActiveX Data Objects (ADO) component to manipulate data stored in databases. ASP ships with several other sample components you can use to enhance your Web pages. Table 17-7 summarizes the included components.

Table 17-7	Components that Ship with ASP
Component	*Description*
MSWC.Adrotator	The Advertisement Rotator component automatically rotates advertisements following a specified schedule and order.
MSWC.BrowserType	The Browser Capabilities component helps you to determine the capabilities, type, and version of the client browser.
ADODB	The ActiveX Data Objects component gives you access to data objects on the sever.
MSWC.Nextlink	The NextLink component can be used to help create a table of contents for the Web pages in your application.
MS.TextStream	The TextStream component allows you to read and write to text files on the server.

The following code from browser.asp makes use of the Browser Capabilities component to display a table describing the capabilities of the Web browser being used to browse the page:

```
<%  Set objBrw = _
  Server.CreateObject("MSWC.BrowserType") %>
<TABLE BORDER=1>
<tr><td><strong>Feature</strong></td>
<td><strong>Value</strong></td></tr>

<tr><td>Browser</td><td><%= objBrw.Browser  %></td></tr>
<tr><td>Version</td><td><%= objBrw.Version  %></td></tr>
<tr><td>Platform</td><td><%= objBrw.Platform  %></td></tr>

<tr><td>Frames</td><td>
<%  If (objBrw.Frames = TRUE) Then  %> TRUE
<%  Else  %>  FALSE
<%  End If  %> </td></TR>

<tr><td>Tables</td><td>
<%  If (objBrw.Tables = TRUE) Then  %> TRUE
```

```
<%  Else  %> FALSE
<%  end if  %> </td></TR>

<tr><td>Cookies</td><td>
<%  If (objBrw.Cookies = TRUE) Then  %> TRUE
<%  Else  %> FALSE
<%  End If  %> </td></TR>

<tr><td>VBScript</td><td>
<%  If (objBrw.VBScript = TRUE) Then  %> TRUE
<%  Else  %> FALSE
<%  End If  %> </td></TR>
<tr><td>JScript</td><td>
<%  If (objBrw.JavaScript = TRUE) Then  %> TRUE
<%  Else  %> FALSE
<%  End If  %> </td></TR>
</TABLE>
```

The Browser Capabilities component identifies browsers using information from the HTTP header. The component then compares this identifying information with a list of browsers and their capabilities that are stored in a file named *browscap.ini* file that's stored on the server. Thus, the Browser Capabilities information is accurate only if this file is kept up to date with the latest browser releases. You can find a current version of this file, which by default is placed in the winnt\system32\inetsrv\asp\cmpnts folder on your Web server, on Microsoft's Web site.

Figure 17-8 shows browser.asp when run against Internet Explorer 3.02 on a Windows NT Workstation machine.

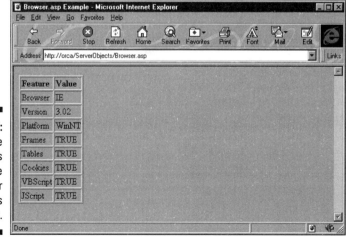

Figure 17-8:
This page demonstrates using the Browser Capabilities component.

Creating your own components

You can use the `Server.CreateObject` method with any ActiveX Automation object. ActiveX Automation objects are components that communicate using the Microsoft Component Object Model (COM) standard. This means that you can use programming languages such as C++, Java, Delphi, and VisualBasic to create server components.

For example, I created a simple VisualBasic 5.0 ActiveX Automation Server to serve as a mortgage loan payment calculator. The VBScript language, which, remember, is a subset of the VBA language, lacks any built-in financial functions. The VBA language that's part of VisualBasic, however, has numerous functions you can use to calculate loan payments and other financial goodies.

With very little work, I created an ActiveX Automation server (mortage.dll included on the CD-ROM) that calculates a mortgage payment amount from three parameters:

- ✔ `AnnualRate`: The annual interest rate
- ✔ `Years`: The length of the loan in years
- ✔ `LoanAmount`: The amount of the loan in dollars

To use the Loan Payment Calculator component in your ASP pages, follow these steps:

1. **Install the mortgage ActiveX Automation server.**

   Because the DLL needs to be registered on the Web server machine, you can't just copy the DLL to your machine and expect it to work. Use the included setup routine on the book CD-ROM.

2. **Collect the three parameters from the user that mortgage.dll needs.**

   For example, the loancalc.asp page collects the needed parameters using an HTML form that is shown in Figure 17-9.

3. **Use the `Server.CreateObject` method to instantiate the Loan Payment Calculator component (`Mortgage.Payment`) and use its single method, `Calculate`, to calculate the loan payment from the passed parameters.**

   A smart move is to include some code that validates the posted form fields before passing along the values to the component.

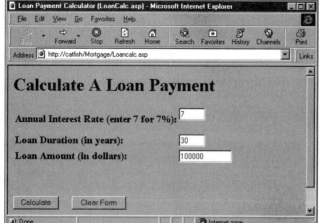

Figure 17-9:
This form
collects the
loan
payment
calculator
parameters.

For example, following is the first part of a sample ASP page, calculate.asp, which I use to call Loan Payment Calculator component. This code retrieves the form fields from loancalc.asp and validates the fields before continuing:

```
<%
Dim objPay
Dim varAnnRate
Dim varNumYears
Dim varLoanAmt
Dim vbCrLf
Dim varError
Dim varPayment


vbCrLf = Chr(13) & Chr(10)

varAnnRate = Request.Form("AnnualRate")
varNumYears = Request.Form("Years")
varLoanAmt = Request.Form("LoanAmount")

If Not (varAnnRate > 0 And varAnnRate < 100) Then
    varError = "The rate must be a percentage " & _
    "greater than 0 and less than 100." & vbCrLf
End If

If Not (varNumYears > 0 And varNumYears < 100) Then
    varError = varError & _
    "The number of years must be greater " & _
    "than 0 and less than 100." & vbCrLf
```

(continued)

(continued)

```
End If

If Not (varLoanAmt > 0 And varLoanAmt < 10000000) Then
   varError = varError & _
   "The loan amount must be greater " & _
   "than 0 and less than 10,000,000." & vbCrLf
End If
If Not IsEmpty(varError) Then
   Response.Write _
   "Problem: One or more required fields was " & _
   "left blank or is out of range. <BR>"
   Response.Write "Resolution: " & varError
Else
```

The following portion of the page creates the `Mortgage.Payment` object as a session-scope variable (also known as a session user-defined property), but only if it hasn't already been created:

```
If IsEmpty(Session("objPayment")) Then
   Set Session("objPayment") = _
   Server.CreateObject("Mortgage.Payment")
End If
Set objPay = Session("objPayment")
```

Finally, the `Payment` object's `Calculate` method is called and the results are sent back to the client (see Figure 17-10):

```
   varPayment = objPay.Calculate( _
      varAnnRate/100, varNumYears, varLoanAmt)
   Response.Write "Your monthly loan payment for "
   Response.Write "a " & varNumYears & "-year "
   Response.Write FormatCurrency(varLoanAmt) & " loan "
   Response.Write "at a " & varAnnRate
   Response.Write "% annual interest rate is "
   Response.Write FormatCurrency(varPayment) & "."
End If
%>
```

The mortgage.dll VisualBasic 5.0 ActiveX Automation Server accomplishes all its magic with the following code:

```
Public Function Calculate(AnnualRate As Variant, _
 Years As Variant, LoanAmount As Variant) As Variant
   Calculate = -Pmt(AnnualRate / 12, _
    12 * Years, LoanAmount)
 End Function
```

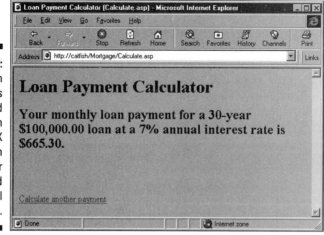

Figure 17-10:
The loan
payment is
calculated
by using an
ActiveX
Automation
Server
created
with Visual
Basic 5.0.

That's it!

As you may imagine, the ability to create and use your own server objects opens up quite a few possibilities.

Is That All There Is to Visual InterDev?

In the chapters of this part, I cover only a portion of the functionality of Visual InterDev. There are several other facets to Visual InterDev that I haven't discussed, including:

- ✔ Client-side scripting
- ✔ Creating pages that employ the HTML Layout control
- ✔ Source code control integration
- ✔ The Visual Database Tools
- ✔ Microsoft Image Composer, Microsoft Music Producer, and Microsoft Media Manager

Part VIII
The Part of Tens

The 5th Wave   **By Rich Tennant**

SEVERAL HOURS PASSED BEFORE WAYNE DISCOVERED THAT HE WAS LOOKING AT HIS SCREEN SAVER AND NOT OUT THE SUBMARINE'S PORTHOLE

"IT'S <u>INCREDIBLE</u>! I'M SEEING LIFE FORMS NEVER BEFORE IMAGINED!! BIZARRE, COLORFUL, ALMOST WHIMSICAL!!!"

In this part . . .

The chapters in this part all have something in common: the number 10. Chapter 18 shares with you ten things to consider when choosing Web publishing software. This chapter helps you decide the best Web publishing solution for you. Chapter 19 introduces ten frequently asked questions about Web database publishing. Here you find answers to age-old questions like "Why can't I get my IDC or ASP page to come up?" and "How come dogs are always scratching themselves?" (Okay, I don't answer that last one.) Chapter 20 answers the ten most common questions about Visual InterDev. In this chapter, you discover why you should buy Visual InterDev and if you should create a data connection or a database project.

Chapter 18

Ten Things to Consider When Choosing Web Publishing Software

• •

In This Chapter

▶ Understanding the questions you need to ask

▶ Deciding which Web server is right for you

▶ Deciding which Web development tool is right for you

▶ Exploring non-Microsoft alternatives

▶ Processing credit-card transactions

• •

*U*ntil this chapter, the book covers publishing data on your intranet or Internet Web server, focusing on Microsoft-centric solutions. Now comes the hard part: Deciding which products to use for your own Web applications.

This chapter includes ten questions to ask yourself when making this important decision.

Which Web Server Are You Running?

The answer to this question generally falls into one of three scenarios:

✔ You're running a Microsoft Web server.

✔ You're running a non-Microsoft Web server on Windows NT or Windows 95.

✔ You're running a non-Microsoft Web server on a UNIX system or another non-Windows operating system.

If your Web server is running on a Microsoft Web server, then you can easily use any of the software and technologies discussed in this book.

If you're using a Netscape, O'Reilly, Oracle, or some other Web server that runs under Windows NT Server, Windows NT Workstation, or Windows 95, then you may still be able to use the dynamic Microsoft technologies discussed in Parts IV through VII. Several vendors ship or will soon be shipping Microsoft-compatible Web servers or Web server add-ons. WebSite Professional 2.0, a Web server from O'Reilly and Associates, includes support for Active Server Pages and other ISAPI applications (www.ora.com). ChiliSoft sells an ASP clone called Chili!ASP that works with Netscape and Lotus Web servers running under Windows NT (www.chilisoft.net) and thus you can run your preferred Web server.

If your Web site, however, is hosted on a UNIX-based server or some other operating system, you probably won't be able to use the dynamic Microsoft technologies discussed in Parts IV through VII. You can, however, still use the static HTML pages generated by the Access Publish to the Web Wizard and the SQL Server Web Assistant. (Also note that ChiliSoft plans other versions of Chili!ASP for UNIX platforms; check out www.chilisoft.net for the latest information on Chili!ASP.)

If your Web site is hosted by your Internet service provider (ISP) off site, you may not have much choice in what Web server it uses. You do have a choice in ISPs, however, and may want to consider moving to an ISP that runs under Windows NT.

If you can't run a Microsoft or a Microsoft-compatible server, you can still use the static pages produced by the Access and SQL Server publishing wizards discussed in Parts II and III of the book. In addition, you may want to consider other non-Microsoft solutions. See the section "What Other Solutions Are Out There?" later in this chapter for more ideas.

Will Your Site Be on an Intranet or Internet?

Whether you're running an intranet or Internet site affects you in at least two ways:

- ✔ With an intranet site, you're more likely to be hosting the Web site internally and thus have more control over which Web server is used.

- ✔ Web sites hosted on the Internet often have many more hits than smaller corporate intranet sites.

If you're running a small, departmental Web server, you may be able to use a product running under Windows NT Workstation or Windows 95, or perhaps even a Mac-based solution. For any intranet or Internet site with a decent amount of traffic, however, you should be using Windows NT Server or a UNIX-based solution.

What Sort of Traffic Are You Expecting?

A site getting only a small amount of traffic (say, less than 100 hits per day) may successfully be hosted on a Web server running under Windows NT Workstation, Windows 95, or the Macintosh operating system, but more than likely these operating systems are best used strictly for interim, development, or server testing.

Most Web sites can benefit from the extra robustness of a Web server running under Windows NT Server or UNIX. In addition, the servers running under Windows NT Server and UNIX usually have features — such as more elaborate security and better usage statistic reporting — that the other operating system-based servers lack.

Where's the Data?

If your data is stored in Microsoft Access, then you may want to employ a solution that keeps the data in an Access database. In these cases, you can use the Access Publish to the Web Wizard (see Parts II, IV, and V) or Visual InterDev (see Parts VI and VII) to produce static or dynamic pages.

Keep in mind, however, that if you're planning on using the IDC or ASP technologies to link your Access database to your Web server, Access will be able to handle only a small number of concurrent user connections. If you think you might get more than 10 or 20 concurrent user connections, you need to think about upsizing the data to a server database such as SQL Server.

If you decide to move from Access to SQL Server, you may find that the Access 97 Upsizing Tools come in handy in helping you make the move. This free set of tools is included on the CD-ROM that comes with this book. If your data is stored in SQL Server, then you may be interested in the static HTML pages produced by the SQL Server Web Assistant (see Part III). If you'd prefer dynamic pages, check out Visual InterDev and Parts VI and VII.

If your data is stored in another ODBC data source accessible from a Microsoft Web server, then you should be able to use Visual InterDev and the solutions discussed in Parts VI and VII.

How Much Time and Money Do You Have?

The Access Publish to the Web Wizard and the SQL Server Web Assistant have very short and flat learning curves. Visual InterDev, however, requires quite a bit more time to master. If you decide to use Visual InterDev, you'll also have to shell out the extra bucks for Visual InterDev on top of the amount of money you spend on your database software.

When it comes to choosing a Web server, Microsoft Windows-based Web servers are among the easiest to set up and configure and cost nothing, which makes them the prime candidate for those on a tight budget.

How Dynamic Do You Need the Data?

If you can live with static read-only pages, then the static HTML pages produced by the Access Publish to the Web Wizard or the SQL Server Web Assistant should satisfy your needs quite nicely. Static solutions also tend to be easier on the Web server too.

If your data needs to be timely but is never updated, you may still be able to get away with static HTML pages that are regenerated on a regular schedule by the Access or SQL Server wizards (see Chapters 5 and 7). On the other hand, this won't work if you want your users to be able to query the database on the fly. In this case, you need to employ one of the dynamic technologies discussed in Parts IV through VII of the book.

What's the Difference Between CGI, IDC, and ASP?

Common Gateway Interface (CGI), Internet Database Connector (IDC), and Active Server Pages (ASP) are all technologies for linking Web pages to dynamic content.

CGI is an industry-wide standard that is difficult to implement and generally slower than the other two technologies. On the positive side, CGI applications can be produced with both compiled languages such as C++ and Visual Basic and interpreted scripting languages such as PERL. CGI applications aren't limited to data access. CGI applications run on all major operating systems and with most brands of Web servers. I don't discuss CGI in this book.

IDC is an older Microsoft standard for connecting Web pages to ODBC data sources. IDC applications are created using two scripting files: the IDC file and the HTML Extension (HTX) file. IDC applications are limited to data access. The IDC standard is only supported by Microsoft and compatible Web servers. I discuss IDC in Part IV of this book.

ASP is the newest Microsoft technology for creating dynamic Web pages. ASP pages can be created using multiple scripting languages, including VBScript and JavaScript (also called JScript). ASP pages aren't limited to data access applications. You can call any ActiveX Automation Server to provide services to an ASP page. You can write these ActiveX components in any Component Object Model (COM — another Microsoft promulgated standard) compiled programming language such as C++, Java, Delphi, or Visual Basic. The ASP standard is only supported by Microsoft and compatible Web servers. I discuss ASP in Parts V, VI, and VII of this book.

What Other Solutions Are Out There?

You can choose from lots of non-Microsoft solutions in both Web servers and Web database application development solutions.

- ✔ **Web servers:** Many Web servers run on a variety of platforms. Apache Server is a free UNIX server from the Apache Project (www.apache.org). Netscape sells several servers, including the industrial-strength Enterprise Server, which runs under UNIX and Windows NT. WebSite Professional, a popular Web server from O'Reilly and Associates (www.ora.com), runs on Windows NT and Windows 95 boxes. For the Macintosh enthusiasts, StarNine Technologies sells WebStar (www.starnine.com). These servers are just a few of the many choices out there.

- ✔ **Web database application development products:** You can find several alternatives to the Microsoft development tools and databases presented in this book. Cold Fusion from Allaire is a popular product for developing dynamic database-based Web sites (www.coldfusion.com). Other alternatives include IntraBuilder from Borland (www.borland.com/intrabuilder), NetDynamics from NetDynamics (www.netdynamics.com), LiveWire from Netscape (www.netscape.com), and Visual Café Pro for Java, Database Development Edition from Symantec (www.symantec.com/vcafeprowin).

What About FrontPage?

FrontPage is a great tool for developing primarily static content, but it doesn't have much, if anything, for the developer needing to develop database-based Web applications. The database wizard included with the newest version of the product, FrontPage 98 is pretty anemic-looking when compared with the wizards that are part of Access, SQL Server, and Visual InterDev.

On the other hand, FrontPage is a good visual tool for creating the static portion of Web sites, so you may want to use it in concert with some of the other products. In fact, Visual InterDev comes with a special edition of the FrontPage editor that you can use with your Visual InterDev projects. (Visual InterDev also includes another editor, the "Source Code Editor" that complements the FrontPage Editor — for more details see Chapter 14.) For more on FrontPage, see *FrontPage 98 For Dummies,* by Asha Dornfest (IDG Books Worldwide, Inc.).

What Do I Use to Process Credit-Card Transactions?

To process credit-card transactions, you need to purchase a full-strength Internet *commerce* server such as Microsoft Commerce Server, a component of the Enterprise Edition of Microsoft Site Server (www.microsoft.com), Domino.Merchant from Lotus (www.net.lotus.com), Netscape Merchant System (www.netscape.com), or Net.Commerce from IBM (www.net.commerce.ibm.com). Expect to pay big money here, in the neighborhood of $2,000 to $100,000.

Chapter 19

Ten Things That Can Go Wrong with Dynamic Web Publishing and How to Fix Them

. . . .

In This Chapter

▶ What can go wrong with dynamic Web publishing

▶ Fixing common publishing problems

▶ Things to ask yourself when that page stops working

▶ Wrestling with virtual directory security

. . . .

*L*ots of things can conspire to make your dynamic pages come crashing down. Perhaps it's a problem with your Web server setup. Or maybe it's your browser. It could even be you — and, actually, it's more likely something you did or didn't do.

In this chapter, I share with you the ten or so things that have gone wrong for me at least once. Lucky for you, it happened to me first.

Why Do I See My ASP Script in the Browser?

If you see your ASP script in the browser, you may have forgotten to start your URL with "http://". You must use this prefix to force the server to process the script.

This problem may also be a symptom of a virtual Web directory security problem (see "Why Do I Get 'Access Forbidden' or 'HTTP/1.0 501 Not Supported' Errors?" later in this chapter for more details on how to resolve this issue).

Another potential cause of this problem: You haven't installed ASP support on your Web server. If you're running IIS or Peer Web Services 2.0, you need to upgrade to Version 3.0 or later — Version 2.0 doesn't include ASP support. If you're running Personal Web Server 1.0, you need to make sure that you remember to separately install ASP support — it's not part of the PWS 1.0 install program.

Why Can't I Get My IDC or ASP Page to Come Up?

If you get an Opening dialog box or some other strange occurrence every time you try to open an IDC or ASP page, then you may have a problem with the beginning or the end of the URL address.

Are you forgetting to begin your URL with "http://"? You must use this prefix to force the server to process the script. Otherwise, the Web client tries to process the page, which tends to confuse browsers because they don't know server scripts from Adam.

For IDC pages, this problem also may occur when you forget to end the URL with a question mark. Add a question mark to the end of the URL and try again.

Why Do I Get "Access Forbidden" or "HTTP/1.0 501 Not Supported" Errors?

"Access Forbidden" or "HTTP/1.0 501 Not Supported" errors may be a sign that you haven't enabled the Script Access permission (the Execute permission on older Microsoft Web servers) for the virtual Web directory that's hosting your IDC or ASP files. See Chapter 2 for more details on setting up the right level of security for your dynamic applications.

Sometimes a bad ASP installation will manifest itself as an HTTP error. This is more than likely to be the culprit if you recently installed beta software on your Web server machine. Try reinstalling ASP support. Failing that, it may be time to reformat the Web server and re-install everything from scratch.

Why Did All My ASP Files Suddenly Stop Working?

If your ASP files suddenly stop working, more than likely you've installed some product — perhaps a beta product — that messed up your ASP DLL files or the registry entries. You may be able to solve this problem with a simple reinstall of ASP support (or the Web server software). If the re-installation doesn't help, then you may need to reformat the machine's hard drive and re-install everything from scratch.

It Works Great On My Development Machine, But . . .

It's common for things not to work when moving a Web application to a different machine. This problem is a sign that something is configured differently on the new machine, but finding the exact difference may take some time. Try asking yourself these questions:

✔ If you're using a DSN, did you define the System DSN on the new machine?

✔ Is the database management software installed on the new machine?

✔ Is the database installed on the new machine?

✔ If you're using SQL Server or some other server database, did you create the correct user and group accounts on the new machine?

✔ If you're using ASP pages, did you install ASP support on the new machine?

These configurations are just some of the things you may have forgotten to do.

I Keep Getting an Illegal Name Error When Accessing SQL Server Data

If you receive an error that looks something like the following when you access SQL Server Data, perhaps you're using double quotes where you need to use single quotes:

```
The name 'somename' is illegal in this context.
Only constants, constant expressions, or variables
allowed here. Column names are illegal.
```

SQL Server uses single quotes as both the text and date delimiter.

How Do I Format a Field Using IDC?

To format a field using IDC, you need to use a database-specific formatting function such as Format() or Convert() in the IDC file's SQL statement. See Chapter 9 for more details.

Why Don't My Access Wizard-Published Parameter Query Pages Work?

Several things can go wrong when you use the Access Publish to the Web Wizard to publish your parameter queries. You need to make sure that you declared your query parameters. If not, declare the parameters and republish the query.

Does your query use the LIKE operator? The Access wizard tends to *munge,* or mess up, the syntax of queries using the LIKE operator. See Chapter 8 for more details.

Why Do I See a Blank Page in the Browser?

If you see a blank page in the browser, you may be using a page that employs an improperly installed HTML Layout Control. Reinstall the HTML Layout Control and try again.

You also may see a blank page if you attempt to use a form published by the Access Publish to the Web Wizard in any browser other than Internet Explorer 3.0 (or later versions).

Why Don't My Access Forms Containing Subforms Work?

If forms without subforms publish just fine, but you can't get that form with an embedded subform to display properly, you may have gotten the Server URL address on page 5 of the wizard wrong. See Chapter 11 for more details on the solution to this problem.

If you're worried that your subform is read-only — welcome to the club — this is not a bug but how the pages produced by the Access Publish to the Web Wizard are supposed to work.

Chapter 20

Ten Common Questions about Visual InterDev

In This Chapter

▶ Understanding some of the nuances of Visual InterDev

▶ Making sense of projects and workspaces

▶ Getting JavaScript to work on your ASP pages

▶ Deciding which editor to use

*V*isual InterDev is a powerful Web development tool for creating dynamic, database-based Web sites. Its power, however, can be a little disorienting at first.

In this chapter, I cover ten frequently asked questions about Visual InterDev. And, nice guy that I am, I include the answers, too.

Why Should I Buy Visual InterDev?

If you already own a copy of FrontPage, you may be asking why you should buy Visual InterDev. Although FrontPage is a great tool for developing static Web content, it can't do much for you in the area of dynamic, database-based Web publishing. Microsoft built Visual InterDev, on the other hand, with the express purpose of helping you develop interactive, server-side, data-driven Web sites, using the Active Server Pages and ActiveX Data Objects techologies. FrontPage doesn't work with any of these technologies.

What's the Difference Between a Project and a Workspace?

A Visual InterDev Web *project* has a one-to-one relationship with a Web (or Web site). Your Visual InterDev Web project consists of a Web plus the associated Web project file. A *workspace,* on the other hand, is a container for one or more projects. A single workspace may contain multiple Web projects or a Web project together with other (non-Web) Visual Studio projects.

For example, you can create a workspace that contains a Web project, a Java project, and a database project.

The Developer Studio IDE allows you to open only one workspace at a time, but that workspace may contain multiple projects.

What the Heck Is this Default.asa File?

Every Active Server Web has the optional Default.asa file that you can use to create user-defined session and application properties. You can place code in a session or application event procedure that's executed every time a session or application is created or destroyed.

A Web may have only one Default.asa file, which sits in the Web's root directory. See Chapter 17 for more details on Default.asa.

Should I Create a Data Connection or a Database Project?

A *database project* allows you to manipulate a database and its schema. Adding a database project to your workspace, however, doesn't tie it in any way to your Web project. On the other hand, when you add a *data connection* to your Web project, you're telling Visual InterDev that you want to establish a connection to a data source that you plan to use on one or more pages of your project.

You can use the Visual Database Tools with both database projects and data connections. In most cases, you want to create a data connection, not a database project. The one exception: Create a database project when you want to manipulate a database without linking it to a Web site.

How Do I Get Visual Database Tools to Process My Database Schema Changes?

This one took me a while to figure out, especially because the Table design window doesn't have a close icon. To process your database schema changes, simply close the document window by choosing File➪Close. You're then prompted with a "Do you want to save changes?" dialog box. Select Yes to have Visual InterDev generate a script of the changes and execute that script to make your design changes.

Why Don't the Data Range Controls Display Anything When I Browse the Page?

The Data Range controls don't, by themselves, make up a whole page. You must create references to the data fields somewhere between the code produced by the Data Range Header control and the code produced by the Data Range Footer control. See Chapter 16 for more details.

How Do I Use JavaScript in My ASP Files?

VBScript is the default ASP scripting language. If you prefer JavaScript (or JScript, the Microsoft implementation of JavaScript) to VBScript, you can override this default for a single script or the whole page by using the SCRIPT tag. You also can change the default scripting language for a particular server to JavaScript by making a change to the registry. See Chapter 14 for more details.

How Do I Check My Links?

Visual InterDev includes *link view* for displaying the hyperlinks to and from a page and for checking the integrity of those links. Simply right-click a Web page in the Project Workspace window and choose View Links from the pop-up menu to display link view.

Which Editor Should I Use: FrontPage or Source Editor?

Are you a coder at heart, or do you prefer to do things more visually by clicking and dragging? Visual InterDev can handle both situations because it comes with two — count 'em — two editors.

The built-in Source Editor is a lean-and-mean color-coded editor that knows a few things about HTML and scripting tags but lacks the visually-oriented niceties of the FrontPage Editor.

On the other hand, the FrontPage Editor is a much more user-friendly tool that tries to shield you from the code. The editor, however, is kind of stupid when it comes to scripts. In fact, the FrontPage Editor may rearrange your pages without asking your permission — or even worse — it can sometimes break your scripts by inserting or deleting stuff in its overzealous effort to assist you.

Ultimately, it's your call, but I like to think that there's room in most Web projects for using both editors at different times. FrontPage is great for HTML tables and forms (see the following section), but the Source Editor is a better tool for coding scripts.

How Do I Visually Lay Out an HTML Table, Form, or Frame?

The Visual InterDev Source Editor can't help you with laying out HTML tables or forms. You need to use the FrontPage Editor, which is quite adept at laying out HTML tables and forms.

Neither FrontPage nor the Source Editor knows squat about HTML frames. When it comes to HTML frames, you're on your own.

Appendix

About the CD

*F*ollowing are highlights of what you can find on the *Intranet & Web Databases For Dummies* CD-ROM:

- ✔ All the sample databases and sample code discussed in the book
- ✔ Microsoft Internet Explorer 4.0, the newest release of this popular Web browser
- ✔ The Access 97 Upsizing Tools, a great wizard for helping you move your Access data to SQL Server

System Requirements

Make sure that your computer meets the following minimum system requirements. If your computer doesn't match up to most of these requirements, you may have problems in using the contents of the CD.

- ✔ A PC with a 486 or faster processor.
- ✔ Microsoft Windows 95 or later or Microsoft Windows NT 4.0 or later.
- ✔ At least 8MB of total RAM installed on your computer. For best performance, I recommend that your PC have at least 16MB of RAM installed.
- ✔ At least 20MB of hard drive space available to install all the sample databases and code from this CD. (You need more space if you install every program.)
- ✔ A CD drive — double-speed (2x) or faster.

The software on this CD cannot run on the Windows 3.*x* operating system.

How to Use the CD

The CD that comes with this book contains an assortment of sample files, shareware, and free software that I have copied to a bunch of different folders. To install one or more of these items from the CD to your hard drive, follow these steps:

1. **Insert the CD into your computer's CD-ROM drive and close the drive door.**

2. **What you do next depends upon the contents of the particular folder. If the folder contains an install program, go to Step 3. If the folder contains sample files, go to Step 4.**

3. **Those folders containing programs (for example, WinZip, the Upsizing Tools, and Internet Explorer) have setup programs that you need to run before you can use them.**

   Double-click the setup program file (usually named setup.exe) to start the program's setup program. The setup program should guide you from this point.

4. **Those folders containing sample files need to be copied to your hard drive before you can use them.**

   To make it easy, we created a self-extracting archive for each set of sample programs. The self-extractors are at the root of the CD and are called Ch09.exe, Ch12.exe, Ch13.exe, and Ch17.exe. Simply run these extractors, and the sample files will get copied to your hard drive (to subfolders named for the chapters in a folder called c:\INTR_WEB).

5. **Follow the instructions in the next section or the chapter that discusses the sample files for more details on using the files.**

What You Find on the CD

Following is a summary of the software on this CD.

Sample Access database

Most examples used throughout the book involve a fictitious Internet meal delivery business called Web_Meals.Com. The Microsoft Access 97 version of this database is named Meals.mdb. You can use this database to try out the examples from Parts II and IV–VII. You must own a copy of Access 97 (or a later version) to use this sample database. It's on the CD at D:\Dbaccess\Meals.mdb. If your CD-ROM drive is not D:\, be sure to use the appropriate letter for your drive.

Sample SQL Server database

I also created a Microsoft SQL Server 6.5 version of the Meals database. However, before you can use this version of the database, you must run a script that creates the database. Take the following steps to accomplish this:

1. **Start up SQL Enterprise Manager and log in.**

   If you don't know how to do this step, you need to consult with your SQL Server administrator or the SQL Server documentation.

2. **Create a new database named Meals, consisting of at least 10MB, on the device of your choice.**

   Again, if you don't know how to do this step, you need to consult with your SQL Server administrator or the SQL Server documentation.

   If you want to minimize the amount of space taken up by the sample database, don't select a log device for the Meals database.

3. **Start the SQL Query Tool by choosing Tools⇨SQL Query Tool from the menu.**

4. **Load the meals1.sql script file from the CD-ROM. (It's on the CD at D:\Dbsqlsrv.)**

   This script creates the schema (structure) of the Meals database.

5. **Execute the meals1.sql script.**

   This script may take a few minutes to run.

6. **Load the meals2.sql script file from the CD.**

   (The file is also located in the D:\Dbsqlsrv folder.)

   This script creates the records of the Meals database.

7. **Execute the meals2.sql script.**

   This script may take several minutes to run. Be patient.

8. **Close the query tool when the script is done, and you're ready to use the database.**

You first use this sample database in Part III and then in several other parts of the book.

Sample IDC files

The Ch09 folder on the CD contains lots of sample Internet Database Connector (IDC) pages that correspond to examples from Chapter 9 of the book. These IDC files retrieve data from the sample Access and SQL Server databases. I've created a home page named default.html that you can use to navigate to each of the sample IDC pages in this folder.

See Chapter 9 for more details on using these sample IDC files.

Sample ASP files

The Ch12 folder on the CD contains lots of sample introductory Active Server Pages (ASP) pages that correspond to examples from the chapter that bears the same name. I've created a home page named aspmenu.html that you can use to navigate to each of the sample ASP pages in this folder.

See Chapter 12 for more details on using these sample ASP files.

Sample ADO files

The Ch13 folder on the CD contains lots of sample Active Server Pages (ASP) pages that use the ActiveX Data Objects model to retrieve data from the sample Access and SQL Server databases. The ASP pages correspond to examples from the chapter that bears the same name. I've created a home page named adomenu.html that you can use to navigate to each of the sample ASP pages in this folder.

See Chapter 13 for more details on using these sample ASP files.

Sample Active Server object files

The Ch17 folder on the CD contains several sample Active Server Pages (ASP) pages that demonstrate using Active Server objects. Some pages retrieve data from the sample SQL Server database. The ASP pages correspond to examples from the chapter that bears the same name. I've created a home page named objectsmenu.html that you can use to navigate to each of the sample ASP pages in this folder.

The Ch17 folder also includes two subfolders, Mortgage and Mortsrc. Mortgage contains a setup program you can use to install the sample Mortgage ActiveX Server used on the loancalc.asp and calculate.asp sample pages. Run this setup program before you try the loancalc.asp and calculate.asp pages. The Mortsrc folder contains the Visual Basic 5.0 project file and source code I used to create Mortgage ActiveX Server. See Chapter 17 for more details on using these sample files.

Access Upsizing Tools

While you can start out testing your intranet and Internet Web sites using Access 97 as your database program, a time may come where Access doesn't quite have the horsepower you need to keep your Web site data happy. In this case, you need to consider moving on up to a server database program such as SQL Server. The free Access Upsizing Tools from Microsoft make this move a piece of cake.

Run the wzcs97.exe file found in the \Accup folder to install this valuable tool.

Internet Explorer 4.0

Internet Explorer 4.0 is the next-generation Web browser from Microsoft. This baby supports all the latest Web browser innovations including channels, dynamic HTML, and an improved user interface.

Run the setup.exe program in the \IE4 folder to install Internet Explorer.

Job Forum sample application

The folks in the Access group at Microsoft created a great sample Web site that uses Access 97 and the Internet Database Connector (IDC). The sample application includes a "white paper" (Jobforpa.doc) that explains in detail how it works.

Follow the instructions found in the readme.txt file in the \jobforum folder to install the job forum application.

Microsoft Office 97 viewers

Microsoft has given us permission to distribute three Office 97 file viewers. The viewers, which you can find in the \Off97Vwr folder of the CD, are for Microsoft Word 97, Microsoft Excel 97, and Microsoft PowerPoint 97 files. Each Office 97 file viewer allows you to view and print a Word, Excel, or PowerPoint document without having to have a copy of that Office 97 application installed on your machine.

Run the viewer install programs found in the \Off97vwr folder to install one or more of the viewers.

System DSN tester

You can use the files you find in the \DSNTest folder to make sure your ODBC System Data Source Name (DSN) works correctly.

Copy the TestDSN.HTM and TestDSN.ASP to your Web server's root directory and follow the instructions in the readme.txt to test and debug a System DSN.

WinZip

WinZip, from Nico Mak Computing, is a very cool shareware utility for *zipping* (compressing) and *unzipping* (expanding) files to save disk space. The shareware system provides this indispensable utility program. If you like the program and continue to use it after a brief trial period, you need to register and pay for it.

To install WinZip, run the winzip95.exe install program. See the included documentation for more details on WinZip and registering it.

If You Have Problems (Of the CD Kind)

I tried my best to compile programs that work on most computers with the minimum system requirements. Alas, your computer may differ, and some programs may not work properly for some reason.

The two likeliest problems are that you don't have enough memory (RAM) for the programs you want to use, or you have other programs running that affect installation or running of a program. If you get error messages like Not enough memory or Setup cannot continue, try one or more of the following methods and then try using the software again:

- ✔ **Turn off any antivirus software that you have on your computer.** Installers sometimes mimic virus activity and may make your computer incorrectly believe that it's infected with a virus.

- ✔ **Close all running programs.** The more programs you run, the less memory is available to other programs. Installers also typically update files and programs. So if you keep other programs running, installation may not work properly.

- ✔ **Add more RAM to your computer.** Your local computer store can do this step. Admittedly, this step is drastic and somewhat expensive. However, adding more memory can really help the speed of your computer and allow more programs to run at the same time. If you still have trouble with installing the items from the CD, please call the IDG Books Worldwide Customer Service phone number: 800-762-2974 (outside the U.S.: 317-596-5430).

Index

IDG Books Worldwide, Inc., End-User License Agreement

READ THIS. You should carefully read these terms and conditions before opening the software packet(s) included with this book ("Book"). This is a license agreement ("Agreement") between you and IDG Books Worldwide, Inc. ("IDGB"). By opening the accompanying software packet(s), you acknowledge that you have read and accept the following terms and conditions. If you do not agree and do not want to be bound by such terms and conditions, promptly return the Book and the unopened software packet(s) to the place you obtained them for a full refund.

1. **License Grant.** IDGB grants to you (either an individual or entity) a nonexclusive license to use one copy of the enclosed software program(s) (collectively, the "Software") solely for your own personal or business purposes on a single computer (whether a standard computer or a workstation component of a multiuser network). The Software is in use on a computer when it is loaded into temporary memory (RAM) or installed into permanent memory (hard disk, CD-ROM, or other storage device). IDGB reserves all rights not expressly granted herein.

2. **Ownership.** IDGB is the owner of all right, title, and interest, including copyright, in and to the compilation of the Software recorded on the disk(s) or CD-ROM ("Software Media"). Copyright to the individual programs recorded on the Software Media is owned by the author or other authorized copyright owner of each program. Ownership of the Software and all proprietary rights relating thereto remain with IDGB and its licensers.

3. **Restrictions on Use and Transfer.**

   (a) You may only (i) make one copy of the Software for backup or archival purposes, or (ii) transfer the Software to a single hard disk, provided that you keep the original for backup or archival purposes. You may not (i) rent or lease the Software, (ii) copy or reproduce the Software through a LAN or other network system or through any computer subscriber system or bulletin-board system, or (iii) modify, adapt, or create derivative works based on the Software.

   (b) You may not reverse engineer, decompile, or disassemble the Software. You may transfer the Software and user documentation on a permanent basis, provided that the transferee agrees to accept the terms and conditions of this Agreement and you retain no copies. If the Software is an update or has been updated, any transfer must include the most recent update and all prior versions.

4. **Restrictions on Use of Individual Programs.** You must follow the individual requirements and restrictions detailed for each individual program in the Appendix of this Book. These limitations are also contained in the individual license agreements recorded on the Software Media. These limitations may include a requirement that after using the program for a specified period of time, the user must pay a registration fee or discontinue use. By opening the Software packet(s), you will be agreeing to abide by the licenses and restrictions for these individual programs that are detailed in the Appendix and on the Software Media.
   None of the material on this Software Media or listed in this Book may ever be redistributed, in original or modified form, for commercial purposes.

5. **Limited Warranty.**

   (a) IDGB warrants that the Software and Software Media are free from defects in materials and workmanship under normal use for a period of sixty (60) days from the date of purchase of this Book. If IDGB receives notification within the warranty period of defects in materials or workmanship, IDGB will replace the defective Software Media.

   (b) IDGB AND THE AUTHOR OF THE BOOK DISCLAIM ALL OTHER WARRANTIES, EXPRESS OR IMPLIED, INCLUDING WITHOUT LIMITATION IMPLIED WARRANTIES OF MER- CHANTABILITY AND FITNESS FOR A PARTICULAR PURPOSE, WITH RESPECT TO THE SOFTWARE, THE PROGRAMS, THE SOURCE CODE CONTAINED THEREIN, AND/OR THE TECHNIQUES DESCRIBED IN THIS BOOK. IDGB DOES NOT WARRANT THAT THE FUNCTIONS CONTAINED IN THE SOFTWARE WILL MEET YOUR REQUIREMENTS OR THAT THE OPERATION OF THE SOFTWARE WILL BE ERROR FREE.

   (c) This limited warranty gives you specific legal rights, and you may have other rights that vary from jurisdiction to jurisdiction.

6. **Remedies.**

   (a) IDGB's entire liability and your exclusive remedy for defects in materials and workmanship shall be limited to replacement of the Software Media, which may be returned to IDGB with a copy of your receipt at the following address: Software Media Fulfillment Department, Attn.: *Intranet & Web Databases For Dummies,* IDG Books Worldwide, Inc., 7260 Shadeland Station, Ste. 100, Indianapolis, IN 46256, or call 800-762-2974. Please allow three to four weeks for delivery. This Limited Warranty is void if failure of the Software Media has resulted from accident, abuse, or misapplication. Any replacement Software Media will be warranted for the remainder of the original warranty period or thirty (30) days, whichever is longer.

   (b) In no event shall IDGB or the author be liable for any damages whatsoever (including without limitation damages for loss of business profits, business interruption, loss of business information, or any other pecuniary loss) arising from the use of or inability to use the Book or the Software, even if IDGB has been advised of the possibility of such damages.

   (c) Because some jurisdictions do not allow the exclusion or limitation of liability for conse- quential or incidental damages, the above limitation or exclusion may not apply to you.

7. **U.S. Government Restricted Rights.** Use, duplication, or disclosure of the Software by the U.S. Government is subject to restrictions stated in paragraph (c)(1)(ii) of the Rights in Technical Data and Computer Software clause of DFARS 252.227-7013, and in subparagraphs (a) through (d) of the Commercial Computer–Restricted Rights clause at FAR 52.227-19, and in similar clauses in the NASA FAR supplement, when applicable.

8. **General.** This Agreement constitutes the entire understanding of the parties and revokes and supersedes all prior agreements, oral or written, between them and may not be modified or amended except in a writing signed by both parties hereto that specifically refers to this Agreement. This Agreement shall take precedence over any other documents that may be in conflict herewith. If any one or more provisions contained in this Agreement are held by any court or tribunal to be invalid, illegal, or otherwise unenforceable, each and every other provision shall remain in full force and effect.

Installation Instructions

To install one or more of these items from the CD to your hard drive, follow these steps:

1. **Insert the CD into your computer's CD-ROM drive and close the drive door.**

2. **What you do next depends upon the contents of the particular folder. If the folder contains an install program, go to Step 3. If the folder contains sample files, go to Step 4.**

3. **Those folders containing programs (for example, WinZip, the Upsizing Tools, and Internet Explorer) have setup programs that you need to run before you can use them.**

   Double-click the setup program file (usually named setup.exe) to start the program's setup program. The setup program should guide you from this point.

4. **Those folders containing sample files need to be copied to your hard drive before you can use them.**

   To make it easy, we created a self-extracting archive for each set of sample programs. The self-extractors are at the root of the CD and are called Ch09.exe, Ch12.exe, Ch13.exe, and Ch17.exe. Simply run these extractors, and the sample files will get copied to your hard drive (to subfolders named for the chapters in a folder called c:\INTR_WEB).

5. **Follow the instructions in the next section or the chapter that discusses the sample files for more details on using the files.**

YOUR ONLINE RESOURCE

WWW.DUMMIES.COM

Discover Dummies Online!

The Dummies Web Site is your fun and friendly online resource for the latest information about ...*For Dummies*® books and your favorite topics. The Web site is the place to communicate with us, exchange ideas with other ...*For Dummies* readers, chat with authors, and have fun!

Ten Fun and Useful Things You Can Do at www.dummies.com

1. Win free ...*For Dummies* books and more!
2. Register your book and be entered in a prize drawing.
3. Meet your favorite authors through the IDG Books Author Chat Series.
4. Exchange helpful information with other ...*For Dummies* readers.
5. Discover other great ...*For Dummies* books you must have!
6. Purchase Dummieswear™ exclusively from our Web site.
7. Buy ...*For Dummies* books online.
8. Talk to us. Make comments, ask questions, get answers!
9. Download free software.
10. Find additional useful resources from authors.

Link directly to these ten fun and useful things at
http://www.dummies.com/10useful

For other technology titles from IDG Books Worldwide, go to
www.idgbooks.com

Not on the Web yet? It's easy to get started with *Dummies 101*®: *The Internet For Windows*®*95* or *The Internet For Dummies*®, 4th Edition, at local retailers everywhere.

IDG BOOKS WORLDWIDE

Find other ...*For Dummies* books on these topics:

Business • Career • Databases • Food & Beverage • Games • Gardening • Graphics Hardware • Health & Fitness • Internet and the World Wide Web • Networking Office Suites • Operating Systems • Personal Finance • Pets • Programming • Recreation Sports • Spreadsheets • Teacher Resources • Test Prep • Word Processing

IDG BOOKS WORLDWIDE BOOK REGISTRATION

We want to hear from you!

Register This Book and Win!

Visit **http://my2cents.dummies.com** to register this book and tell us how you liked it!

- ✔ Get entered in our monthly prize giveaway.

- ✔ Give us feedback about this book — tell us what you like best, what you like least, or maybe what you'd like to ask the author and us to change!

- ✔ Let us know any other ...*For Dummies* topics that interest you.

Your feedback helps us determine what books to publish, tells us what coverage to add as we revise our books, and lets us know whether we're meeting your needs as a ...*For Dummies* reader. You're our most valuable resource, and what you have to say is important to us!

Not on the Web yet? It's easy to get started with *Dummies 101*®: *The Internet For Windows*® *95* or *The Internet For Dummies*®, 4th Edition, at local retailers everywhere.

Or let us know what you think by sending us a letter at the following address:

...*For Dummies* Book Registration
Dummies Press
7260 Shadeland Station, Suite 100
Indianapolis, IN 46256
Fax 317-596-5498

BUSINESS AND
GENERAL
REFERENCE
BOOK SERIES
FROM IDG

COMPUTER
BOOK SERIES
FROM IDG